the S

MW01603210

and the

Cross

A History of the Church in Lithuania

Dr. Saulius Suziedelis

Preface by Bishop Paul A. Baltakis, O.F.M.

Our Sunday Visitor Publishing Division
Our Sunday Visitor, Inc.
Huntington, Indiana 46750

ISBN: 0-87973-416-7
LCCCN: 88-61211

PRINTED IN THE UNITED STATES OF AMERICA

Cover design by Steve Windmiller

416

ABOUT THE AUTHOR

Saulius Suziedelis was born in Gotha, Germany, in 1945, and grew up in the Lithuanian community of Brockton, Massachusetts. He graduated from Catholic University with a B.A. in 1967, then served two years in Ethiopia with the Peace Corps. In 1972 he received his M.A. in Russian history from the University of Maryland and in 1977 a Ph.D. in Russian and East European history from the University of Kansas. In 1974 and 1975 Dr. Suziedelis conducted research for his doctoral dissertation at the History Institute of the University of Warsaw under an International Research and Exchanges Board Grant. He has worked at Gallaudet College in Washington, D.C., and has taught at the Oklahoma City Community College. Until the spring of 1987, Dr. Suziedelis was a research historian with the U.S. Department of Justice. He was visiting professor at the University of Illinois-Chicago in the spring of 1988 and is a Senior Research Fellow of the Lithuanian Research and Studies Center.

Sibiro tremtį kentėjusių,
Juozo Sužiedėlio (1902-1980)
ir
prel. Bernardo Sužiedėlio (1888-1967)
atminimui

To the memory of two
who suffered Siberian exile:
Juozas Suziedelis (1902-1980)
and
Msgr. Bernardas Suziedelis (1888-1967)

CONTENTS

Preface

If France is traditionally known as the eldest daughter of the Church, Lithuania may rightly be characterized as the youngest daughter of the Church in Europe, since she was the last to be Christianized. The sixth centenary celebration just concluded was a time of great grace to the Lithuanian community in the homeland and in the diaspora. It gave us an opportunity to reflect on what life under the sign of the Cross has meant these six hundred years. The Lithuanians were always spiritual people even while pagans, and their naturalistic religion provided them with a good preparation for the gospel. The Lithuanian nation is fiercely independent and hence its resistance to would-be baptisms at the point of the sword. The Lithuanian people know the meaning of commitment; therefore, once they made their decision for Christ — as late as it was — they have never wavered.

Dr. Saulius Suziedelis's work should not be of interest only to Lithuanians or to those concerned with Eastern European affairs; rather, the history of the Church in Lithuania should serve as a model for reflection on any country's acceptance of and fidelity to Christ, his gospel, and his Church — or for any individual believer, for that matter.

May this book be a stimulus to prayer and action alike. To prayer, so that all Christians would thank Almighty God for having called them in Christ to live in the company of the redeemed and that those persecuted for their faith in Christ would come to know that true freedom befitting the dignity of the children of God. To action, so that those who are blessed with religious freedom would use that gift wisely and similarly work in and through the political process to ensure this fundamental human and civil right for all peoples.

When another generation of Lithuanian Catholics

faces another centennial observance, may they look to *The Sword and the Cross* not only as a source of enlightenment but as the catalyst that helped make Lithuanians free to "worship in Spirit and truth" (John 4:24).

Most Rev. Paul A. Baltakis, O.F.M.
Bishop for the Spiritual Assistance
of Lithuanians Outside Lithuania

Introduction

In his apostolic letter to the Lithuanian bishops, "On the Occasion of the Sixth Centenary of the 'Baptism' of Lithuania" (June 5, 1987), Pope John Paul II stressed his vision of the importance of the Catholic Church for the Lithuanian people:

> The Church was so immersed, and I would say identified, with the reality of the Nation that in every age your forefathers stood firmly together around her, especially in times of trial, in the dark, sad hours, which even in recent times have marked the history of your land.
>
> In the Church, in her teaching, in her evangelizing and sanctifying work, in her service of unity and truth, your people always found the meaning of their own history, their particular identity, their reasons for living and hoping.

Of course, the pope spoke from a position of committed faith. But one does not have to be deeply religious (or even a believer, for that matter) to appreciate the significant role of the Catholic Church in the history of Lithuania.

This history is intended for the English-speaking reader unfamiliar with the details of Lithuania's past. It is an introduction, a survey of the history of Lithuania and its Catholic Church; this book does not pretend to be a comprehensive work, nor is it an academic monograph. I have assumed that the reader is not closely acquainted with Lithuanian history; thus a portion of the book deals with background not strictly related to the history of the Lithuanian Catholic Church. In general, the approach here has been one of concentrating on the mutual interaction of the Lithuanian people and the Catholic Church from an institutional, political, and cultural perspective. This book is history, not theology; hence I have avoided strictly religious value judgments that cannot be proved by accepted historical methodology.

The history of Lithuania and its Church has been the object of differing opinions and interpretations. I have not avoided giving my own, since I do not believe that it is possible to write serious history by simply presenting data without comment. It is my hope that two decades of professional training and experience in East European studies lend some validity to the points of view expressed herein. To those who read this history, it will become clear that it is written from a "Lithuanian" point of view — that is, I have stressed the uniqueness of the Lithuanian historical experience within the East European context. It seems obvious that the Lithuanian experience is vastly different from that of, say, Americans even when both peoples were involved within the same broad historical event, such as the Second World War. Yet it is surprising how often this elementary fact, this vast difference in historical experience between peoples, eludes even professional scholars who are too often ignorant of many features of the East European past. It is my contention that one of the most important aspects of Lithuanian history is the acquisition of Western cultural values, a process in which the Catholic Church was a driving force. I should like to add that this work is intended to inform rather than proselytize. Thus both positive and negative aspects of Lithuanian history are acknowledged: conscious avoidance of unpleasant truths is self-defeating and pointless.

This survey is being published at a time when new developments are taking place in Lithuania. Some of them have been reported in the major American newspapers. For example, not too long ago the Soviet regime addressed one of the major grievances of Lithuania's Catholics by announcing that it will return the Queen of Peace church in Klaipeda that had been seized in 1960. More important, even the Soviets no longer deny that the Church has broad popular support in Lithuania, and there has been a more open discussion of religious matters. However, despite the release of a number of Catholic ac-

10

tivists from camps and exile, reports of repression continue. There is disagreement concerning the extent and genuineness of Gorbachev's *glasnost*, or openness. What this all means will not be obvious for a considerable time, but the potential for change is there and some people are hopeful.

Frequent political changes as well as Lithuania's multinational character have resulted in various spellings and versions of personal and place-names over the years. With few exceptions, I have utilized the present-day spellings of place-names as employed by the National Geographic Society's maps. As a general rule, in handling personal names I have tried to adhere to the spelling peculiar to a given person's nationality except where widely accepted in English-language works dictated otherwise. In such cases, and especially for persons who lived before the twentieth century it seemed to me that practicality and expediency were preferable to absolute consistency (thus Radziwill rather than Radvila, for example).

I would like to express my thanks to the Committee of the Lithuanian Christianity Jubilee, particularly Mr. Jonas Kavaliunas and Dr. Linas Sidrys, who supported my work and arranged for my trip to Rome to observe the impressive celebration of the sixth centenary of Lithuanian Christianity at the Vatican. Special thanks go to Dr. Rasa Mazeika, who read the section on medieval history and offered suggestions, thereby saving the manuscript from errors concerning a period with which I am less familiar. Rev. William Wolkovich-Valkavicius provided valuable suggestions for the history of Lithuanian-Americans and the Church in the United States. Rev. Casimir Pugevicius graciously consented to review and criticize portions of the manuscript. I also owe a debt to Prof. Marija Gimbutas of UCLA for her assistance on the pre-Christian period as well as to the critical insights of Prof. V. Stanley Vardys of the University of Oklahoma, whose work on the Catholic Church in Lithuania under Soviet rule is an indispensable reference. The Most Rev. Vincentas Brizgys and Dr. Adolfas Damusis took time to share their reminiscences and reflections on the recent past. I appreciate the assistance of all those who provided illustrations. Dr. Jonas Rackauskas of the Lithuanian Research and Studies Center helped overcome some of the technical hurdles. While many kind persons contributed to this study, I alone take responsibility for the facts and interpretations presented here. Naturally, every historical work has its errors, omissions, and misstatements. I hope that these will be pointed out to me, since dialogue invariably facilitates better understanding.

Dr. Saulius Suziedelis

CHAPTER 1

The Eastern Baltic Before Christianity

The Early Balts

The Lithuanians speak a language belonging to the Baltic group, which in turn is one of the branches of the giant Indo-European family of languages that encompasses most of Europe and extends into Asia, including much of the subcontinent. In fact, many linguists consider Lithuanian the most conservative living Indo-European tongue (Sanskrit is the oldest known written form) and thus the language has been of great interest to scholars.

The exact origin of the Lithuanian people has been debated over the years, but it is clear that between 3000 and 2500 B.C. stable agricultural communities were well established in what is now Lithuania and Latvia by people we call "Balts." In order to avoid confusion, we should stress that the term Balt has acquired two basic meanings: (1) a term for the ethnically and linguistically related group of peoples of whom only the Lithuanians and Latvians survive in today's world; (2) a political and geographic definition for the population hailing from the Baltic States, including the Estonians, who are ethnic relatives of the Finns rather than the Latvians and Lithuanians.

The Balts had achieved their greatest expansion during the Bronze Age between circa 2000 and 1500 B.C., when they inhabited all of what is now Belorussia, much of central Russia, and in the west, an area stretching to East Germany; in the south, they reached the upper Vistula. The eastern Balts, who inhabited regions as far east as present-day Moscow, eventually disappeared during the

Slavic expansion northward between the seventh and thirteenth centuries A.D. In the west there were the numerous Prussian tribes, including the Yotvingians (Sudovians), while the central Balts encompassed the Samogitians, Selians, Latgallians, and the Curonians among others. The central Balts were the ancestors of modern Lithuanians and Latvians whose vernaculars are the only surviving Baltic languages (although some Old Prussian texts from the medieval period have been preserved). Most of the Baltic tribes vanished through either assimilation or conquest. Only the Lithuanians managed to create a unified state before the twentieth century.

The early Balts maintained fairly extensive economic and cultural relations with their neighbors, including the Finno-Ugric tribes to the north and especially with the various cultures of Central Europe. The economic ties were apparent in the amber trade that flourished since ancient times: the December 1987 issue of *National Geographic* described evidence of Baltic amber in the remains of the world's oldest known shipwreck (dating back to the fourteenth century B.C.) that was recently discovered near Ulu Burun on Turkey's Mediterranean coast. Caches of Roman and Arabic coins uncovered by archaeologists in Lithuania indicate that Baltic commercial ties with the outside world continued during the classical and early medieval periods. On the other hand, like the other Balts, the Lithuanians lived in relative political isolation from the rest of Europe until the thirteenth century. Hence the peoples of the eastern Baltic were not decisively influenced by such events as the collapse of the Western Roman Empire or the emergence of Charlemagne.

Pre-Christian Worship

Archaeological research has revealed a good deal about the material culture of the prehistoric Balts. Unfortunately, we know considerably less about the spiritual and religious aspects of Baltic pre-Christian culture. Ancient sources are meager. Herodotus refers to a group called the Neurians, who may have been the eastern

Balts. In his work *Germania* (first century A.D.), Tacitus mentions the "gentle Aestians" living on the east coast of the Baltic Sea. He wrote that these amber-gathering people "worship the mother of the gods and carry figurines in the shape of a boar as an emblem of her worship." In the ninth century the Anglo-Saxon traveler Wulfstan described the customs and mores of the Baltic "Aestians," who were ruled by regional princes and lived in a socially stratified society. The name "Lithuania" first appeared in a German chronicle that has been dated to 1009. However, in early medieval times, this name referred only to a part of the modern ethnographically Lithuanian lands. In general, since they left no written records, little is known of the cultural and political history of the early Lithuanian tribes.

Earlier historians based their views of pre-Christian religion in the Baltic region on medieval sources. However, it is now clear that such records must be treated with caution. Investigation of archaeological and folkloric evidence indicates that before the Indo-European advance into the eastern Baltic region, there existed an older culture based on a matristic religion in which a woman, not a man, constituted the creative force in the world. The powerful influence of this "Old European" (as opposed to "Indo-European") religion is evident in the goddesses of the ancient Lithuanians: Laima, the giver of life; Ragana, the goddess of destruction and regeneration; Zemyna, the Mother Earth, concerned with fertility and multiplication. Customs and rituals associated with these deities survived among the peasantry until the beginning of this century. In general, Old European religion celebrated the unity, sacredness, and mystery of life in nature, characteristic of a peaceful and relatively egalitarian society.

The Indo-European ancestors of the modern Lithuanians brought with them a religion more suited to a warlike people, and the new culture gradually fused with that of Old Europeans into a hybrid, multilayered religious system. The new gods were male: Dievas, the god of heavenly light; the Thor-like Perkunas, or god of thunder

15

and lightning; Velinas, the god of the underground, who was transformed into a devil during Christian times. Ancient Lithuanians believed that various supernatural beings dwelt in the forests and swamps. For example, the *laume*, a kind of semidivine wood nymph, exercised a fateful role in a person's life and is still a well-known figure in Lithuanian folklore. Much of Baltic religion, culture, and folklore is closely associated with reverence for the forest, which served as a vital economic resource and a protection against enemies. Worship revolved around a fire in a sacred grove. The pre-Christian Lithuanians had a special awe for certain animals, apparently dating back to the Old European period and still evident in folklore — for example, the grass snake (*zaltys*), which was a benevolent protector of the hearth, and the industrious bee. It is known that the ancient Lithuanians believed in an afterlife, a conviction reflected in the country's numerous excavated burial sites. A person continued his or her existence in a mysterious realm known as *dausos*. Early Lithuanians believed that the spirits of their ancestors dwelt within plants and animals near the locales where they once lived. Some scholars think that customs associated with cemetery visits on All Souls' Day reflect remnants of this ancestor cult.

It should be said that in general the historical view of religion in pre-Christian Lithuania has varied greatly over the years. Medieval sources and nineteenth-century romantic writers often posited the existence of a high priest, a caste of ordinary "clergy," and even a group of nunlike vestal virgins. In reaction to occasionally erroneous descriptions and exaggerations, some twentieth-century Lithuanian authors perceived the ancient Lithuanians as animists who did not practice what we would call organized religion and who did not possess large temples or a clear-cut religious hierarchy, except for various diviners. However, it seems that we may now have to revise this appealingly naturalistic outlook and strike a new balance in evaluating traditional Lithuanian religion. New excavations in Lithuania suggest the existence of tribal sacred centers. In 1986 archaeologists announced the discovery in Vilnius of the foundation to a non-Christian temple; the ruins were sandwiched between the remains of two Catholic cathedrals, the first dating back to the thirteenth century, and the second to the late fourteenth century. Interestingly, such a temple had been described by a formerly discredited "romantic" historian. Thus while we do not have detailed knowledge about the religion of the old Lithuanians (such as we have, for example, about that of the Greeks and Romans who left written records), there is now hope that we will uncover more information in the near future.

The pre-Christian religion of ancient Lithuania is now a distant memory. However, many of its creative aspects have shown remarkable persistence in the culture of the Lithuanian people and have even blended with the Christian experience. In her paper on pre-Christian Lithuanian religion delivered at the International Colloquium of Church History in June 1987 commemorating the six hundredth anniversary of Lithuania's Christianization, Prof. Marija Gimbutas of UCLA made this observation:

> The countryside of Lithuania with its sacred rivers, trees, and groves still brims with ancient spirit. One cannot erase the memory of the past, even by revolutions and cruel wars; that memory continues in our psyche and dreams as archetypes. Human nature does not tolerate sudden breaks.
>
> In spite of history's cruel game, Lithuania today blossoms as a Christian flower. Yet it has its own scent and color. Only in Lithuania do wooden crosses raised high on a pole shine like suns with the rays of lush plant shoots or snakes; only in Lithuania do thousands of roofed poles two or three stories high stand like life trees in cemeteries, at roadsides and farmsteads. In Lithuania still flourish wood carvings of gods and saints — sorrowful Christs, Madonnas, Matres Doloroses, Johns, Georges, and others — made by gifted village artists. This creative force comes from deeper local roots than 600 years of Christianity.

Before the first contacts with Christianity, the relative political isolation of the Lithuanians and other Balts enabled them to maintain a stable religious, cultural, and social structure, at least until early medieval times. The Lithuanian tribes engaged in raiding and warfare with the surrounding Slavs, but it does not seem that this activity was outside the norms current for the Europe of that age. The trade and cultural interaction with surrounding peoples influenced but did not undermine the traditional way of life. In the end, it was the advent of Christianity that launched the transformation of the ancient Baltic world.

CHAPTER 2

First Contacts With Christianity

Early Martyrs and Colonists

The old Lithuanian tribes and their Baltic brethren came into contact with Christian Europe well before the fourteenth century. Given the nature of Baltic trade, it can be assumed that the Balts were acquainted with people of other religions since the days of the Roman Empire. The first recorded contact of a Baltic people with Christianity occurred in the tenth century when the unfortunate St. Adalbert (known in Czech as Vojtech), the bishop of Prague, traveled to Prussia with two companions to preach Christianity in Pomerania, the westernmost region of Old Prussia. Medieval chronicles relate that Adalbert and his companions entered a sacred grove forbidden to foreigners and, as a result, the trio were martyred in 997. A few years later the Benedictine monk St. Bruno of Querfurt was named bishop of Prussia and arrived there from Poland in 1008. Bruno and his eighteen companions were killed the following year during a Prussian war with the now Christian Poles. A German chronicle of that year reported that the missionaries had died on the border of Lithuania, the first time the country's name appears in a historical source. Further attempts at peaceful conversion were made by the Cistercian monk called Christian who succeeded in establishing small Christian communities in Prussia by the beginning of the thirteenth century.

At the same time, somewhat more ominous developments were occurring to the north. Since the middle of the twelfth century, German colonists had been building settlements at the mouth of the Daugava River, where they eventually founded the city of Riga; meanwhile, the Christian Danes initiated the conquest of most of present-day Estonia. In 1202 the bishop of Riga founded a crusading order under the name of the Brothers of the Army of Christ, better (and more aptly) known in history as the Knights of the Sword. Their purpose was to protect the interests of the German colonists and subdue the "pagan" natives in the region that became known as Livonia (which consisted of what is now Latvia and, after 1346, included the Danish possessions in Estonia). The Latvian and Estonian tribes resisted the invaders, but in the end the indigenous peoples were unable to halt the conquest and Christianization of their lands. These Livonian knights tried to expand southward, but they were decisively defeated by an alliance of Lithuanian tribes at the battle of Saule, or Siauliai, in 1236.

Peaceful missionary activity posed little threat to the Lithuanians. The German conquests in the north were worrisome but in themselves did not initially constitute a mortal danger. Lithuanian tribes had already come into contact with Christians among their eastern Slavic neighbors whose lands they gradually acquired, a process made easier after Kievan Rus fell into disarray because of the Tatar invasions. Beginning with the late thirteenth century, the Lithuanian princes who were sent out to rule the conquered Slavic territories generally adopted the customs and religion of the local inhabitants, and thus a part of the medieval Lithuanian nobility came to profess Orthodox Christianity. However, this development had little effect on the Lithuanian tribes inhabiting the homeland; here the traditional religion and culture held sway.

The Prussian Crusade

The single event that, more than any other, forced Lithuania to confront Christianity was the arrival in the Baltic region of an army of crusading knights known as the Teutonic Order. This Christian army's rapid subjugation of Lithuania's neighbors was a watershed in the history of Eastern Europe and therefore deserves closer scrutiny. The Teutonic invasion of the eastern Baltic had its origins in the rather innocuous founding of the "Order of the Hospital of St. Mary of the Germans" in Jerusalem in 1190. It was incorporated as a military order a few years later. Knights from the German nobility formed the elite of this army, also manned by ordinary soldiers, chaplains, and servants of the knights. The failure of the Crusades in the Holy Land left this well-equipped and aggressive force with little opportunity to fulfill its vow of fighting the enemies of Christ. For a while, King Andrew of Hungary employed the Teutonic knights to battle the Cumans in Transylvania. The Hungarians soon grew to resent the independent and arrogant ways of the knights and consequently drove them out of the country. Interestingly, the German settlers who had accompanied the knights to Transylvania initiated a community there that survived until 1945.

At this point, a Polish prince, Conrad of Mazovia, inadvertently came to the rescue of these "knights without a country." Conrad had been fighting the troublesome Prussian tribes to the north and he appealed to the now unemployed German crusaders for assistance in 1226, a decision that future generations of Poles would come to regret. The first Teutonic knights arrived at the Prussian borderland about 1230. In order not to repeat their ill-fated experience in Hungary, the Teutonic Order acquired a charter from Holy Roman Emperor Frederick II granting the grand master of the knights the status of a prince of the empire as well as ownership of the lands conquered during the crusade. This paved the way for the creation of a powerful and aggressive German state in the eastern Baltic; the Livonian Knights of the Sword federated with the Teutonic Order in Prussia under the latter's leadership in 1237.

The Teutonic Order's crusade against the Prussians quickly degenerated into a war of subjugation. Within fifty years, the crusaders managed to conquer all of Old Prussia to the Nemunas River despite fierce resistance by an alliance of Prussian tribes. The Prussians simply could not long resist a technologically more powerful enemy who was reinforced by aid from West European princes eager for a share of the spoils in Europe's borderlands. The Teutonic knights buttressed their castles with settlements of German farmers, merchants, and craftsmen. These early fortress settlements eventually grew into Hanseatic towns such as Thorn (Torun), the birthplace of Copernicus, Koenigsberg (now Kaliningrad), and Marienburg (Malbork), the capital of the Teutonic Order. The main castle in Malbork has been preserved and is today a popular tourist attraction in northern Poland. The local Prussians were either enserfed or killed; by the seventeenth century the Prussian language and culture had disappeared. It is a bitter irony that these Baltic people left behind only their name, "Prussian," which, as an adjective, came to denote a particularly strident form of German militarism.

Mindaugas and the First Attempts
to Christianize Lithuania

The Lithuanian princes viewed the fate of their Prussian relatives with apprehension. They had been able to stave off the harassment of the Livonian Order, but the Teutonic knights based in Prussia proved to be a more formidable enemy. As the Lithuanians rose to meet this challenge they developed two basic modes of resistance. The first combined military and political aspects: the German threat impelled the Lithuanian tribes to seek unified leadership and spurred them to coordinate their defenses against the invading knights. The second consisted of both a sustained diplomatic opening to other powers in the West, whom the Lithuanians perceived as having influence over the Teutonic Order, and attempts to find allies in Eastern Europe. For its part, the Order sought to portray Lithuania as a land of savage heathens whose successful conversion required military conquest. The Teutonic knights augmented their forces through periodic appeals for assistance to knights in the West who, attracted by the possibilities for religious salvation and plunder, assisted in the "baptism" of the natives in the Baltic. One such crusader is the adventurous English knight of Chaucer's *Canterbury Tales*: "Above all nations' knights / In Prussia, in Lithuania he raided / And in Russia. . ."

Aside from some limited assistance to the Prussians, the Lithuanians made the first attempt to counter the advance of the Teutonic Order in the mid-thirteenth century. This period coincided with the emergence of Mindaugas as the preeminent Lithuanian ruler, considered by some historians as the founder of the Lithuanian state. Mindaugas sought to unify the Lithuanian lands, but he faced pressure from the Livonian knights and was hard-pressed by political enemies at home. He tried to strengthen his position by accepting Christianity, together with his immediate family and some members of his court, probably sometime in 1250 or 1251. Pope Innocent IV later wrote that a "multitude" of Mindaugas's subjects accepted Christianity, but there are indications that the Lithuanian ruler's baptism hardly affected the religious practices of the Lithuanian population at large. Mindaugas's apparent purpose was to gain the pope's protection against the expansionist aims of the Teutonic Order in the Baltic. It is recorded that Mindaugas was crowned king of Lithuania in 1253 at the behest of the Holy Father. In return for his baptism, Mindaugas was obliged to compensate the Teutonic Order with lands in Samogitia (the historic western region of Lithuania known as Zemaitija). This "appeasement" may have been intended to give Mindaugas a free hand in consolidating his own power among the recalcitrant Lithuanian princes and extending his rule to the east.

At the very outset, this early attempt at the Christianization of Lithuania was beset with certain political problems reflecting the difficult and complex situation facing the Lithuanians of that time. Although reliable information concerning Mindaugas's relations with the Church is scarce, available sources indicate considerable rivalry over the juridical status of the nascent Lithuanian diocese. Both the archbishop of Riga and the Teutonic Order in Prussia sought ecclesiastical jurisdiction over Christian, the newly invested bishop of Lithuania. After some intrigue, the new bishop was formally placed directly under the pope's authority, thereby making the Lithuanian diocese independent of the surrounding powers. In practice, however, the Lithuanian bishop came under the influence of the Teutonic knights, and the latter now attempted to further extend their political and military sway over the lands granted to the bishop in western Lithuania. One can guess that Mindaugas found this situation distasteful; faced, however, with rebellious princes at home and a turbulent situation in the east, he had no choice but to tolerate circumstances that forestalled, at least for the time, the Teutonic threat.

Having gained a somewhat illusory respite from the danger in the west as well as the prestige of a royal crown, Mindaugas now turned to his major political aim: the defense of Lithuanian interests in the east and the conquest of new Russian lands. Mindaugas successfully defended Lithuania from Prince Daniel of Volhynia, his major regional rival, and extended Lithuanian rule to much of present-day Belorussia. Yet while Mindaugas expanded Lithuanian power eastward, the western flank continued to deteriorate, despite his newly professed Christianity. The Samogitians simply refused to accept the suzerainty of either Bishop Christian or the Teutonic knights and launched a series of rebellions against the foreigners. There is evidence that the new bishop of Lithuania never really gained any substantial control over his intended flock and was forced to leave Lithuania within a few years. In 1260 the Samogitians destroyed a massive expedition of the knights at the battle of Durbe and initiated a widespread revolt, which soon spread into Prussia, threatening the very existence of the Teutonic Order.

These developments forced a crisis in Mindaugas's relations with the Christian West. Historians think that he secretly assisted the Samogitians in their war with the Teutonic Order. Some chronicles suggest that at this point Mindaugas became an apostate; other sources state that he remained a Christian. In any case, by 1261 the Lithuanian king turned against the Livonian knights and even concluded an alliance with Alexander Nevsky, the famous grand duke of Vladimir, who had once defeated the combined forces of the Teutonic and Livonian knights at the battle of Lake Peipus in 1242. In 1262 Mindaugas supported Treniota, the leader of the Samogitians, in the latter's attempts to assist the Prussians' revolt against the Teutonic knights. Yet Mindaugas seemed unwilling or unable to exploit this historic opportunity against the knights, and opposition to his rule in Lithuania grew. Treniota abruptly turned against Mindaugas and, together with other conspirators who were dissatisfied with the king's ruthless attempts at consolidating the Lithuanian state, assassinated the king and two of his sons in 1263. Mindaugas's violent end terminated the process of transforming Lithuania into a stable Christian monarchy.

Mindaugas's assassination initiated a period of internecine bloodshed. Treniota finally succeeded in overcoming his rivals, but he too was killed in 1264 or 1265 by followers of the dead king. Mindaugas's son Vaisvilkas, a devout Eastern Orthodox prince who had become a monk and was reported to have traveled to the sacred Mount Athos in Greece, now assumed leadership, apparently trying to continue his father's policies. However, he abdicated in 1267 and was murdered by a brother-in-law the following year. The internal strife abated about 1270 with the accession of Traidenis, a strong military leader who waged a vigorous campaign against the knights in both Livonia and Prussia, continuing the consolidation of the Lithuanian lands. Despite all of Traidenis's efforts, the Teutonic Order was finally able to overwhelm the Prussian uprising by the mid-1270s. A more or less unified Lithuania was now the last non-Christian stronghold facing the knights. There ensued a bitter military and diplomatic struggle that was to last for a century and a half.

There is very little information concerning the late thirteenth century, except that the Lithuanian war with the Teutonic and Livonian Orders continued and that about 1295 a certain Vytenis emerged as Lithuania's ruler. Vytenis attempted to defeat the Teutonic threat by exploiting divisions among the Christians themselves: in this case, the conflict between the archbishop of Riga (the nominal sovereign of Livonia) and the Livonian knights (the real military power in that region). For several years, Vytenis joined with the archbishop and the burghers of Riga in an alliance against the knights. He also defended Samogitia from the frequent attacks of the knights based in Prussia. In addition, Vytenis consolidated Lithuanian gains in the east and made successful incursions into Poland. When he died in 1315 or 1316 under as-yet-undetermined circumstances, Vytenis bequeathed his throne to his brother Gediminas, the founder of a new dynasty and a ruler who transformed Lithuania into a major power in Eastern Europe.

Thus, by the beginning of the fourteenth century, the Lithuanians had a tradition of extensive though often hostile relations with both the "eastern" and "western" Christian worlds. However, except for Mindaugas's immediate retinue and the Lithuanian princes in the east who adopted the Orthodox rite, the Lithuanians had resisted conversion to the new faith. Yet the influence of Christianity grew. Lithuania's increasing commercial contacts with the Hanseatic towns (particularly Riga) meant that Christian merchants, especially Germans, traveled and even settled in Lithuania. Franciscan monks arrived during the time of Mindaugas and they maintained a small and intermittent presence during subsequent reigns; they were allowed to build churches in Lithuania well before 1387. The behavior of the Lithuanian rulers themselves seems to indicate their understanding that the traditional religion was no longer politically tenable. However, while Christianity seemed irresistible to the farsighted, the immediate alternatives were far from clear: the country's unique political and geographic position made a choice between the Latin West and Orthodox East a particularly painful dilemma.

CHAPTER 3

Lithuania's Turn to the Christian West

Gediminas

The accession of Grand Duke Gediminas around 1316 began a period of growth and expansion for the fledgling Lithuanian state. Gediminas was also the founder of a dynasty that prospered for almost three centuries. During Gediminas's reign Lithuania's contacts with the Christian world expanded greatly. The grand duke hoped to terminate the menace posed by the Teutonic Order through diplomatic means by an "opening to the West." At least six copies of Gediminas's letters survive; the originals date from the period between 1322 and 1325. One of them was addressed to Pope John XXII, then residing in Avignon. While there has been some doubt as to the authenticity of these letters, recent scholarship tends to support the thesis that they are genuine. In his letters Gediminas stressed three basic themes: (1) a promise to convert to Christianity; (2) a wide-ranging invitation to foreigners, particularly merchants, craftsmen, and artisans, to settle in Lithuania; and (3) an indictment of the Teutonic knights for obstructing the Christianization of Lithuania. Gediminas also invited Franciscans and Dominicans to settle in his country; the letters indicate that at least two churches, one of them in Vilnius, were operating in Lithuania during the early fourteenth century.

Responding to Gediminas's apparent willingness to accept the Christian faith, Pope John XXII sent two Church dignitaries, Bishop Bartholomew and Abbot Bernard, to Riga in 1324. Frederick, the archbishop of

Riga and a political ally of the Lithuanians, accompanied the delegation, which intended to negotiate the Christianization of Lithuania. However, when an advance party of papal envoys arrived in Vilnius to confirm Gediminas's intentions, they encountered a confusing situation. Gediminas now evaded the Christianization issue, explaining that he had really meant to proclaim a policy of religious tolerance: he "did not forbid the Christians to worship God according to the manner of their faith, the Russians according to theirs, and the Poles according to theirs." The Lithuanians, he said, would continue "worshiping God according to our customs: and we all have one God." Gediminas accused one of his Franciscan scribes, whom he employed for writing Latin diplomatic correspondence, of misinterpreting his wish to be baptized. It seems that Gediminas was reluctant to accept baptism after realizing that this would not grant Lithuania respite from the attacks of the German knights. The disappointed papal delegates returned to Avignon while the angry archbishop of Riga placed an interdict on the Order whom he blamed for the failure to convert the Lithuanians.

The collapse of the papal mission led to renewed war between Gediminas and the crusading Orders. Since Livonia and Prussia had now been conquered, the knights were able to concentrate their efforts on the subjugation of Lithuania itself. Both the Livonian and Prussian branches of the Order launched a series of attacks into Lithuania, justifying their aggression by pointing to Gediminas's refusal to accept Christianity. In return, the Lithuanians launched several ambitious expeditions into Prussia and Livonia; in 1329 they reached the city of Riga itself. In 1330 the knights forced the archbishop of Riga to come under their rule, thus putting an end to the latter's alliance with the Lithuanians. During the 1330s, the Teutonic Order intensified its forays into Lithuania, which abated only during the last years of Gediminas's reign. The knights received military assistance from important rulers in Central and Western Europe (such as King John of Bohemia and Duke Henry of Bavaria) as well as political support from the Holy Roman Emperor Louis IV. The bitterness of this conflict is revealed in the dramatic episode at the castle of Pilenai in 1336, which was recorded by chronicler Wigand von Marburg in the fifteenth century. The Lithuanian defenders, besieged by a superior force of knights, reportedly set fire to their fortress and perished at their own hands in a suicidal conflagration rather than surrender to the enemy.

Ironically, the pressure from the crusaders in the west led Gediminas to closer ties with his Christian neighbors to the south and east. The Teutonic threat in the Baltic tended to drive the Poles and Lithuanians together. Gediminas married two of his daughters to prominent Polish princes; one of them, Aldona, eventually became the wife of the Polish king Casimir III and reigned as queen under her Christian name Anne. However, Gediminas's alliance with the Poles did not produce any really valuable military assistance against the Teutonic Order; as a result, toward the end of the reign, Lithuania's relations with Poland deteriorated.

Gediminas is perhaps better known for his more successful policy of expanding Lithuanian power in the Orthodox East, a feat he accomplished more through diplomacy than war — especially through the marriages of his numerous children. He titled himself "the King of Lithuania and of many Russians," and it is thought that his ultimate aim was to become suzerain of all Russia. Gediminas's brother Theodore occupied the throne of Kiev, the capital of the old state of Rus, and the first center of Russian Christianity. Lithuanian princes were to rule Kiev and most of Ukraine for the next two centuries. Gediminas also made Smolensk, an important Russian city west of Moscow, a Lithuanian dependency, and allied himself with Tver, at that time the chief rival of Moscow for control of central Russia; this foreshadowed centuries of conflict between the Lithuanian state and Muscovy. Lithuania's expansion to the east was facilitated by the fact that the Russians preferred Lithuanian rule to that of the Tatars, but it also brought new conflicts with the khans, particularly the ruler of the Golden

Horde, a powerful Tatar state centered in the southeast Ukraine and the northern Caucasus. In the northeast, Gediminas extended Lithuanian influence over the old Russian cities of Pskov and Novgorod, important cultural and trading centers.

Finally, one must mention Gediminas's historic decision to locate the Lithuanian capital in Vilnius, a settlement at the confluence of the Neris and Vilnia Rivers that had been growing in importance since the beginning of the thirteenth century. A famous legend has it that Gediminas, obsessed with a dreamlike vision of a howling iron wolf, had been informed by his diviners that it signified the gods' command to build a powerful fortress city (hence the iron), whose fame was to carry throughout the world (thus the howling). In any case, it is clear that by the end of Gediminas's reign, Vilnius was established as Lithuania's seat of government and it was to become an important cultural and religious center. The surviving castle tower, located on a steep hill named after the capital's founder and overlooking the city, is possibly the best-known tourist landmark in Vilnius and an important symbol of Lithuanian statehood.

Few persons can approach the stature of Gediminas as an important and decisive figure in Lithuania's history. While Mindaugas had initiated the centralization of the Lithuanian lands and had made it a kingdom, most historians consider Gediminas the true founder of the Lithuanian state that played an important role in the history of Eastern Europe during the late medieval and early modern periods. In retrospect, Gediminas also laid much of the foundation for Lithuania's eventual acceptance of Western Christianity. He employed Franciscan monks in his chancery, where Latin became an important language of diplomacy. Gediminas realized the importance of speaking to the West in terms it could understand; he recognized that it was essential to detach Western support from the Teutonic knights if Lithuania was to successfully oppose Germanic expansion. While he rejected baptism, there is no evidence that Gediminas held any animosity toward Christianity, permitting its practice within the non-Christian part of Lithuania. He actively courted the technology and economic benefits that flowed from increased contacts with the West. In a word, Gediminas's policies set the stage for Lithuania's Christianization. Furthermore, it was the country's fortune that Gediminas's successors included, for several generations, rulers of exceptional ambition, foresight, and ability to face the 1300s, that "darkest of centuries."

Algirdas and Kestutis: Facing Challenges East and West

Gediminas died about 1341; his manner of death is uncertain, since there are conflicting reports of doubtful reliability. A recent study published in Lithuania suggests that like Mindaugas he may have been murdered by forces inimical to Christianity. Gediminas left seven sons of whom the majority ruled principalities in the Russian lands; however, the youngest, Jaunutis, inherited the Vilnius region and thus laid claim to the throne. Unfortunately, Gediminas's death was accompanied by fierce attacks from the Teutonic Order and territorial disputes with the Poles over Volhynia; these developments threatened the defense of the realm in the west and Lithuania's recent gains in the east. Fearing that Jaunutis was too weak and inexperienced to handle the new crises, Gediminas's older sons carried out what amounted to a palace coup and, after some fraternal argument, elevated Algirdas (Olgerd in Russian and Polish), the former ruler of Vitebsk, to the throne in Vilnius in 1345. For his part, Algirdas's brother Kestutis reigned from the nearby castle of Trakai. While Algirdas was the grand duke, the two men operated in tandem: Algirdas took on Gediminas's dream of conquest in the east while Kestutis, the ruler of Lithuania's western borderlands, was primarily concerned with managing Lithuania's defenses against the Teutonic Order.

The war against both the Livonian and Prussian knights intensified dramatically during the mid- and late fourteenth century. In 1344 the Order commenced an ambitious campaign to subjugate Lithuania with the participation of the kings of Bohemia and Hungary as well as numerous nobles from Western Europe. Algirdas and Kestutis reciprocated with a counterinvasion of Livonia that carried the Lithuanian forces to the outskirts of Riga in 1345 — a defeat of the knights that led to the dismissal of the Order's grand master. For a while, the Teutonic knights engaged in a successful war of attrition: between 1345 and 1382, they made sixty-six incursions into Lithuania while the Livonian branch of the Order made thirty attacks. The invaders pillaged and devastated much of western Lithuania, seizing booty and taking thousands of local inhabitants into captivity. In 1362 the Teutonic knights succeeded in destroying the important fortress of Kaunas on the Nemunas River; in succeeding years they twice laid siege to Vilnius and Trakai, the capitals of Algirdas and Kestutis, but failed to capture them. The Lithuanians retaliated by launching numerous counterattacks into Prussia and Livonia, but it is clear that by the time of Algirdas's death (1377), Lithuania was very much on the defensive.

While Kestutis held on against the Teutonic threat in this difficult seesaw contest, Algirdas continued his father's policy of expansion in Russia. It was during Algirdas's reign that Muscovy emerged as Lithuania's chief rival in the competition for conquering and uniting the fragmented Russian lands. Algirdas's convenient connections and marriages to Orthodox Russians (his second wife, Juliana, was the sister of Michael of Tver, Moscow's hostile neighbor) as well as his military skills enabled him to seriously pursue his ambitious political goal, which is recorded, in his own words, by a chronicler of the Teutonic Order: "All Rus [Old Russia] must simply belong to the Lithuanians." By the time of his death, the grand duke had managed to firmly annex Kiev, already under Lithuanian influence during Gediminas's reign, and extend Lithuanian dominion toward the Black Sea, pushing back the troublesome Tatars. This expansion to the east and southeast placed the majority of the eastern Slavs under the rule of Lithuania. Algirdas and his allies made attempts to overrun Moscow itself, but their attacks on the city were repulsed. Algirdas's lasting political legacy was Lithuania's increasing involvement in Russian and Tatar affairs resulting in a long-term struggle with Muscovy over the unification of the Russian lands.

During this period of joint rule by Gediminas's sons, Lithuania's relations with both Eastern and Western Christianity grew more complicated. More clearly than his predecessors, Algirdas understood the practical advantages of becoming involved in the politics of the Orthodox Church, an important factor in establishing the legitimacy of Lithuanian rule in Russia. He sought to undermine Moscow's claims to the spiritual leadership of eastern Slavic Christendom by establishing the metropolitanate of all Rus in Kiev, the original center of Russian Orthodox Christianity and now under Lithuanian control; this plan, however, was dependent on the consent of the patriarch of Constantinople, who was considered the "first among equals" among the patriarchs of the Eastern Orthodox Church. At the very least, Algirdas aimed to establish a separate metropolitanate in Kiev independent of Moscow. This led to conflicting claims of jurisdiction within the Russian Church. In the long run, the "eastern" Christian policy of the Lithuanians failed and was an important reason for Muscovy's eventual success in wresting leadership of the Russian lands from the grand duchy of Lithuania.

While most of Algirdas's twelve sons became Orthodox Christians for primarily political reasons, Lithuania's rulers saw no advantage in seeking a respite from the Teutonic knights by adopting Eastern Orthodoxy for all of Lithuania. Negotiations continued for conversion to the Latin Rite. In 1349 King Casimir of Poland wrote to the Holy Father that Kestutis and his brothers were willing to be baptized. At least twice, in 1349 and 1373, Popes Clement VI and Gregory XI wrote to the Lithuanian rulers urging them to convert. (At that time, the pontiffs were guiding the Catholic Church from Avignon. Gregory XI eventually returned the papacy to Rome.) As far as we know, there was no direct answer from the Lithuanians, who apparently preferred dealing with powerful secular rulers. Serious attempts to negotiate a baptism were conducted with Holy Roman Emperor Charles IV in 1358. This effort is of interest, since Algirdas and Kestutis set forth two conditions for Christianization that revealed Lithuanian political hopes concerning the adoption of Latin Christianity: first, that the knights cede to Lithuania much of Prussia and all of Livonia west of the Daugava and, second, that the Teutonic Order leave the eastern Baltic and transfer its "crusading" activities to the goal of converting the Tatars in the remote steppes of southern Russia. Since these proposals meant the end of the knights' hard-fought territorial gains in the Baltic, there was, of course, no realistic hope that the emperor could arrange Lithuania's Christianization.

These negotiations emphasized an important political fact: no Lithuanian ruler was willing to accept a formal baptism of the country if it meant subjugation to the Teutonic knights. This was especially the case during the latter half of the fourteenth century when the Teutonic Order, under its great grand master Winrich von Kniprode (1351-1382), reached the height of its temporal power. On the other hand, it made little sense for Lithuania's rulers to adopt a hostile attitude toward Christianity as such when their eastern Slavic subjects and growing numbers of townspeople were themselves Christians. Algirdas continued his predecessors' policy of friendliness and tolerance toward both the Orthodox East and the Latin West. Both of his wives and most of his children were Orthodox, whereas his son Jogaila was reportedly befriended by the learned Franciscan Peter of Candia (later Pope Alexander V). Algirdas himself never adopted Christianity, but his death in 1377 led to a series of dramatic events that were to ultimately result in Lithuania's emergence as a Catholic nation.

Civil War and Interregnum: Choices East and West

Algirdas's death in 1377 commenced a period of both internal strife and foreign wars, which constituted a turning point in the history of Lithuania and concluded with the country's formal acceptance of Latin Christianity. As successor, Algirdas had named his son Jogaila (Jagiello in Polish), who was born about 1354. However, the succession proved anything but smooth. Jogaila's older brothers claimed a right to the throne; the eldest, Andrew of Polotsk, actually enlisted the grand duke of Moscow and the Knights of the Sword in Livonia in an attempt to seize power in Vilnius. Faced with these difficulties and impressed with the seemingly invincible military power of the Teutonic Order, Jogaila determined to end the exhausting war with the knights. Unfortunately, in negotiating a peace treaty with the Order, Jogaila sought to undermine his uncle Kestutis, whose relations with his deceased brother's family in Vilnius were already strained. Familial tensions soon broke into the open when Kestutis, claiming that he had proof of Jogaila's collusion with the Order, marched on Vilnius and, after banishing his nephew to rule Vitebsk, proclaimed himself grand duke in 1381. However, Kestutis and his son Vytautas (Vitovt in Russian, Witold in Polish) proved unable to quell the rebellions of Algirdas's nephews and the dissatisfaction of Vilnius's townspeople, whose merchants were wary of the commercially ruinous wars with the Order. Medieval chronicles agree that while Kestutis and Vytautas assembled a large force to defend the throne against an alliance of Algirdas's heirs and Teutonic knights, a battle never took place; apparently, Jogaila was able to lure Kestutis away from his army by a treacherous promise to negotiate and then promptly arrested his uncle and cousin. A few days later Kestutis met a violent end at the old princely residence in Kreva, but Vytautas managed to escape, vowing to reclaim his patrimony. In retrospect, the passing of Kestutis marked a dramatic historical milestone for the Lithuanian people. He was Lithuania's last "pagan" ruler, indeed the last of a major European state, the last to die as an adherent of the traditional religion, and, according to medieval chronicles, the last to be ritually cremated in accordance with ancient custom. At the time, however, Kestutis's death was overshadowed by the violent confrontations of Vytautas and

Jogaila and the complicated political maneuvers, which were leading up to the Christianization of Lithuania.

It was no small measure of Vytautas's desperation that he sought support against Jogaila from his father's implacable foes, the Teutonic knights, who seemed to have become suspicious of Jogaila and now were only too happy to abet divisions among the feuding Lithuanians. Vytautas accepted baptism as a Catholic along with two of his brothers in 1383. Jogaila now faced not only increasing opposition from his cousin and the latter's new-found Teutonic allies but resistance from Kestutis's followers, who were embittered by the new ruler's harsh methods. In 1384 the situation took a new twist: the two cousins abruptly reconciled and Vytautas turned against the knights. There is some evidence that at this juncture or at some later time Vytautas may have professed Orthodoxy for political purposes, although the details are not clear. In any case, the combination of civil conflict and foreign threat was moving Lithuania decisively toward a new political arrangement.

Since 1383 Jogaila had been conducting negotiations with neighboring states concerning the Christianization of Lithuania through some sort of dynastic union. On the one hand, a pro-Orthodox party (which probably included Jogaila's mother, Juliana) advocated an alliance with the grand duchy of Moscow; this would be accomplished through a marriage with Sofia, the daughter of Dmitrii Donskoi, the victor over the Tatars in the battle of Kulikovo, and, naturally, baptism into the Eastern Orthodox Church. Inasmuch as Lithuania now ruled vast lands inhabited by Orthodox Slavs, there were obvious benefits to such a course. However, there was another, more startling choice: concurrently, Jogaila was also engaged in talks with the Poles. Historians disagree on which party initiated the negotiations for a dynastic Polish-Lithuanian union; however, it is known that a Polish delegation visited Vilnius and that in January of 1385 a Lithuanian mission headed by Jogaila's brother Skirgaila arrived in Cracow. It was decided that Jogaila would marry Jadwiga, Poland's child-queen who had been crowned in October of 1384, assume the Polish crown as Wladyslaw IV, Christianize Lithuania under the Latin Rite, and keep Lithuania united with Poland. The Polish and Lithuanian nobility documented these and other provisions by the Act of Krewo in August of 1385.

The decision to choose an alliance with Poland and thus accept the Western form of Christianity was doubtless influenced by many reasons, including Lithuania's long and complex prior relationship with the Latin West, previous missionary activity, important economic ties, and the like. Yet there were significant cultural and political advantages to accepting Orthodox Christianity in view of Lithuania's interests in Russia. Clearly, one of the most important motivations in the Lithuanian decision to turn to the West (and, it should be remembered, an inducement for the Poles) was the obvious military and diplomatic advantage to be gained in the life-and-death struggle against the Teutonic Order. In contrast, a turn to the east might gain Lithuania valuable military assistance, but it would also undermine the grand duchy's political posture in the West.

It is recorded that Jogaila's coronation took place in Cracow on March 4, 1386, only a few days after his baptism as Wladyslaw and the marriage to the youthful Jadwiga. The new king was accompanied by his brothers Skirgaila and Lengvenis as well as by his cousin Vytautas with whom he had worked out a temporary reconciliation. There is speculation that at this juncture Vytautas renounced Orthodoxy and was rebaptized under the Latin Rite, retaining the name Alexander. In any case, the time had come for Lithuania to be formally inducted into the Christian world. In practice, it should be remembered that this meant the introduction of Catholicism only into the ethnographically Lithuanian lands, since the eastern Slavic regions of Lithuania had already been part of the Orthodox Christian world for centuries.

The Meaning of 1387

At the beginning of 1387, Jogaila arrived in Vilnius to fulfill his promise of baptizing the Lithuanian nation. Unfortunately, this historic event is obscured by a good deal of nationalist myth and questionable scholarship; hence it is difficult to determine the actual course of events. Most of the detailed information concerning Lithuania's baptism comes from the Polish chronicler Jan Dlugosz (1415-1480), the author of an imposing twelve-volume history of Poland. According to Dlugosz, Jogaila and Vytautas presided over mass conversions and baptisms: crowds of Lithuanian "pagans" were collectively given names, sprinkled with holy water, provided with gifts of clothing, and then sent home as new followers of Christ. Such fancifully embellished accounts contradict common sense: we simply do not know how quickly the non-Christian masses in Lithuania were converted and baptized, but it seems probable that the process did not occur overnight. What is certain is that King Jogaila arrived in Vilnius in early 1387 with a group of clergy (mostly Poles along with a few Czechs) and succeeded in establishing the nucleus of a Western Christian ecclesiastical establishment. In February of 1387 the king issued a series of decrees by which he donated lands for the sustenance of the Church and initiated the construction of a new cathedral and a number of other churches, thereby obligating all of his Lithuanian (but not Russian) subjects, or "the entire Lithuanian nation," regardless of status, to adopt the Catholic faith, and prohibiting them from marrying Orthodox believers. In this way Jogaila began the process of tying the ethnically Lithuanian lands firmly to the religious and cultural traditions of the West, setting them apart from the Slavic territories in the east.

The Teutonic Order was quick to perceive the Christianization of Lithuania as a grave danger; the military threat of a Polish-Lithuanian alliance was bad enough, but "heathen" Lithuania's entry into the world of Western Christendom threatened the knights' very reason for existence. It is not surprising, then, that the German crusaders attempted to hinder Lithuania's baptism, but without success. In March of 1388 Andrew Jastrzebiec, formerly the auxiliary bishop of Gniezno, was appointed the bishop of Vilnius by Pope Urban VI at Jogaila's request. In Vilnius, Andrew baptized a number of Lithuanian nobles and many of the inhabitants of the area. He also traveled to other locales in later years. There is some evidence that he and some Franciscans prepared Lithuanian translations of the Our Father, the Hail Mary, and other prayers.

Thus in 1387 Jogaila initiated a process by which Catholicism became the dominant form of Christianity in the ethnically Lithuanian lands. This marked a turning point in Lithuanian history for a number of reasons. Most important, the Catholic Church was to become the greatest religious institution in Lithuania. In the centuries that followed, its influence would extend to virtually every aspect of Lithuanian religious, cultural, economic, and political life. And in addition to its obvious spiritual role, the Church had also a temporal function: it served as the medium through which the values of the West became part of the Lithuanian experience. It is difficult to imagine how the Renaissance, the Reformation, and the Baroque could have become part of Lithuania's heritage without Jogaila's turn to the West. One need only walk the streets in Vilnius, to stroll past St. Anne's or the ornate Church of SS. Peter and Paul, to appreciate how much the country's very physical landscape is conditioned by what happened in 1387.

There are some who argue that the advent of Roman Catholicism was a mixed blessing for the Lithuanian people. Most often, they point to the fact that the Church also served as a conduit for the injection of Polish culture into Lithuania to the detriment of the native Lithuanian language and culture. Others claim that the Church was an important factor in the eventual subjugation of Lithuania, particularly after 1569, to the political interests of Poland. Still others, including Marxists, contend that the Church was an important pillar of the upper classes in upholding a feudal system based on the grievous exploitation of the present masses by a landholding elite. Of course, all of these criticisms have some merit. These points of view have been discussed, and even held, by various Catholic scholars. In brief, it can be answered that the Church, like other medieval institutions, was a product of its times and carried within it some of the social inequities and national prejudices of the age. The crusades of the Teutonic knights in the Baltic certainly had little to do with the spirit of the gospels. Yet the Church has never really claimed perfection in the temporal sphere, where its activities are carried out by fallible human beings; it only claims that it embodies the true faith in leading its flock toward salvation of the spirit. In any case, it is difficult to see how a Lithuanian turn to the Orthodox East, the only other viable Christian alternative, would have alleviated any of the problems mentioned above, except to replace Polish domination with Russian cultural hegemony.

There is another problem with Lithuania's Christianization in 1387: some say that the date is an artificial construct; that Mindaugas's baptism of 1251 is in fact the starting point of Lithuanian Christianity and is the real date of Lithuania's baptism. There is some validity to this point of view as well, inasmuch as it is clear that Christianity, both in its Orthodox and Roman Catholic forms, had penetrated Lithuania long before 1387. In 1987 archaeologists in Vilnius discovered the foundations of what would appear to be a large cathedral dating back to Mindaugas's reign, that is, the thirteenth century, and published their findings in the magazine *Kulturos Barai* (*Fields of Culture*). There is evidence that even before the mission in 1387 there were at least three Catholic churches in Vilnius as well as several Orthodox ones. Furthermore, one must agree that the date of 1387, like other historical anniversaries that we commemorate, is somewhat arbitrary; that is, it tends to assume greater significance in retrospect and usually marks a less dramatic beginning of a long and complex process rather than a sharp turn with immediately obvious results. In Lithuania, traditional pre-Christian practices did not disappear in 1387, nor did the majority of Lithuanians become ardent Catholics that year: the process took decades; in some areas, centuries. In 1387 Samogitia was still largely under the rule of the Teutonic Order and hence was not included in the missionary efforts and the establishment of Church administration that was centered in the Vilnius region.

Yet even if the immediate effects of Lithuania's Christianization of 1387 were not overly dramatic, there are still good reasons for considering it a crucial event worthy of commemoration. It is significant that while Mindaugas's successors tolerated and permitted the existence of both Eastern and Western Christianity within Lithuania, they themselves clung to the traditional Lithuanian religion, even when, like Algirdas, they married Christian wives. Before Jogaila, none of the Lithuanian rulers formally acknowledged the pope as the spiritual leader of their state, and the very fact that they continued to negotiate with the West (and the East) for the baptism of their subjects into a "Christian realm" suggests that they considered themselves outside of it. Furthermore, after 1387 there was no official reversion to traditional religion or, if you will, "paganism." If we are to measure historic turning points in terms of choosing alternatives and initiating decisive trends, then 1387 is one such point in Lithuanian history and it is quite justifiable to begin a new chapter at this juncture.

CHAPTER 4

Lithuania and the Catholic Church Before the Reformation

The Age of Vytautas (1392-1430)

Jogaila's accession to the Polish throne and the adoption of Roman Catholicism by Lithuania did not end the country's political turmoil that had commenced with Algirdas's death. As we have seen, Vytautas had made peace with his cousin after receiving some of his father's lands as a vassal of Jogaila. However, he was resentful when Jogaila chose his own brother Skirgaila as viceroy for Lithuania. Vytautas tried to organize opposition to Jogaila both within the country and by making an alliance with Moscow. His plotting was uncovered and Vytautas once again turned to the Teutonic Order; in 1390 he promised to abide by his previous promises to the knights in return for their assistance and even provided the understandably suspicious Order with hostages from among his own family. In the fall of 1390 the combined forces of Vytautas, the Teutonic knights, and numerous West Europeans (including the future Henry IV of England) invaded Lithuania and almost succeeded in seizing the capital. For Jogaila, this alliance between his cousin and the Order proved too dangerous: the king secretly opened peace talks with Vytautas. Once again, the latter betrayed his Teutonic allies and signed a treaty with Jogaila in August 1392, ending the ten-year dynastic war that had afflicted Lithuania. The agreement's provisions effectively transferred control of the entire country to Vytautas. In 1395 he began to title himself grand duke while formally acknowledging his cousin as supreme ruler in both Poland and Lithuania.

This curious familial arrangement placed no real restrictions on Vytautas's power, and in a very short time Kestutis's son commenced a policy of enhancing Lithuania's influence — a policy so successful that some historians have referred to him as Vytautas the Great. The grand duke's policies affected all the important aspects of the time: Lithuanian policy in the east; the struggle against the Teutonic threat; relations with Poland; and the development of new religious, cultural, and social institutions within Lithuania itself. In the east, Vytautas launched an ambitious plan to subject virtually all of Russia to Lithuanian control, including the lands then ruled by Muscovy and the Golden Horde. Vytautas's defeat at the hands of the Tatars in the battle of Vorksla (1399) made this goal (which was perhaps overly ambitious) impossible; yet he still managed to recover and expand Lithuania's eastern possessions beyond the boundaries achieved by his uncle Algirdas. For a time, Lithuania even acquired a strip of the Black Sea coast, and a trading post was established on the site of present-day Odessa. By the end of Vytautas's reign, Lithuania was territorially the largest state in Europe and contained somewhat more than two million inhabitants; in addition, Vytautas had secured considerable influence in Moscow, where his daughter Sofia was grand duchess, as well as in Moldavia (where his sister reigned). However, large parts of the Lithuanian state, particularly in the southeast, were sparsely inhabited and only about ten percent of the territory consisted of ethnically Lithuanian lands.

Victory Over the Teutonic Order

Even after his second turnaround against the Teutonic knights, Vytautas maintained relatively peaceful relations with the Order while he pursued his ambitious plans in Russia. During these years, the Teutonic Order sought to make territorial gains in Samogitia, the strategically important land that separated the Livonian and Prussian branches of the knights' domain. Preoccupied with his Russian policy, Vytautas at first made concessions and, in a so-called "treaty of perpetual peace" in 1398, ceded much of western Lithuania to the Order. Yet the native Samogitians refused to acknowledge Teutonic suzerainty and launched a series of rebellions. In 1408, after a reconciliation with his son-in-law Vasilii I of Moscow, Vytautas began to support the Samogitians against the knights; this made war inevitable. In 1409 Vytautas and Jogaila made plans for a joint campaign against the Teutonic knights. There is evidence that both sides viewed the approaching conflict as decisive, an expectation that was not disappointed.

Jogaila and Vytautas gathered a large army, including troops from virtually every corner of their far-flung empires: Christian and non-Christian Lithuanians, Catholic Poles, Orthodox Russians, Czechs, and even a detachment of Muslim Tatars. This disparate and cumbersome army numbering in the tens of thousands was confronted by a smaller but better-equipped force of Teutonic knights and their usual coterie of West European adventurers. On July 15, 1410, the two hordes faced each other near the village of Gruenwald in the forested lake region of southern Prussia. The ensuing battle — known variously as the battle of Gruenwald, the battle of Tannenberg, and, in Lithuanian, the battle of Zalgiris — was one of the most decisive in European history. The knights suffered a crushing defeat, a disaster so thorough that the Order was never to recover its former political or military prominence. The allied forces then besieged Marienburg (Malbork), the Teutonic capital, but here the previous success was not followed up and the campaign gradually withered. As a result, the knights received unexpectedly generous terms in the Treaty of Thorn (Torun) in 1411. The war was renewed in 1412, but it became clear that the knights were no longer a match for the Polish-Lithuanian forces; another Teutonic defeat followed and the Treaty of Lake Melno in 1422 left Samogitia with Lithuania. The Prussian-Lithuanian boundary established there survived virtually intact for five centuries.

The Order's defeat at Gruenwald (Tannenberg or Zalgiris, depending on one's inclinations) did not eliminate the presence of the knights in the eastern Baltic, but it did halt the German *Drang nach Osten* ("expansion to the East") and put an end to the centuries of "crusading" that had perennially devastated the Lithuanian lands. The defeat of the Order was a precondition for the emergence of Poland and Lithuania as major Catholic powers in Eastern Europe. In subsequent years, the Teutonic Order declined. The Prussian branch came under the Polish crown in 1466 while the Livonian knights placed themselves under the protection of the Holy Roman Emperor. In 1525 the Order's last grand master, Albert von Brandenburg, converted to Lutheranism and, as a vassal of the Polish king, became the first duke of Prussia. The Livonian branch suffered a similar fate in the mid-sixteenth century when, as the duchy of Courland (or Kurland), it came under the control of both Lithuania and Poland.

Lithuania and Poland in the Fifteenth Century

As Vytautas's power grew, relations with Poland became more complicated. After the victory at Gruenwald, new acts of union were signed at Horodle in 1413. The Horodle provisions were somewhat contradictory: on the one hand, the de facto autonomous empire that Vytautas had created for himself was recognized; on the other, the outward political and social structures of Lithuania and Poland were made more uniform when fifty Lithuanian magnates adopted Polish coats-of-arms. After the peace treaty of Lake Melno in 1422, which ended Lithuania's last war with the Teutonic Order, Vytautas's relations with the Poles steadily deteriorated. Much of the Polish nobility (headed by Zbigniew Olesnicki, the bishop of Cracow) feared that the grand duke's power and prestige would lead to a formal separation of Lithuania and Poland. Their suspicions were confirmed when it became clear that Vytautas intended to assume a royal crown as king of Lithuania.

It must be remembered that following the assassination of Mindaugas in 1263, subsequent Lithuanian rulers had avoided baptism and hence were not crowned, as was the custom for Christian monarchs in the West. While in Western Europe it was not unusual for two kingdoms to be united, the Poles rejected such an outcome. The escalating conflict over whether Vytautas should assume a royal crown became an international controversy. Holy Roman Emperor Sigismund favored the coronation, whereas Pope Martin V opposed it, fearing that a collapse of the Polish-Lithuanian alliance would hinder the campaign against the Hussite heretics in Bohemia. The dispute finally reached its conclusion in 1430: the coronation of Vytautas was to take place in Vilnius late in the year after an agreement with Jogaila and the Poles. However, Vytautas died in October of 1430 and his cousin Jogaila passed away in 1434. Thus the project of actually creating a Catholic Lithuanian kingdom came to naught.

Vytautas left no male heirs. The Lithuanian nobility then chose Svitrigaila, Jogaila's younger brother, as the new grand duke. An aggressive and ambitious man, Svitrigaila tried to complete Vytautas's plans to make Lithuania an independent kingdom. When the Poles opposed these endeavors, Svitrigaila went to war but was defeated by a Polish-Lithuanian army in 1432. Vytautas's younger brother Sigismund was then elevated to the throne in Vilnius. Svitrigaila fought on for a few more years but was eventually forced to withdraw. While Sigismund had seized power with the aid of the Poles, he himself wished to gain the royal crown and was organizing an alliance against Poland when he was assassinated in 1440 by Lithuanian nobles who opposed his anti-Polish plans.

Sigismund was followed by Casimir, the thirteen-year-old youngest son of Jogaila; at this time, Casimir's older brother Wladyslaw was king of Poland. The Poles protested that Casimir's election as grand duke violated the acts of the Polish-Lithuanian union; for all practical purposes, however, Lithuania was ruled as a separate state until 1447 when the Poles chose Casimir king of Poland to replace Wladyslaw who had been killed in Bulgaria while fighting the Turks. The Lithuanians agreed to their grand duke's coronation only after Casimir issued a series of decrees protecting the privileges of the Lithuanian nobility and safeguarding the Lithuanian lands from Polish interference. Yet Casimir maintained both the title of grand duke and king in his person, appointing his sons as viceroys in Lithuania. In general, despite the rapidly emerging power of Muscovy, Lithuania's chief rival in the east, and continuing Polish-Lithuanian friction, Casimir's reign was one of relative peace and prosperity. Upon Casimir's death, his younger son Alexander was enthroned grand duke while an older son was made king of Poland. The early years of Alexander's reign were preoccupied with Lithuania's increasingly difficult conflict with Moscow, now ruled by the energetic and aggressive Ivan III. Neither military efforts nor diplomacy (Alexander married Ivan's daughter Elena) proved enough to reverse Muscovite expansion, and the Lithuanian position in Russia now began a long process of decline. Upon King John Albert's death in 1501, his younger brother Alexander was called from Vilnius by the Polish nobility to assume the royal throne in Cracow. This was a political event of some significance: from this time every king of Poland was also appointed grand duke of Lithuania, that is, the two states were henceforth invariably ruled by the same monarch. When Alexander himself died in 1506, the two thrones passed to his youngest brother, known in history as Sigismund the Old.

The Catholic Church and the New Society: The Vilnius Diocese

The reign of Vytautas (1392-1430) saw the beginning of important changes in the religious, social, and cultural life of Lithuania. This was a time when the Catholic Church gained a firm institutional foothold in the grand duchy. As mentioned earlier, after the Christianization of central Lithuania in 1387, Andrew Jastrzebiec was installed as bishop of Vilnius. The papal bull of Urban VI officially creating the diocese of Vilnius was brought to Lithuania in June of 1388. Bishop Andrew had traveled widely in Eastern Europe; he once headed the Moldavian see of Sereta and had served as auxiliary bishop of Gniezno. At the outset, the new bishop was faced with a shortage of priests and churches. Most of the available priests could not speak Lithuanian. Yet Andrew not only established a solid basis for Church administration but became active in political affairs as well, participating in the drawing up of treaties and commercial agreements with foreign powers.

The mission of 1387 resulted in the baptism of only a part of the population (estimates of twenty thousand to thirty thousand have been suggested) and one of its main purposes was political: to show the outside world, particularly the West, that the "heathen" Lithuanians had now embraced Roman Catholicism. However, the permanent establishment of Catholicism required more sustained missionary work; for this, it was necessary to create a network of parishes. While Jogaila had commenced the work of founding the first parishes as well as granting them the lands and wherewithal for economic survival, it was Vytautas who did the most in expanding the parish network. During the thirty-eight years of his reign (1392-1430), he established eleven new parishes, the first Benedictine house in the country (founded in Old Trakai), and at least two churches in Kaunas, the city that was to become such an important future center of Lithuanian culture. After Vytautas's death, the creation of new parishes was continued at an accelerated rate. During the 1431-1500 period an estimated sixty-five parish churches were founded through private grants. By the mid-sixteenth century, there were some one hundred sixty-six Catholic parishes in the ethnically Lithuanian part of the diocese of Vilnius.

One should remember that Eastern Orthodoxy, in addition to pre-Christian traditional religion, was still quite strong in some of the lands included in the diocese of Vilnius until the seventeenth century. A noted specialist in Lithuanian medieval history, Jerzy Ochmanski, has found that during the first half of the sixteenth century the city of Vilnius contained fifteen Orthodox churches and fourteen Catholic ones. In Nowogrodek, an ethnically mixed area to the southeast, there were ten Orthodox churches and only one Catholic church. It is probable that the spread of Catholicism to the east of Vilnius was in large part the work of Lithuanian Catholic nobles who established new estates in this area. One historical result of this process was the predominance of Catholicism and Polish culture in what we now call western Belorussia until very recent times. However, Roman Catholicism never spread to the Orthodox areas of eastern Belorussia and the other Russian lands that were ruled by native Orthodox nobles and princes. In effect, western Belorussia proved the easternmost limit of Roman Catholicism in Europe.

The Christianization of Lithuania was hampered by the lack of native Lithuanian priests and missionaries who knew the language of their intended flock. It is known that the first Capitula, the clergy's executive council in the diocese, was made up of Poles, Germans, and Czechs: only Matthew, the pastor of Trakai (Vytautas's residence), hailed from Lithuania. Queen Jadwiga had established a Lithuanian college at the University of Prague, but it was not fully utilized for some time. There is no record of a central school for Lithuanian clergy during the first years after 1387; in most cases, the Cathedral School in Vilnius and the parish schools of the diocese prepared the Lithuanian secular priests. At first, the level of the clergy's education was low: there is evidence that only the initial trivium (that is, reading, writing, and singing) of the traditional medieval curriculum (which was also supposed to include grammar, rhetoric, and dialectic) was followed. It was only during the Reformation that the education of the clergy was considerably expanded. Contemporary records make it clear that the training of the native clergy lagged: a privilege issued by Grand Duke Alexander in 1501 complains of priests who lack knowledge of their parishioners' language. The linguistic problem had two adverse effects: culturally, it encouraged the Polonization of the people to the detriment of the native culture and,

49

religiously, it hindered the Christianization of the Lithuanian peasantry.

The Christianization of Samogitia

While much of Lithuania was receiving baptism after 1387, most of Samogitia remained resistant to the new religion. There were several factors that retarded the Christianization of this region. The Samogitians had carried the brunt of the war against the Order and, as neighbors of the Teutonic knights, they tended to experience Christians at their worst. Understandably, more than any other Lithuanians, they showed the most reluctance to accept baptism. Between 1401 and 1409 the Order ruled Samogitia but showed little interest in converting the inhabitants. The Samogitian rebellion of 1409, which eventually developed into the full-scale war that culminated in the defeat of the knights at Gruenwald in 1410, opened the way for the conversion of Samogitia. In the autumn of 1413 Vytautas and Jogaila, together with a delegation of clergy, traveled to western Lithuania to preach the Catholic faith; Canon Matthew of Trakai was placed in charge of the region's Christianization.

However, the baptism of the Samogitians was not without some peculiar difficulties. Hoping to restore its suzerainty in Samogitia, the Teutonic knights sought to revive their previous function as a crusading power by undermining Vytautas's position in Samogitia. The political struggle over the Christianization of Samogitia was fought at the Council of Constance, an ecumenical gathering that had been called to heal the schism of the Western Church (1378-1414). The Lithuanian-Teutonic controversy over Samogitia was presented to a special committee of the council for arbitration. The Polish-Lithuanian delegation repeated the old charges against the Teutonic Order, accusing the knights of obstructing the Catholic mission in the east through their campaign of aggression. For its part, the Order claimed that the Lithuanian conversion was a superficial charade and implied that Vytautas was a pagan at heart. In 1415 sixty recently baptized Samogitians appeared before the council and read a proclamation listing the wrongs their people had suffered at the hands of the Teutonic Order; it is reported that they made a good impression. While the Council of Constance, deeply preoccupied with the split within Western Christendom and under pressure from Emperor Sigismund, did not formally resolve the Samogitian question, it made a decision that amounted to a serious diplomatic setback for the Order. The council authorized the creation of the diocese of Samogitia with its seat in the town of Varniai (historically known as Medininkai), and in 1417 the aforementioned Matthew of Trakai became its first bishop. Yet even now, difficulties abounded. In 1418 the Samogitians revolted, threatening the gains that Vytautas had painstakingly achieved. While the dissatisfaction was fueled by the anti-Christian opposition of hard-core adherents to the old ways, it also reflected the resistance of the peasantry to the privileges granted to newly-Catholic nobles, which made easier the exploitation of the villagers on their estates. The Samogitian example revealed that the coming of Roman Catholicism to Lithuania was a complex process not without its economic and social costs to the people. In any case, the conversion of the Samogitians proceeded slowly, especially in the more remote rural areas: at the beginning of the sixteenth century, there were less than forty churches in the region and reports indicated that many inhabitants still practiced the traditional pre-Christian religion. However, over time, Samogitia became one of the strongest centers of Catholicism in Lithuania.

Catholicism and the Western Heritage

Several other aspects of the fifteenth century should be briefly mentioned. Vytautas and his successors continued to use religious policy to strengthen their political power. In the early 1420s the grand duke sent part of the country's army to fight on the side of the Hussites who had rebelled against the Holy Roman Emperor, thus causing outrage in Catholic circles in Western Europe; however, he soon abandoned his ill-advised project of seeking to establish himself in Bohemia. In the east,

Vytautas once again attempted a union of the Catholic and Orthodox Churches but later became reconciled to the fact that the medieval Lithuanian state would remain religiously divided. Lithuania's turn toward Roman Catholicism went through a complicated maze of political struggles.

Yet, if the beginning of Lithuania's history as a formally Catholic power was full of contradictions, the foundations of Latin Christendom became stronger with each passing decade. One of the greatest symbols of Lithuania's entry into the Catholic world is St. Casimir (1458-1484), whom the Church has declared the patron saint of Lithuania. Born at the royal palace in Cracow, the son of Casimir IV and Elizabeth of Hapsburg (therefore, Jogaila's grandson), the younger Casimir showed signs of early devotion. One of his teachers, the Italian humanist Callimachus Buonacorsi, remembered him as a "holy youth." As a young man, Casimir traveled widely, often at his father's side, and took a direct part in affairs of state. While carrying out his difficult duties, the young prince led an ascetic life, damaged his health, and contracted tuberculosis. In the spring of 1483 he arrived in Lithuania to represent his father and take over the chancery of the grand duchy. For a while, he lived in Vilnius and Trakai, but his health deteriorated and he died in Grodno on March 4, 1484, at the age of twenty-seven. He was buried at the cathedral in Vilnius (the remains were transferred to the Church of SS. Peter and Paul in 1953). The cult that grew up around St. Casimir illustrated the increasing importance of Catholic belief and culture in Lithuania. The conviction that he had made a miraculous appearance on behalf of the Lithuanians in their victory over the Muscovites at Polotsk in 1518 led to his popularity as a patron saint of the wars against Russia. In later years, the Jesuits did much to spread the veneration of St. Casimir in Lithuania and surrounding countries. When Pope Clement VIII announced permission to celebrate the saint's feast (March 4) in 1602, there were solemn manifestations in Vilnius. The growth of St. Casimir's cult paralleled the development of Catholic devotion among the Lithuanian people of all social strata.

The establishment of Catholicism in Lithuania was a varied process involving not only the spread of religious devotion but political and social change as well. In addition to the more obvious political and religious transformations in the country, historians have noted other definite though gradual changes that increasingly determined the cultural landscape of Lithuania for centuries to come. One was the inception of Western-style education, however modest at first. The Cathedral School of Vilnius was established in 1397 and soon other schools came into being. A few Lithuanian students began to attend universities, such as the one in Cracow. The increasing use of Latin, the universal idiom of educated Europeans of that age, brought Western ideas and concepts into the country. Monasteries and churches became the centers not only of Western-style learning but were also places where Western art made its influence felt.

Another important factor of change was the spread of Polish culture, a more or less direct result of the country's Christianization. It is unlikely that the Polish clergy who surrounded Jogaila actually planned Lithuania's cultural Polonization or in fact even gave it much thought. The deliberate program of assimilation to Polish culture is a much later phenomenon. The penetration of "Polish manners" and speech was initially a gradual and natural process restricted to the magnates. The grand duchy's chancery continued to use a kind of West Russian form of Old Church Slavic as its official language in internal legal documents until 1697, even while the use of Polish gained ground among Lithuania's upper classes, clergy, and townspeople. In time, it became the native language of the aristocracy — for example, of such famous families as the Radziwills (Radvila in Lithuanian). By the early nineteenth century, Polish was adopted, with few exceptions, by most of Lithuania's non-peasant population, a situation that changed only at the turn of this century. The Lithuanian language was never lost; it was just that the native idiom came to be confined to progressively lower social strata. For its part, Latin became the official language of the Church and of education.

This complex condition prevailed, since there was little linguistic compulsion in the medieval grand duchy of Lithuania and virtually no nationalism in the modern sense. While Lithuanian was widely spoken, it proved more practical to write things down in languages that already had a written tradition. No native literature developed until the Reformation, and Lithuanian did not become the country's official language until the twentieth century. Eventually, the identification of Catholicism with Poland became so strong that, until recently, villagers in some areas of Lithuania and western Belorussia often referred to Catholics as people of the "Polish faith." In modern times this political and cultural heritage has resulted in a good deal of conflict between Lithuanians and Poles as well as between Poles and their eastern neighbors, the Belorussians and Ukrainians. However, it should be remembered that none of the above-mentioned consequences were obvious to people of the fourteenth and fifteenth centuries. The fact is that medieval politicians would have found the modern European preoccupation with nationality and language difficult to understand.

CHAPTER 5

The Church From the Reformation to the Enlightenment

Lithuania and the Reformation

The Lithuanian Church was, by historical standards, still a youthful institution at the beginning of the sixteenth century. Lithuania had been a Christian state for little more than a century when the religious strife that was to rend Western Christendom began spreading through Europe. It was, of course, the western Catholic part of the grand duchy that was most affected by the Reformation and the accompanying religious wars. Most students are taught that the Reformation began in 1517 when a German Augustinian monk by the name of Martin Luther proclaimed his famous ninety-five theses in Wittenberg and that this initiated a period of religious and national conflict in Europe which culminated in the destructive Thirty Years' War. This war ended in 1648 with the Treaty of Westphalia, an epoch-making event, which is generally considered to have legitimized the religious division of Europe into Catholic and Protestant regions and set up a new international system based on this reality.

Assuming that the reader is familiar with the history of the Reformation, at least in broadest outline, we can now consider this historic movement in Lithuania during the sixteenth and seventeenth centuries. There is an important point to be made here: while Western Christianity had been Lithuania's state religion for just over a century, it would be a mistake to assume that Lithuania, or more specifically its aristocracy and urban population, lived in some sort of cultural backwater. Traditionally, some Catholic commentators have ascribed the early success of the Reformation to the institutional weaknesses of Roman Catholicism in Lithuania: the persistence of pre-Christian beliefs; the poorly educated clergy, many of whom did not know Lithuanian; the bishops' preoccupation with political affairs; the system of parishes too often "founded" and controlled by nobles. While true, such explanations are incomplete; the speed of the Reformation's advance (as well as its remarkable diversity in Lithuania) also testifies to the educated elite's cultural Westernization in the Roman Catholic regions of the country, and the resulting receptiveness to new ideas current in Western and Central Europe. In other words, the temporary success of the Reformation in Lithuania was a tribute to the country's "Europeanization."

Protestantism penetrated Lithuania from the same direction as had Catholicism. In 1521 Grand Master Albert of the Teutonic Order began a trip through Germany and while there came under the personal influence of Martin Luther who suggested that Albert resign from the Order, marry, and become a secular prince. As the teachings of Luther gained ground in Prussia, this notion came to make sense, and the secularization of the Order was formally enacted in April 1525 when Polish King Sigismund I received his vassal Albert as the secular duke of Prussia. The entrenchment of Lutheranism in Prussia was to have important consequences not only for the history of Eastern Europe but, as we shall see, for the development of Lithuanian culture as well. In Livonia, the rise of Protestantism became violently evident as early as 1522 when the burghers of Riga seized the monasteries, banned Catholic worship, and expelled the archbishop. In 1527 Lutheran unrest spread to Tartu.

It was not long for the consequences of these events in neighboring lands to reach Poland and Lithuania. In 1520 King Sigismund banned Luther's works from the kingdom of Poland. In 1527 the diocesan synod of Vilnius expressed its concern over the spread of what it termed the "heresy of the Lutherans." The synod sought to prevent suspect persons, especially those arriving from Germany, from assuming teaching positions. In fact, it appears that Lutheranism found its first adherents among Lithuania's German merchants and craftsmen. Not surprisingly, King Sigismund issued a decree in 1537 forbidding Lithuanian students from attending the University of Wittenberg, but it had little effect, and the spread of Lutheranism proceeded apace. One of the very first known propagators of Lutheranism in Lithuania was Father Jonas Tartila who began preaching Luther's theses in Silale (western Lithuania) about 1535; however, on account of the royal ban on the teaching of Lutheran and Anabaptist doctrines, he was forced to flee to Prussia.

Bans and decrees proved of little help in stemming the appeal of Protestantism. It is reported that in 1540 some Franciscans began to preach Protestant doctrines at St. Anne's in Vilnius, where services were held for the local German community. Perhaps the best-known Lithuanian intellectual of the early Reformation was Abraomas Kulvietis, who was born into an old Lithuanian noble family on a small estate near Kaunas, probably around 1510. He studied at the Universities of Cracow, Leipzig, Wittenberg, and Siena (some of his biographers maintain that Kulvietis studied under Erasmus, but this is not certain). A favorite of Queen Bona Sforza, the influential Italian wife of Sigismund the Old, Kulvietis was given support to establish a school of classical languages in Vilnius in 1539. However, as he began to propagate Protestant ideas, Kulvietis soon fell from Bona's grace, as the queen was a devout Catholic. Under attack from the bishop of Vilnius, Kulvietis found his way to Prussia where he became a professor of Greek and Hebrew at the newly founded University of Koenigsberg (1544). In 1545 Kulvietis briefly returned to Lithuania when conditions for the Protestants improved, but he died of tuberculosis the same year.

In general, while interest in the Reformation spread quite rapidly among segments of the clergy and especially among the Lithuanian nobility, the Catholic authorities held firm against the new doctrines during the reign of King Sigismund the Old (1506-1548). However, in 1544 the elder Sigismund transferred power in the grand duchy of Lithuania to his son Sigismund Augustus, who had been educated in the spirit of Italian humanism and was sympathetically inclined to many of the concepts of the Reformation. Upon his father's death in 1548, the younger Sigismund became king of Poland. Lacking his father's aversion·to Reformist doctrines, the new ruler presided over a period when the tide of the Reformation reached its height in both Poland and Lithuania. It was during this time that Calvinism rather than Lutheranism became the most powerful current of the Reformation in the grand duchy itself.

This new development was stimulated not only by the somewhat ambiguous sympathies of the new king but also by the emergence of the powerful Lithuanian Radziwill family as the preeminent magnates in the realm. The power of the Radziwills was further enhanced by the legendary romance of Sigismund and the beautiful Barbara Radziwill, immortalized in literature and most recently the subject of a Polish film. Proclaiming her the love of his life, the king married Barbara over the bitter opposition of his mother and many Polish nobles. In any case, the new queen, crowned in December of 1550, reigned only six months; it was rumored that her early death was due to a plot carried out by her jealous Italian mother-in-law, Bona Sforza. The power of the Radziwills, however, was undiminished. Nicholas Radziwill the Red remained grand hetman (or chief military leader) of Lithuania while his cousin Nicholas Radziwill the Black enjoyed prestige as chancellor of the grand duchy.

In the meantime, Calvinism was gaining support and sympathy in the country. In 1554 and 1555 Calvin himself sent the king letters from Geneva urging him to "free himself from the oppression of the Pope." There is evidence that Sigismund had certain leanings toward the Protestant cause and that he wavered when Calvinist nobles urged him to divorce the childless Catherine of Hapsburg (whom he had married after Barbara's death).

But he was no Henry VIII and, although the couple separated, Sigismund never broke with the Church: he did not marry again. Thus, in the end, Sigismund Augustus remained loyal to the Catholic cause and, most important in terms of the history of the Reformation, he approved the settlement of the Jesuits in Vilnius in 1569. On the other hand, Sigismund refused to use the power of the sword against the Protestants; in 1563 he equalized the rights of all Christians, allowing non-Catholics to occupy high office. In this, the king showed unusual tolerance for the age.

The legal status acquired by Protestant believers enabled Calvinism to make further gains. They found their champion in the Lithuanian chancellor Nicholas Radziwill the Black, one of the country's most able and energetic politicians who was Lithuania's de facto ruler during the fifteen years before his death in 1565. Like many other Protestant reformers of the time, Nicholas the Black began by attacking the abuses current in the Church and, at first, probably thought of himself as a critic "within the system." Eventually, he became one of the foremost spokesmen of the Reformation in Lithuania. Nicholas the Black corresponded with John Calvin and other theologians in Geneva (although he questioned some of the Calvinist teachings), made large endowments to build Protestant churches, established the first synod of the Lithuanian Evangelical Reformed Church, and aided persecuted coreligionists in other countries. In Poland, this Radziwill became famous for commissioning the famous Bible of Brest (1564), a Polish translation of the Scriptures, which is now recognized as a milestone in the history of Polish literature. Nicholas Radziwill the Red, Barbara's brother, who followed his cousin as chancellor in Vilnius, was no less committed to the Reformation. He reopened the classical school established by Kulvietis, intending it as a training center for Calvinism; a second such school was established on the Radziwill estate in Birzai (northern Lithuania). Unlike their cousins, the Red Radziwills persisted as faithful Protestants. The town of Birzai and its environs have remained the most important center of the Lithuanian Evangelical Reformed Church to this day.

Thus, by the second half of the sixteenth century, the Reformation had engulfed much of Lithuania. One indication of its influence is that in 1563 the Lithuanian Council of Lords, the king's advisory body in the grand duchy, seated ten Calvinists out of eighteen members. While Lutheranism and Calvinism provided the mainstream of the Reformation in the country, other more radical groups also appeared. The strongest were the Arians, who represented one of the earliest Christian heresies, which denied the divinity of Christ. Among the Lithuanian nobility, the most prominent advocate of Arianism was John Kiska of Samogitia. There were sizable communities of Arians in Vilnius, Kedainiai, and Taurage, and their most extreme members propagated a radical social program, urging the abolition of social classes, taxes, and military service. In addition there were the Anabaptists, Antitrinitarians, Unitarians, the Czech Brethren, and other radical Christian groups. One of the more interesting Lithuanian offshoots that emerged during this age of religious fervor were the so-called "Judaizers," a sect that was fascinated by the various aspects of Jewish and Eastern learning, including both its occult and rational elements (for example, the teachings of Maimonides). This movement had appeared in Novgorod in the late fifteenth century and may well be the only reform movement in Lithuania that came from the East. The distance between Lutherans and Judaizers was a great one indeed and was illustrative of the growing diversity of the anti-Catholic movement. The fragmentation of Protestantism in Lithuania proved an important element in the weakening of the Reformation, since the various internal divisions promoted an atmosphere of suspicion and unrest within the movement.

It is difficult to gauge the true extent of the Reformation at its height, or to answer the question of how close Lithuania came to becoming a Protestant country, like Latvia and Estonia. However, it is obvious that the Reformation, in both its Lutheran and Calvinist forms, appealed strongly to the Lithuanian nobility and the urban population during the sixteenth and part of the seventeenth centuries. Certainly, political and social considerations played an important part in the success of Protestantism. There was also the economic factor: as elsewhere in Europe, Church properties proved an attractive target for the nobility. Yet some historians claim that this last element should not be overemphasized in the case of Lithuania; according to one estimate, the Catholic Church held only five percent of the grand duchy's arable land on the eve of the Reformation. The Lithuanian nobility's exposure to Western culture and education was at least as important a factor in the spread of the Reformation. The fact is that the history of the Reformation in Lithuania has been largely written by Catholic scholars who, it must be said, have exhibited a certain and perhaps inevitable bias. Protestant accounts have also suffered from partiality. Unfortunately, an objective and comprehensive history of Lithuania's Reformation in either Lithuanian or a Western language has still not appeared (although there is a Polish study that was published in 1978). However, the Reformation had an obviously important impact on Lithuanian life and culture. This impact can be better understood in terms of the Counter-Reformation in Lithuania.

The Catholic Response: The Counter-Reformation

The reaction of the Catholic Church to the rise of Protestantism is traditionally referred to as the Counter-Reformation, although this designation is somewhat unfair. The series of both theological clarifications and administrative reforms carried out in the sixteenth century was not simply a response to the challenge of the Reformation but was reflective of a profound desire within the Church to address the abuses that had emerged with particular force during the reign of the Renaissance pontiffs. Perhaps, with some justification, the Church's own reform movement could better be described as the Catholic Reformation. In any case, it is generally accepted that this Reformation, whether one terms it Counter or

Catholic, gathered force during the Council of Trent, which was convened, with a number of interruptions, between 1545 and 1563. While there was considerable pressure to come up with a compromise solution to Lutheranism and therefore preserve the unity of the Church, the Tridentine Reforms reaffirmed the traditional authority of the Catholic Church regarding Scripture and explained much of Catholic dogma in a rational manner. The Church also established institutions (such as the Inquisition and the Index of Forbidden Books) in order to enforce discipline among Catholics and especially the clergy. It should be noted that the Inquisition, whose Spanish branch developed a justifiably unfortunate reputation, was instrumental in reforming some of the more corrupt practices among the clergy. The Council of Trent recognized the poor training of the Catholic clergy as a major problem and stipulated that priests in the future would be trained in special seminaries that were to be established in each diocese.

If we define the Counter-Reformation in Lithuania as the Catholic response to the rise of Protestantism, then it was a process that lasted almost two centuries and went through a number of interesting phases. At the outset, it must be remembered that while the Reformation made deep inroads into Lithuania its extent has been exaggerated by chroniclers of the time and by popular tradition. The notion that by the mid-sixteenth century only a handful of Catholic faithful held out against the tide of the Reformation (and then restored Lithuania to Catholicism in a dramatic upsurge of religious fervor) may be dramatically appealing; however, it does not hold water historically. Ironically, Protestantism suffered from the same handicap as early Lithuanian Catholicism: there was a shortage of qualified ministers. Furthermore, while Lutherans tended to address their flock in Lithuanian, official Calvinism was culturally under Polish sway and thus its appeal to the Lithuanian peasant masses must have been limited. In general, while the Reformation made spectacular progress among the nobility and elements of the urban populace, there is some doubt as to its hold on the "people," that is, the petty gentry and the peasantry, even in Protestant-dominated areas. Nor is there much merit to the view that Lithuania's Calvinists had seized most of Lithuania's Catholic churches; such seizures, while they did occur, were not easy to accomplish and generally did not take place in Vilnius and Kaunas. Furthermore, even while Lithuanian Protestantism was still in its expansive stage, the Catholic hierarchy resisted fiercely, even though at times this amounted only to a holding action. Paul Holszanski, the bishop of Vilnius from 1536 to 1555, was adamant in opposing the ambiguous flirtations of Sigismund Augustus with Protestantism and even urged him to use the sword against the opponents of the Church. As we have seen, King Sigismund the Old and his queen, Bona Sforza, had opposed the Reformation with decrees and bans. Thus, even when the Church was in retreat, it did not lack powerful defenders within Lithuania.

From the point of view of combating Protestantism, the more effective period of the Counter-Reformation began with the conclusion of the Council of Trent. In 1564 King Sigismund Augustus endorsed the Tridentine Reforms. This new phase of the Catholic response coincided with disillusion and fragmentation within the Protestant movement in Lithuania. It must be remembered that the Lithuanian nobility had less economic stake in the Reformation than their counterparts in other European countries; conversely, this made their return to the Catholic fold easier. The most dramatic turnaround occurred in the family of Nicholas Radziwill the Black, Lithuania's most powerful Reformation statesman: all four of his sons converted to Catholicism, and in 1568 the oldest, Michael Christopher Radziwill, reportedly burned copies of his father's treasured project, the Polish Bible of Brest. In one of the greatest ironies of the Reformation of Lithuania, another son of Nicholas the Black, George Radziwill, went on to become the bishop of Vilnius and subsequently Cracow. When George died in 1600, this son of a zealous Calvinist — and the only ethnic Lithuanian to become a cardinal before 1988 — was buried in a Jesuit church in Rome. Another important defection from Calvinist ranks was that of Jonas Katkevicius (Chodkiewicz in Polish), the Elder of Samogitia, and an able Lithuanian military leader.

The arrival of the Jesuits in Lithuania signaled a more determined Catholic response to Protestantism. The Society of Jesus was a religious order founded by Ignatius of Loyola and confirmed by Pope Paul III in 1540. Bound by a vow of absolute obedience to the Holy Father, the Jesuits became the intellectual soldiers of the Counter-Reformation. Their rigorous discipline, fine education, and devotion made the Jesuits extraordinarily influential. They did not wear a distinctive monastic habit and were often independent of the local political powers; understandably, they were feared by the Protestants. Even some Catholic rulers, suspicious of the Jesuits' devotion to the papacy and their alleged subversion, did not welcome them. In some ways, the Jesuits became larger than life. The enemies of the Jesuit Order have since laid the blame for various political intrigues and other calamities at the door of Ignatius' followers, so much so that during early modern times the myth of the international "Jesuit menace" acquired a mystique as irrational and powerful as that of any of the "conspiracy theories" current in extremist politics of the twentieth century.

In September of 1569, the year of the fateful Union of Lublin (which will be expanded on shortly), the first four Jesuits arrived in Vilnius at the invitation of Bishop Valerian Protasewicz (Protasevicius in Lithuanian). A college was established in Vilnius in 1570; it was raised to the rank of a university in 1579 by King Stephen Batory and Pope Gregory XIII when it became known as the Academy. This latter date is commonly held to mark the beginning of the University of Vilnius. St. John's Church, surrounded by the Academy buildings, became the center of the Jesuit Order in Lithuania. In 1608 a separate province of the Jesuit Order was established for Lithuania, which included Livonia and Prussia. Initially, the Jesuits' apostolic work was directed at preventing the spread of Protestantism and persuading the nobility to return to the Catholic fold. Another important aspect of their work was the preparation of priests with a good grasp of Lithuanian. By the early seventeenth century the Order had almost three hundred members in Lithuania as well as an impressive network of colleges, residences, and missions. Eventually, more than half of the Jesuit priests worked in education and administration. They received most of their support in the form of land, with the congregation maintaining a number of estates.

The Jesuits inaugurated other projects and reforms. In keeping with the provisions of the Council of Trent, Bishop George Radziwill established the first diocesan seminary in Vilnius in 1582, assigning the Jesuits as the first teachers. It is recorded that in 1586 about three hundred nobles returned to the Catholic faith, including the powerful Leon Sapieha (Sapiega in Lithuanian), the future chancellor of Lithuania. The Jesuits also proved an important factor in rolling back the Reformation in Samogitia where Protestantism had struck deeper roots than elsewhere in the grand duchy. Here Bishop Merkelis Giedraitis, a descendant of an aristocratic family and a graduate of German universities (Koenigsberg, Tubingen, and Wittenberg), provided vigorous leadership when he ascended to the episcopate in 1574. A serious advocate of Tridentine Reforms, Giedraitis increased the number of priests, established new Catholic parishes, and sponsored the publication of religious books in Lithuanian. He sent a number of young men to study in Vilnius and sought to open a seminary in Samogitia, a project realized after his death. However, Bishop Giedraitis faced additional troubles. During the sixteenth century, Samogitia was racked by social unrest as the peasantry and petty gentry resisted the economic encroachments of the powerful magnates. Since the former contained a large number of Catholics, Giedraitis drew on their support to strengthen the Counter-Reformation. The bishop of Samogitia also initiated a number of court cases intended to effect the return of ecclesiastical properties seized by the Calvinist nobility. The legal process was a tedious one, but there were some Catholic successes: the Jesuits were settled in the historic town of Kraziai, and Catholic properties were restored in other communities such as Kedainiai and Kelme.

The Catholic-Protestant struggle, which was at its height from the mid-sixteenth to the mid-seventeenth centuries, is symbolized in the famous story of Our Lady of Siluva, a small town in Samogitia. In 1457 a local noble, Petras Gedgaudas, built a Catholic church there dedicated to Mary. It contained a popular painting of the Blessed Virgin and soon began to draw crowds of worshipers on the feast of Mary's Nativity. During the Reformation, the Calvinist Sofia Wnuczko (Vnuckiene in Lithuanian) acquired the town and surrounding estate, confiscated the Catholic holdings, and established a school for Protestant ministers. Around 1606 the local Catholics, under the leadership of Father Jonas Kazakevicius, sued for the return of their properties. Tradition holds that in 1608 a weeping apparition of Our Lady appeared before a Calvinist catechist and some shepherds on the spot where Catholics had once worshiped. The Siluva parish chronicle indicates that soon afterward there followed the remarkable discovery of parish records, including the original deed, which enabled the Catholics to win their court case in 1622. A grateful Father Kazakevicius built a chapel on the site of the apparition and restored the local Catholic church; eventually, successively larger structures were built, until in 1786 a large brick church was consecrated before a throng of thirty thousand. The cult of Our Lady of Siluva grew continuously, and during the years before World War II as many as one hundred thousand pilgrims took part in annual devotions. Even today, the yearly festivities attract thousands, despite Soviet attempts to curtail the celebration. For Lithuanians, Siluva holds much the same religious and historic significance as, for example, Czestochowa does for the Poles. Thus when the Lithuanians constructed a chapel within the massive Shrine of the Immaculate Conception in Washington D.C., in 1966, it was dedicated to Our Lady of Siluva.

The Catholic "restoration" in Siluva became symbolic of the general retreat of the Reformation in Lithuania. King Stephen Batory's reign (1572-1586) was marked by a decidedly official tilt toward Catholicism; however, Batory himself continued to enforce an official policy of religious toleration. This attitude changed markedly under Sigismund III Vaza, the king and grand duke who reigned from 1587 to 1632. In 1594 Sigismund III also assumed the Swedish throne and was initially well disposed to tolerate Lutheranism. However, after losing his Swedish crown in 1604, he turned decisively against the Protestants and steadily eliminated them from government positions. During this period, litigation between Catholics and Protestants over ecclesiastical properties also intensified; increasingly, the churches were restored to their previous owners. It was not long before the spirit of religious toleration was replaced by persecution. Catholics accused Protestants of acts of desecration, and it is known that Calvinist nobles often discriminated against Catholics on their estates. In turn, there were reports of Catholic violence against Protestants. In 1591 a mob burned the Reformed Church in Vilnius and, when it was rebuilt, Catholic vigilantes destroyed it again in 1611, killing one of the ministers. As the nobility gradually returned to Catholicism, religious discrimination increased further and the previous policy of moderation was abandoned, despite the fact that the Lithuanian grand duchy's legal code — the Third Lithuanian Statute, promulgated in 1588 — mandated religious tolerance. The rights of non-Catholics, including those Orthodox believers who had not submitted to Rome during the Union of Brest (1596), were progressively curtailed and most of their political rights were abolished in 1733. Historians consider that this policy of suppressing the "dissidents," as they were called, heightened political tensions, contributed to foreign intervention, and hastened the collapse of the Polish-Lithuanian Commonwealth at the end of the eighteenth century. However, it should be pointed out that the strife that accompanied the Reformation in Lithuania never gave rise to the kind of bloody religious wars and massacres that erupted in Germany, France, and elsewhere in Europe. In a remarkable display of "modernity," the Lithuanian Reformation was fought largely in the publishing houses, the courts, and occasionally in the streets, but never on the battlefield.

The Cultural Heritage of the Protestant and Catholic Reformations

For Lithuania, the religious conflicts described above brought important cultural changes. With the onset of Christianity, there came the need for written texts in the Lithuanian language. The earliest known written text in the language, an inscription containing Catholic prayers and probably dating from the early sixteenth century, was discovered at the University of Vilnius in 1962. However, it was the Protestants who first emphasized religious works in the vernacular and, as a consequence, the Reformation saw the beginnings of Lithuanian literature. Martynas Mazvydas, a Lutheran pastor, authored the first Lithuanian-language publication, *Chatekismusa Prasty Szadey*, or *Catechism in Plain Words*. The book was published in 1547 in Koenigsberg (present-day Kaliningrad), a center of Lutheranism and the cultural capital of Prussia. A number of other talented Lithuanian authors emerged, most of them Lutheran clergymen. Baltramiejus Vilentas (circa 1525-1587) published Luther's short catechism in 1575, adding a translation of the gospels and epistles four years later. Jonas Bretkunas (1536-1602) published a fine collection of Lithuanian sermons in 1591 and produced a translation of the Bible, which unfortunately remained in manuscript form. Danielius Kleinas (Klein in German) (1609-1666), a native of Tilsit, published the very first Lithuanian grammar in 1653, a highly regarded pioneering work. The Prussian government and German Lutherans tolerated the widespread use of the Lithuanian language in East Prussia for their own political and religious ends, but the results were beneficial for the development of Lithuanian culture. Lithuanian was recognized as an official language in East Prussia's local schools, churches, and government offices. Kristijonas Donelaitis (1714-1780), another Lutheran pastor and Lithuania's classical poet, was the author of the epic *Metai (The Seasons)*, a remarkable description of peasant life and work in East Prussia. The tradition of scholarly interest in the Lithuanian language continued at the University of Koenigsberg after the Reformation. In his introduction to a Lithuanian-German dictionary published in 1800, Immanuel Kant, the university's most famous son, wrote that the beauty of the Lithuanian language was sufficient reason for preserving its use in public life. Most of Prussia's Lithuanians succumbed to rapid Germanization during the late nineteenth and early twentieth centuries, but this fact does not diminish their important role in the history of Lithuanian culture.

The response to the Reformation and its wider use of the vernacular triggered a Catholic interest in the Lithuanian language resulting in the first Lithuanian publications across the border in the grand duchy. These first books were in large part a result of Jesuit efforts. The establishment of the University of Vilnius had somewhat contradictory cultural consequences. While it strengthened the process of Polonization by encouraging the use of Polish (the medium of the educated upper classes in Lithuania), there were factors that encouraged the development of native Lithuanian culture as well. First, since the Academy's major avowed purpose was the battle against the Reformation and the shoring up of a faltering Catholicism among the people at large, it was necessary to encourage the study of Lithuanian, a language still widely spoken among the lesser nobility, the native townspeople, and the peasantry. Even those Jesuits coming from afar, such as the noted Portuguese professor Emmanuel Vega, who taught at Vilnius between 1580 and 1594 and was its first doctor of theology, learned the Lithuanian language (Vega then assisted Bishop Giedraitis in preaching Catholicism to the Samogitians). Second, there was the growing number of Lithuanian students and professors at the Academy, such as Jonas Gruzevskis, its first Lithuanian rector

(1615-1619) and later head of the Lithuanian Jesuit province. These Lithuanians were doubtless more sensitive to the prerogatives of the native language. In addition, this period witnessed the emergence of separatist feelings among some Lithuanians who wished to defend the grand duchy against what they perceived as excessive Polish influence. The study of Lithuanian language and history was partly an expression of this anti-Polish tendency.

The Catholic catechism of Canon Mikalojus Dauksa (circa 1527-1613), which came out in Vilnius in 1595, was the first Lithuanian-language book published in the grand duchy (an earlier Lithuanian publication referenced in historical sources has never been found). In 1599 Dauksa published an additional work, a translation of Polish Jesuit Jakub Wujek's *Postilla*, an explanation of the gospels, which contained a remarkable introduction calling for the wider use of Lithuanian in public life and for its equality with other languages. The Jesuit teacher Konstantinas Sirvydas (1579-1631) published the first secular work in the language in 1629, a well-regarded trilingual dictionary (Lithuanian, Polish, and Latin) used widely until the nineteenth century. His *Punktai Sakymu (Gospel Points)*, published in the same year, was the first extensive, original work in the Lithuanian language. The new center of learning in Vilnius was also instrumental in producing the first historical surveys of Lithuania. The best known was *Historia Lituanae*, in two volumes (1650 and 1669), authored by the Jesuit historian Albert Wijuk-Kojalowicz (Kojalavicius in Lithuanian), based in part on a previous work by Matthew Stryjkowski. In addition to the work in Lithuanian language and history, the Jesuit publishing house of the Academy of Vilnius performed a great service in producing numerous works not only in theology but also in science and the humanities, mostly in Polish and Latin. More than half of the published works were secular in nature.

It would be wrong to give the impression that only the Jesuits made contributions to Lithuanian culture and education during this period; however, their work provides the best example of the cultural heritage of the

Counter-Reformation in Lithuania. One should also remember that during the eighteenth century, some cultural advances were made under difficult conditions. The Cathedral of Vilnius, built by the architect Laurynas Stuoka-Gucevicius, was one of the outstanding architectural achievements of the time in Lithuania. In 1773 the National Education Commission instituted an educational reform quite progressive for its time. Unfortunately, the eighteenth century also saw a dramatic decline in the quality of Lithuanian publications both in terms of linguistic quality and content. Awkward Slavic borrowings increasingly dominated the language and grammar, whereas the religious content of many books tended toward ritualistic devotionalism, a situation that improved only during the nineteenth century under the leadership of Bishop Motiejus Valancius. This decline mirrored other worrisome developments, which need to be briefly discussed, namely the political collapse of Poland and Lithuania and their subsequent disappearance from the map of Europe.

The Rise and Fall of the Polish-Lithuanian Commonwealth

As we have seen, the Act of Kreva in 1385 had initiated a Polish-Lithuanian dynastic alliance, and after 1501 the thrones of the king of Poland and the grand duke of Lithuania were invariably held by the same person. Despite the growing cultural and political influence of Poland, however, the two states remained quite distinct: each had its own army, monetary system, gentry diets, and administrative system. As a rule, Poles were forbidden to acquire Lithuanian estates. This state of affairs greatly irritated many Poles who considered that the Lithuanians had simply reneged on previous acts of union. For their part, much of the Lithuanian nobility (for example, the Radziwills) distrusted Polish intentions and frequently asserted Lithuanian independence in political matters. Eventually, however, various pressures, chiefly the growing power of Moscow and the desire for some of the petty gentry for Polish-style privileges, forced the

Lithuanians into dependence on Poland. This problem grew more acute during the reign of Sigismund Augustus, the last of the Jagiellonian kings, indeed the last ruler to trace his origins to the House of Gediminas. The Russian capture of Polotsk in 1563 forced the Lithuanians to turn to the king, and many Poles now saw an opportunity to attach Lithuania firmly to Poland. Acrimonious and heated negotiations followed over the next six years and culminated in the Union of Lublin, which in 1569 established a confederation usually referred to as the Polish-Lithuanian Commonwealth. As a result of the Union of Lublin, Lithuania lost its Ukrainian lands (more than a third of the grand duchy's territory) but retained most of what is now Belorussia. While its political independence was much reduced and the pace of the country's Polonization accelerated, the grand duchy of Lithuania remained a separate administrative unit virtually until the end of the commonwealth in 1795.

Despite its political and military weaknesses, Lithuania displayed considerable vitality during the mid-sixteenth century, a period of intellectual ferment, cultural development, economic growth, and administrative reform within the grand duchy. Sigismund Augustus's great land reform of this time defined the Lithuanian agrarian world and thus its economy well into the nineteenth century. The reform, which determined the boundaries of the crown domains and established villages on the Western model, helped make Lithuania a major European grain exporter and indirectly stimulated urban growth. However, the insidious political debilities grew progressively more serious. One problem was the declining power of the monarchy and the growing influence of the nobility; eventually, the Polish-Lithuanian Commonwealth became an increasingly anarchic "Gentry Republic." The selfishness and greed of the nobility became legendary and undermined the attempts of public-spirited men. The "rugged individualism" of the gentry was symbolized by the ludicrous liberum veto, the practice by which the decisions of the commonwealth's ruling diet had to be unanimous so that a single noble could obstruct, at least in theory, any decision of the legislature. This semi-anarchic political system emerged at a time when the other major European states were developing modern, centralized bureaucracies, and when both Poland and Lithuania faced grave foreign dangers. Under Ivan the Terrible, Moscow continued its expansion westward and for a time even occupied Livonia. During Moscow's "Time of Troubles" in the early seventeenth century a Polish-Lithuanian army had seized Moscow, but this advantage was fleeting. The emergence of the Romanovs in 1613 signaled a new period of steady Russian expansion.

The kings and grand dukes who led the commonwealth into the seventeenth century were of little help in reversing the domestic and foreign dangers. Sigismund Augustus died in 1572, ending the Jagiellonian Age; he was briefly followed by Henry Valois (brother of French King Charles IX) who left in 1574 to assume the French throne as Henry III. The monarchy had now become elective: the Hungarian Stephen Batory was chosen king in 1576. Batory's successor was the son of Swedish King John III, who took the throne as Sigismund III Vaza (1587-1632) and was, for a while, concurrently king of Sweden. Sigismund was followed by his son Wladyslaw (1632-1648) and a nephew, John Casimir (1648-1668). Most historians consider that except for Batory none of these men provided decisive leadership in what unfortunately proved to be an extraordinarily complex and volatile epoch in Eastern Europe.

By the mid-seventeenth century a series of disasters struck the commonwealth. Lithuania became embroiled in war with Sweden, whose power was coming to its height in the northern Baltic. Cossack uprisings, particularly the famous rebellion of Bohdan Chmelnicki, devastated the Ukraine and large parts of Poland. Lithuania's fortunes reached a nadir in 1655 when a Russian force seized Vilnius and virtually destroyed the city, the first time Lithuania's capital had fallen to the enemy. At the same time, the Swedes also occupied much of the commonwealth. King John Sobieski (1674-1696) became famous for his role in saving Vienna from the Turks, but he failed to seriously address the debilitating political crisis threatening Poland and Lithuania. The election of the king became the object of bribery, international intrigue, and foreign coercion aptly demonstrated in the choice of the inept Augustus II of Saxony in 1697 and even more disturbingly in the 1733 "election" of his son, Augustus III, who was elevated to the throne in a session of the ruling diet surrounded by Russian troops. Internal disorder became endemic as political alliances of nobles, known as "confederations" and often inspired by foreign powers (chiefly Russia), battled one another for influence. The inevitable economic decline was accompanied by a series of plagues that culminated in the epidemics (1708-1711) during the Great Northern War, spelling an unprecedented demographic catastrophe, particularly for western Lithuania. In eastern Prussia the plague killed at least half of the predominantly Lithuanian population, leaving vast areas of vacant farmland for subsequent German colonization and permanently altering the ethnic balance of the region.

During the second half of the eighteenth century, there were some encouraging signs of recovery. Agriculture and commerce revived to a considerable degree. Perhaps more important, there were now serious calls for the reform of state and society. In part, these strivings were stimulated by the ideas of the Enlightenment, or Age of Reason. But an even more important consideration was survival: even the less perceptive could see that the Polish-Lithuanian Commonwealth could no longer survive under the prevalent chaotic conditions. Oddly enough, on the eve of its dissolution, the grand duchy of Lithuania accomplished one of its noteworthy reforms: the abolition of the Jesuit school system and the establishment of a secular national commission of education, in effect a ministry of education, the first such institution in Europe. The commission initiated a comprehensive school system based on Enlightenment principles, including primary schools for peasants.

However, these positive achievements were overshadowed by the approaching debacle. Russia (which since the times of Peter the Great openly interfered in the commonwealth's internal affairs), along with Prussia and Austria, simply could not abide a strong Polish-Lithuanian state and effectively hampered any reform, invariably supporting the most reactionary and anarchic factions of the nobility. The last king of Poland, Stanislaw August Poniatowski (1764-1795), was a well-intentioned but indecisive leader and the compromised lover of Empress Catherine the Great of Russia. In 1772 came the first partition of the Polish-Lithuanian Commonwealth: Austria, Prussia, and Russia simply seized land they desired. Sobered, much of the Polish and Lithuanian nobility now made a determined effort to save the commonwealth. The famous Four-Year Diet (1788-1792) passed a number of reforms, including a relatively liberal constitution, which was approved on May 3, 1791. The diet was suppressed by Prussian and Russian troops: in 1793 they forced the Poles and Lithuanians to accept further losses of territory in a second partition. Unable to accept further humiliations and partly inspired by the French Revolution, Polish and Lithuanian forces launched a revolutionary campaign in 1794 under the leadership of Thaddeus Kosciuszko, who had served under George Washington during America's war for independence. The insurrection had no chance: Kosciuszko was wounded and captured by the Russians.

In 1795 Prussia, Russia, and Austria partitioned Poland and Lithuania for the third and final time. Even by the notoriously avaricious standards of contemporary realpolitik, the cynicism and greed of the three powers in eradicating an important and historic European state evoked consternation in the rest of the Continent. The Poles and Lithuanians did not meekly accept the loss of their statehood; neither, in fact, did much of Western European opinion, and for these reasons the "Polish Question," as it became known, confounded European diplomacy for decades to come. Most of Lithuania came under the rule of Orthodox Russia, except for the southwestern part of the grand duchy, which passed, at least for the time, to the Prussians. Neither Poland nor Lithuania would reappear as independent states until after the First World War, but by then their relationship would be very much different.

BALTIC TRIBES

(Twelfth and Thirteenth Centuries)

BASED ON MAP IN
LITUANAS (VOL. 33, NO. 4)

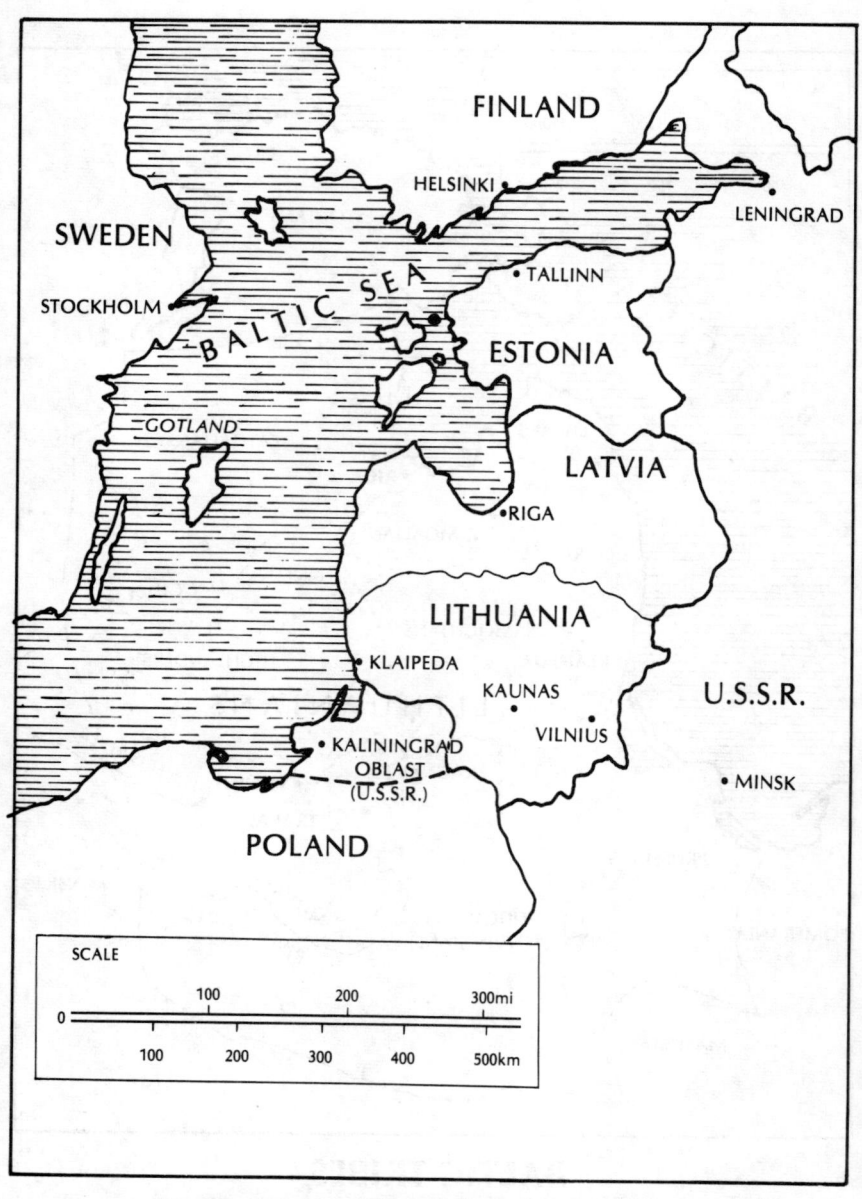

THE BALTIC REGION TODAY

BASED ON MAP IN
THE BALTIC STATES: THE YEARS OF DEPENDENCE

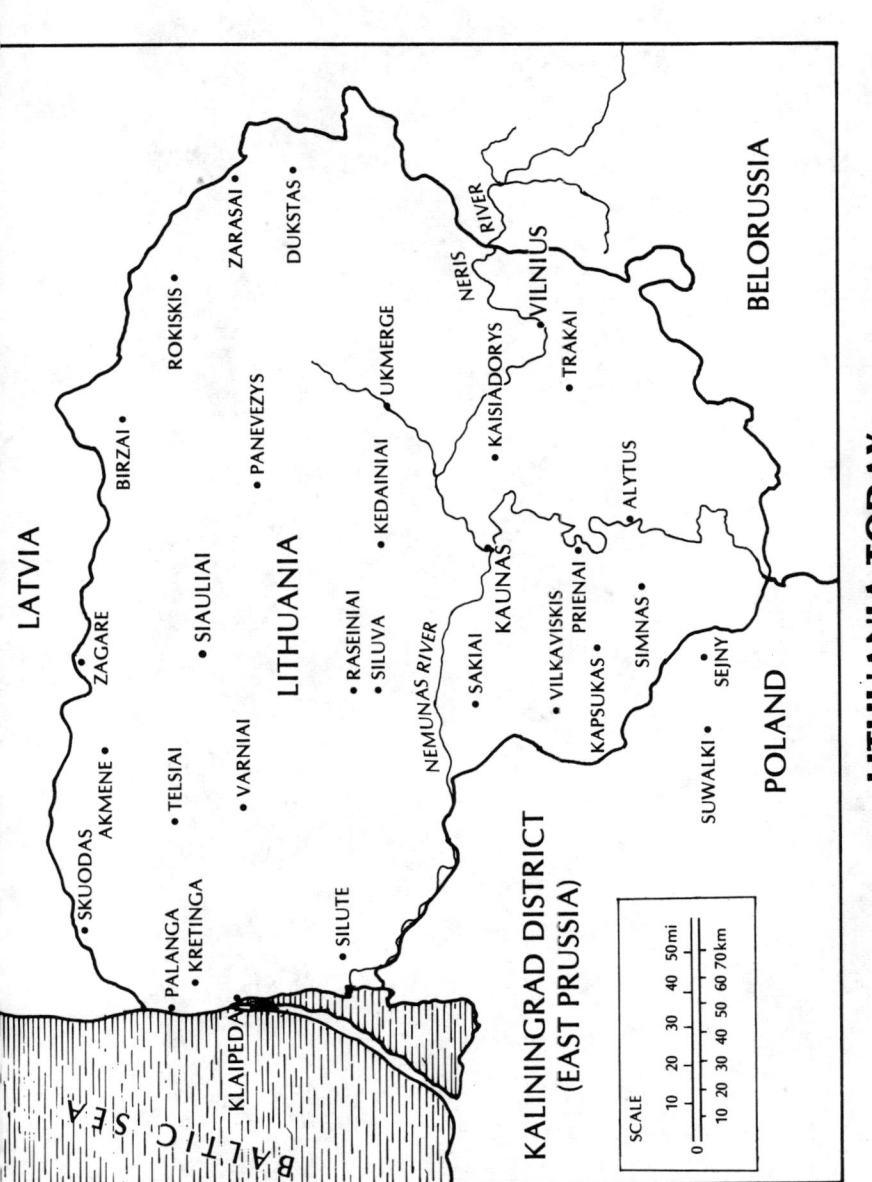

LITHUANIA TODAY

BASED ON MAP IN

THE CATHOLIC CHURCH, DISSENT AND NATIONALITY IN SOVIET LITHUANIA

Vilnius, Lithuania's capital, as seen from the castle tower of Gediminas.

Vilnius: A view of the Old Town.

The Cathedral of Vilnius, now an art gallery, as seen from Gediminas Square.

VICTOR KUCAS

Vilnius: An Old Town street scene.

The fourteenth-century castle of Trakai: Residence of Grand Dukes Kestutis and Vytautas.

The University of Vilnius: The old observatory.

The University of Vilnius: St. John's Church, now a museum.

The palace of Verkiai, built in the eighteenth century for the bishop of Vilnius.

St. Anne's Church in Vilnius, built in the sixteenth century.

**St. Casimir's Church, completed in the early sixteenth century,
now the Museum of Atheism.**

The Madonna: The famous painting of Our Lady of Ausros Vartai (or the Gates of Dawn) in Vilnius.

JONAS KAVALIUNAS

St. Casimir (1458-1484), viceroy of Lithuania and the country's patron saint.

SISTERS OF ST. CASIMIR

SISTERS OF ST. CASIMIR

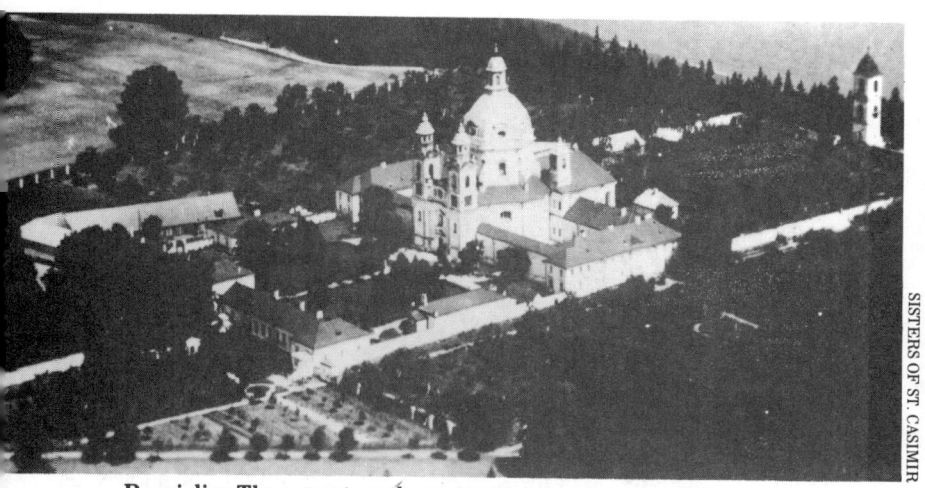

Pazaislis: The seventeenth-century monastery near Kaunas.

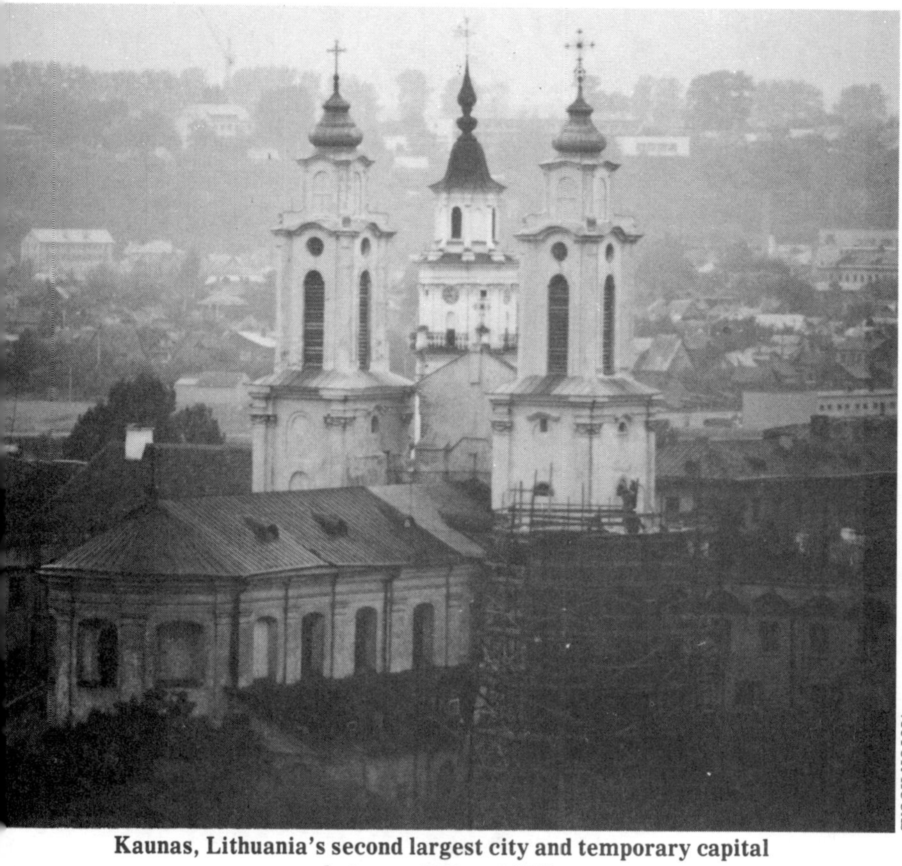
VICTOR KUCAS

Kaunas, Lithuania's second largest city and temporary capital between 1920 and 1939.

JONAS KAVALIUNAS

Commemorative medal of the six hundredth jubilee of Lithuanian Christianity depicting King Mindaugas (who died in 1263), Jogaila (circa 1354-1434), and Grand Duke Vytautas (1350-1430) as well as the Cathedral of Vilnius.

SISTER ANN MIKAILA

Blessed Jurgis Matulaitis (1871-1927), the bishop of Vilnius and apostolic visitator to Lithuania.

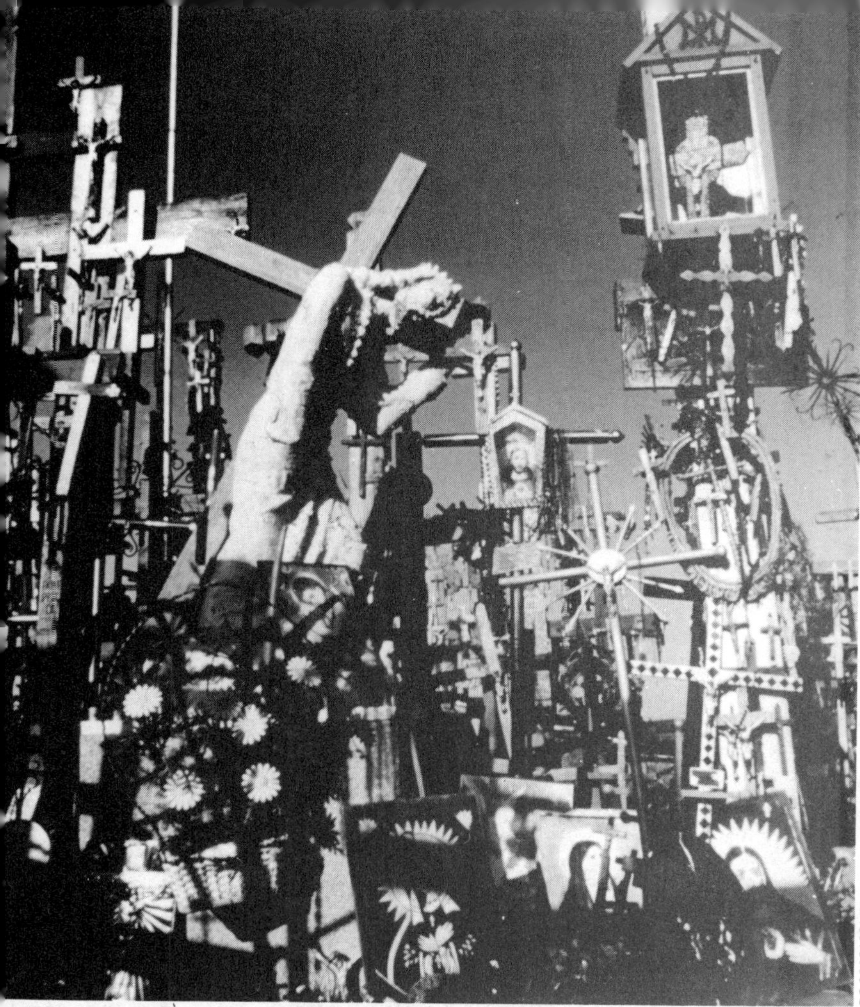

ANONYMOUS

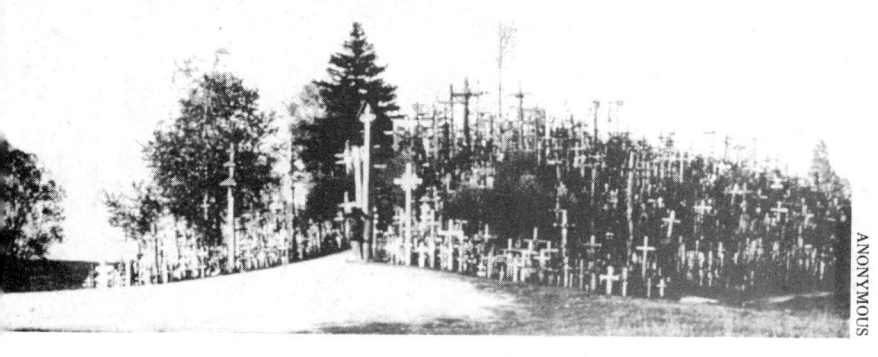

The famous Hill of Crosses near Siauliai, where pilgrims continue to erect crosses and shrines as examples of personal and national devotion.

ANONYMOUS

Wayside shrine, one of the relatively few that survive
in the Lithuanian countryside today.

The Kaunas theological seminary in 1980.

VICTOR KUCAS

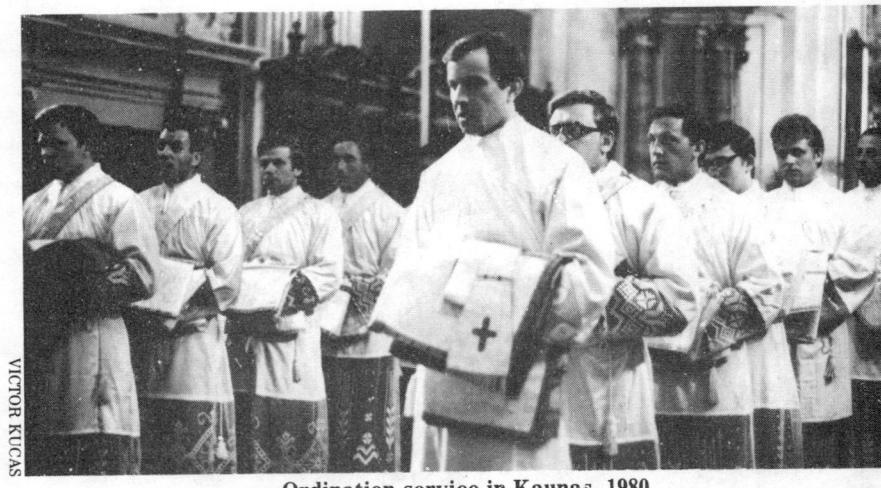

Ordination service in Kaunas, 1980.

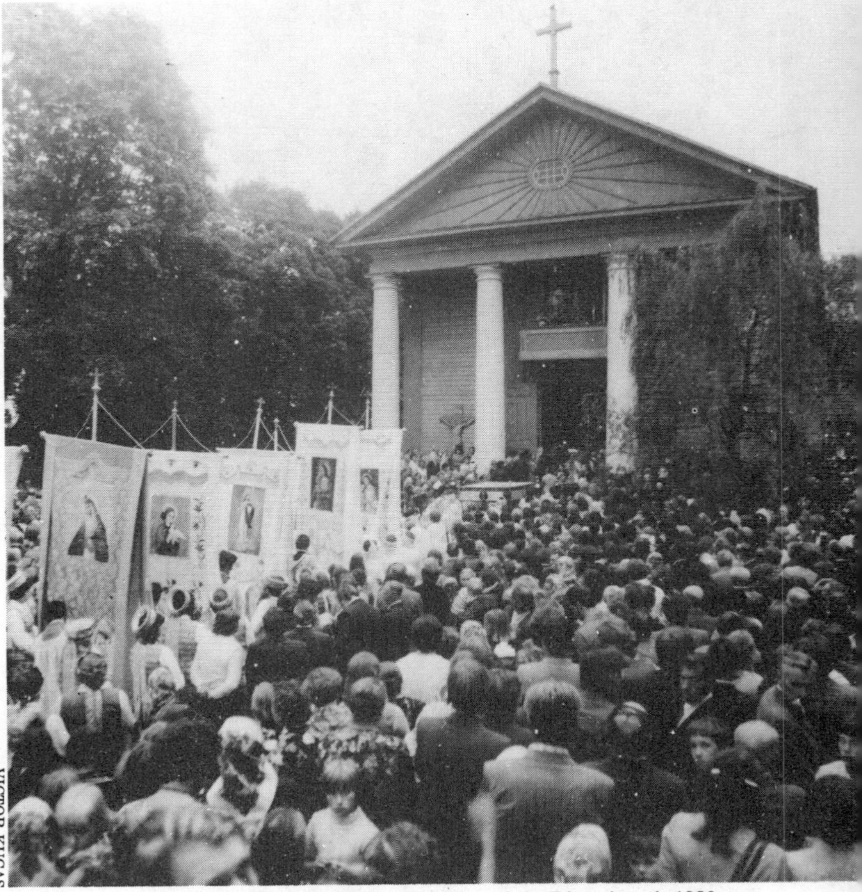

VICTOR KUCAS

Faithful gathered at the church in Pivariunai, 1980.

Young girls preparing for a procession in 1980 at the Queen of Angels Church in the village of Tytuvenai.

Outside the Gates of Dawn chapel on Lithuanian Independence Day, February 16, 1988.

The celebration of the six hundredth anniversary of Lithuania's Christianization in Telsiai, August 30, 1987. Gathered are Bishop Antanas Vaicius, Bishop Juozas Preiksas, and other Lithuanian clergy.

Lietuvos Krikšto 600 metų Jubiliejus 1387-10..

The bishops of Lithuania concelebrating the six hundredth anniversary of
Christianity in their country, June 1987. Exiled Bishop Julijonas
Steponavicius is at left; Archbishop Liudvikas Povilonis is at center.

Former prisoner of conscience Father Alfonsas Svarinskas, member of the Lithuanian Committee to Defend the Rights of Believers, was released in 1988.

Antanas Terleckas enjoying a moment with his grandchildren after his release.

Catholic activists and friends relax after Mass in Vilnius, July 1987. From left: Petras Cidzikas, Julius Sasnauskas, Nijole Sadunaite, Andrius Tuckus, Vytautas Bogusis, and Mr. Bogusis' father.

Journalists at the August 23, 1987, demonstration against the Molotov-Ribbentrop Pact (also known as the Nazi-Soviet Pact).

Gediminas Square in Vilnius is the scene of this protest in Lithuania on June 14, 1988. The tricolor of the independent Republic of Lithuania is raised during the commemoration of the Stalinist deportations of 1941.

KGB Col. Cesnavicius (white hair, foreground) mingles with the crowd during the June 14, 1988, demonstration at the historic Vilnius Cathedral (Gediminas Square).

Bishop Antanas Vaicius of Telsiai (second from right) hands Cardinal Joseph Bernardin of Chicago a plaque commemorating the six hundredth anniversary of Lithuania's Christianization during the festivities in Rome, June 1987.

LITHUANIAN INFORMATION CENTER

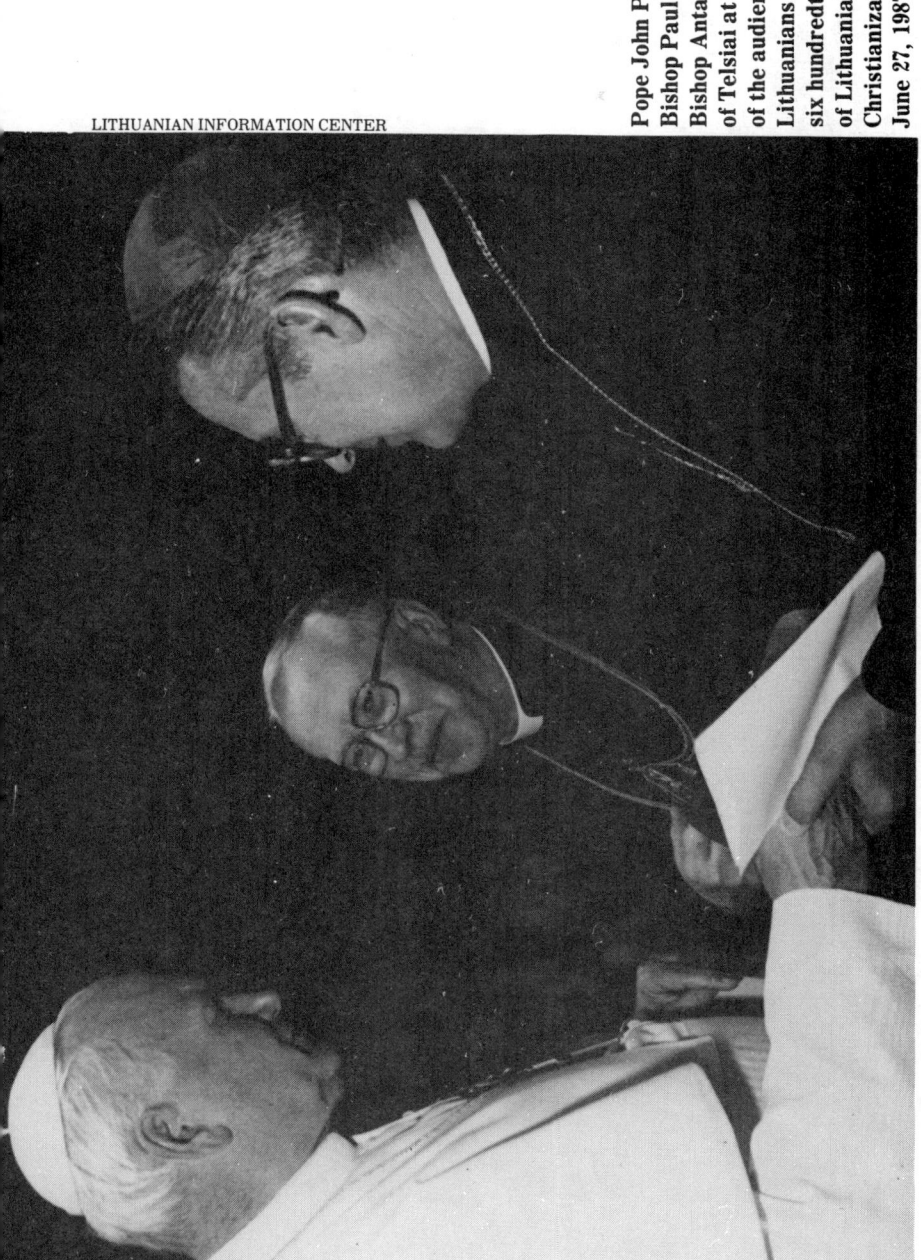

Pope John Paul II greets Bishop Paul Baltakis and Bishop Antanas Vaicius of Telsiai at the beginning of the audience for Lithuanians attending the six hundredth anniversary of Lithuania's Christianization, June 27, 1987.

The Lithuanian Choir, directed by Rita Kliorys, performs at the Maria Maggiore Church in Rome during the commemoration of the six hundredth jubilee of Lithuanian Christianity in June of 1987.

GIOBERTI (ROME)

The West Roseland, Illinois, Council of Knights of Lithuania, 1917.

Representatives of the Knights of Lithuania convention in Marquette Park, Chicago, 1938.

PAUL AND SUSAN BINKIS

Young Lithuanian immigrants at a picnic in the Chicago area, circa 1914.

Maria High School in Chicago.

SISTERS OF ST. CASIMIR

The motherhouse of the Sisters of St. Casimir in Chicago.

The monastery of the Lithuanian Marian Fathers in Chicago.

Our Lady of Sorrows Convent, home of the Sisters of Jesus Crucified, Brockton, Massachusetts.

The Lithuanian Youth Center complex in Chicago, which houses cultural institutions, libraries, and archives, and hosts numerous social and cultural activities.

PAUL AND SUSAN BINKIS

Holy Cross Parish in Town of Lake, Illinois, one of the
oldest Lithuanian Catholic communities in America.

JONAS KAVALIUNAS

The new Church of the Transfiguration, Maspeth, New York,
built in the 1960s. The Lithuanian parish was founded in 1908.

Pope John Paul II greets the president of the Lithuanian bishops' conference and a new member of the College of Cardinals, Vincentas Sladkevicius, at the Vatican, June 1988. At far left is the pope's aide Monsignor Stanislaw Dziwisz; at far right is the Lithuanian envoy to the Holy See, Stasys Lozoraitis, Jr.

Vincentas Cardinal Sladkevicius during a visit to
St. Casimir's College in Rome, June 1988.

The Lithuanian Church Under the Tsars

Culture and Society in the Early Nineteenth Century

The partition of 1795 transformed the Lithuanians into a stateless people, but it did not at first greatly affect their social and cultural life. Under Tsar Paul I (1796-1801) and the enigmatic Alexander I (1801-1825), the Lithuanian nobility preserved its power and influence within the society. There were greater changes in southwestern Lithuania, the region on the left bank of the Nemunas River known as Uznemune (also Suduva, Suvalkija, and, today, the Suwalki region), which had passed to the Prussians (1795-1807) and was later included in the duchy of Warsaw (1807-1815), one of Napoleon's vassal states. The Lithuanian population of this area, which included about a fifth of ethnic Lithuanians, lived under somewhat different juridical and administrative conditions because the Napoleonic Code mandating the abolition of serfdom had been introduced here in 1807. The Napoleonic invasion of 1812 briefly stirred hopes of change and liberation from Russia; some nobles even planned to reestablish the grand duchy. However, the French emperor's defeat and the subsequent Congress of Vienna in 1815 left most of Lithuania within the Russian Empire. The aforementioned Uznemune region was included within an autonomous kingdom of Poland (also known as Congress Poland) ruled by the Russian tsar.

At first, the Church did not suffer persecution and retained unhampered control over its institutions, such as the parishes, schools, and monasteries. However, the status of the Church was different from that which it had enjoyed in the old Polish-Lithuanian Commonwealth. In the Lithuanian lands of the grand duchy, Catholicism had become in essence the state religion. After the partitions, the Church found itself under the rule of an Orthodox sovereign; thus it was no longer routinely entitled to the protection and assistance of the authorities. In addition, the support of some Church leaders — for example, Bishop Ignacy Massalski (1729-1794) of Vilnius — for the pro-Russian reactionary factions of the nobility during the last days of the commonwealth had aroused animosity toward the hierarchy among the younger patriotic supporters of Kosciuszko.

After the late eighteenth century, the Church also lost its monopoly of higher education. The early part of the nineteenth century became especially noteworthy for an intense cultural renaissance centered on the University of Vilnius, which accelerated the secularization of Lithuanian life. In 1773 the Jesuit Order was closed by Pope Clement XIV, and the Academy of Vilnius (renamed the Principal School of the Grand Duchy of Lithuania) was taken over by the National Education Commission. The study of the natural sciences, particularly mathematics, physics, and astronomy, was expanded. In 1803 Alexander I established the Principal School as an imperial university, and for the next three decades it flourished, becoming the most important seat of learning in the lands of the old commonwealth and a major center of science and scholarship in Eastern Europe.

The imperial University of Vilnius radiated the various liberal, even radical, social, and political ideas then current in Western Europe. Modeled after the German *Burschenschaften* and the Italian *Carbonari*, Lithuanian secret societies emerged, imbued with the ideas of romanticism and republicanism. They attacked serfdom, ridiculed the backward social structure, and eventually plotted against the autocratic Russian government. A network of Masonic lodges also spread throughout Lithuania, disseminating their brand of rationalism and deism. In addition, the university became the focus for the diffusion of Polish scholarship and literature, which

122

now reached a level of unprecedented excellence and vitality. Joachim Lelewel (1786-1861), a well-known democrat and professor of history, stressed the role of critical scholarship and historical studies, condemning the prevailing social system. Adam Mickiewicz (1798-1855), a student at Vilnius from 1815 to 1819 and Poland's best-known poet, took his themes from a romanticized version of the history of Lithuania, which he called his "fatherland" in the famous epic *Pan Tadeusz* (1834), depicting the life and times of the Polonized Lithuanian gentry on the eve of Napoleon's invasion. As a Romantic poet and leader of one of the secret societies, Mickiewicz epitomized the revolutionary mystique of the age. In summary, during this period Vilnius experienced a lively intellectual life characterized by the presence of a large group of intelligentsia as well as several excellent journals and publishing houses. Situated on the route connecting Western Europe with St. Petersburg, the society of Vilnius and the Lithuanian-educated strata absorbed the progressive currents of Western Europe.

It should be remembered that this unique period in Lithuania's intellectual history was predominantly a contribution to the development of Polish culture and the Polish national movement.* Men such as Mickiewicz and Kosciuszko may have waxed nostalgic about the heroic deeds of their Lithuanian ancestors, and insisted on the need to bring justice and freedom to the oppressed (Lithuanian and Belorussian) peasant masses, but culturally and linguistically, they were Poles. Like Lord Byron, the young radicals of Lithuania's secret Patriotic Association drew inspiration from the revolutionary outbreaks in Spain, Italy, and Greece, but they were "patriots" of a democratized ideal of the old gentry commonwealth. Paradoxically, as typical Romantics of the age, the Polonized students of Vilnius were fascinated by Lithua-

---

*The Polonization of public life and culture has been emphasized in this history because of its importance in grasping much of the subsequent history of Lithuania, including the role of the Church in the emergence of modern Lithuanian nationalism.

nia's ancient mythology and heroic past, but they could not speak the language of the very peasantry whom they sought to defend against the evils of serfdom. Some saw little use in preserving the dying "village dialect." It is characteristic of the time that the University of Vilnius, which provided courses in Hebrew, Arabic, and Persian, remained indifferent to suggestions for establishing a department of Lithuanian studies.

Yet it would be a mistake to view this cultural renaissance as entirely bereft of value for the development of native Lithuanian culture. In fact, one of its unintentional effects was to stimulate the very beginnings of the modern Lithuanian national movement. This occurred when increasing numbers of Samogitian petty gentry enrolled in the university. (By the early nineteenth century, they were Lithuania's only significant non-peasant social group to still speak Lithuanian.) Inspired by the spirit of romantic nationalism, they took an interest in Lithuanian history, built up an idealized view of the despised peasantry, and initiated a revival of Lithuanian literature. The foremost of the Samogitian literati were Dionizas Poska (1757-1830), whose poetry revealed a deep sympathy for the Lithuanian peasant and who dreamed of introducing the Lithuanian language into public life, and Simonas Stanevicius (1799-1848), who displayed the development of a Lithuanian national consciousness separate from that of the Poles. Two other important personages who studied at Vilnius were Motiejus Valancius (1801-1875), who will be described in more detail below, and Simonas Daukantas (1793-1864), the first historian to write in Lithuanian. His best-known work, *Budas senowes letuwiu Kalnienu ir Zamajtiu (The Customs of the Ancient Lithuanians, Highlanders, and Samogitians)*, was published in 1845. Although most Samogitian Romantics glorified the past, idealized traditional Lithuanian village life, opposed serfdom, and had few sympathies for the Polonized magnates, Daukantas was the first to coherently formulate anti-Polish attitudes. Unlike Mickiewicz and Lelewel, he perceived the Polish-Lithuanian union as a historic mistake rather than as a positive factor in Lithuania's development. This anti-Polish attitude grew and became, in one form or another, one of the most persistent features of Lithuanian nationalism to this day. Although it was an important element in the emergence of modern Lithuanian secular culture, this movement of the early nineteenth century failed to develop into modern nationalism, partly because many of the early Lithuanian Romantics, despite their budding national awareness, still hoped for the restoration of the Lithuanian state within the traditional confines of the old commonwealth.

Revolution and Reaction After 1825

The death of Alexander I in 1825 and the failed plot of the Russian Empire's liberal officers known as the Decembrists commenced the reign (1825-1855) of the reactionary Nicholas I. The relatively tolerant political and cultural policies of Tsar Alexander were replaced by Nicholas's obsession with stamping out liberalism and turning Lithuania, which until then had enjoyed a considerable degree of local autonomy, into a genuine "Russian province," in fact as well as in name. This repressive policy provoked increasing dissatisfaction, and when the army of Congress Poland launched a rebellion, seizing Warsaw in November of 1830, students at the University of Vilnius and officers of the Empire's Lithuanian military corps plotted their own insurrection. Open warfare between the Lithuanian rebels and the Russian Army began in the spring of 1831. Within a short time, the insurgents were in control of most of the country; by April, the tsar's authority was restricted to the besieged Russian garrisons in Vilnius and Kaunas.

Everywhere, the rebels proclaimed their independence from the Russian Empire on the principle of a federal union of Poland and Lithuania. Perhaps the most charismatic military leader then in Lithuania was Emily Plater (1806-1831), a young noblewoman (and an ardent admirer of Joan of Arc) who led her force of gentry and peasants against the Russians. Most of the rebel military leadership consisted of former Napoleonic and tsarist officers, while the rank and file included numerous peasants who, despite their deep differences with the landowners, had even less regard for the Russians (particularly the onerous tsarist military draft, which entailed service for as long as twenty-five years and was often viewed as a veritable death sentence). A common Catholic faith persuaded many villagers to join the manor in attempting to expel the foreign Orthodox invaders. At its height, the Lithuanian rebel force numbered between twenty thousand and thirty thousand fighters; but, despite early successes, neither its equipment nor training could long withstand the superior power of the Russian Army. The insurgents were decisively defeated in July of 1831 and, soon after, guerrilla activity also came to an end.

The Russians had suppressed the insurgency with harsh methods, including the massacre of civilians, and after the war the policy of repression continued. The University of Vilnius was closed in 1832 and the remaining institutions of higher learning were liquidated within ten years. The secondary schools underwent Russification. The Lithuanian Statute, which had formed the basis of the legal code for three centuries, was abolished in 1840 and a Russian administrative system was introduced. The estates of the landowners who were suspected of supporting the uprising were confiscated and distributed to Russians. The treatment of the petty gentry, who were perceived as the most troublesome anti-Russian element, was particularly severe. Some forty thousand were deprived of their charters of nobility; many were deported to the Caucasus and the Russian interior. The Russians were also aware of the role of Catholicism in inspiring anti-tsarist sentiments and they acted accordingly. For the first time in Lithuania's history, the government subjected the Church to systematic persecution: two hundred ninety Catholic priests were arrested in the province (or guberniya) of Vilnius alone. In the diocese of Samogitia thirty-four Catholic monasteries and churches were closed between 1832 and 1850.

Dissident activity was no longer viewed with the

semi-indulgence of Alexander I. When a new conspiracy was discovered in the late 1830s, its leader, Szymon Konarski, was executed. Poles and Lithuanians now confined political expression to the thousands of activists, predominantly from among the nobility, who had fled to the West, including the aforementioned Lelewel and Mickiewicz. There, particularly in France, expatriates continued the debate over freedom and independence. Within the tsar's Empire, however, Nicholas's doctrine of "official nationality" — a reactionary blend of autocratic power, religious intolerance, and Russian chauvinism — became the guiding light of government policy.

The Church and Society Before 1861

Despite the new tsarist policy, the Catholic Church was able to contribute to the cultural progress of Lithuania, although in a different manner than in the past. Christianity was no longer the only major factor in the development of Lithuanian literature, as had been the case during the Reformation. However, Catholicism continued to play a role in preserving the language among the peasantry, although this role, as we shall see below, was ambiguous and even contradictory. One significant factor was the maintenance of the parochial school system, especially in Samogitia. Bishop J. A. Giedraitis (1754-1838), a scholarly man whose Lithuanian translation of the New Testament was published in 1816, directed every parish to maintain a primary school.

The system was greatly improved by Motiejus Valancius, who became bishop of Samogitia in 1850. An educator, an able Church administrator, a historian and ethnographer, as well as a talented writer, Valancius is undoubtedly one of the most versatile figures in Lithuanian history. Born in 1801 to a prosperous Samogitian peasant family, he attended the theological seminary in Vilnius. He met many fellow Samogitians in the city, including Simonas Daukantas, who was to become Valancius' friend. After graduation, Valancius spent several years in a remote parish in Belorussia, but his abilities were soon noticed and in 1845 he was appointed rector of the Varniai theological seminary. At that time, Valancius had enjoyed relatively good relations with the Russian authorities and they did not object when his name was proposed by the Holy See for the Samogitian episcopate, which had been vacant since 1838. Valancius was consecrated in 1850, the first peasant to hold the office, heretofore reserved for sons of the nobility. Some of the Polonized clergy and nobility openly scorned this peasant churchman who insisted on conversing with the villagers in their own language. Valancius was the first Samogitian bishop to publish Lithuanian pastoral letters in which he warned the peasants against various superstitions and coaxed them into learning to read. He devoted considerable energy to systematizing the Samogitian parish school system by demanding financial accounts and lists of students, personally supervising the building of new elementary schools, and keeping records on peasant literacy rates.

Effectively blocked from higher education, the Church was instrumental in stimulating the progress of popular Lithuanian literature. A much-admired author of the early nineteenth century was Antanas Strazdas (1760-1833), whose hymns and poems became immensely popular among the peasants; everywhere in Lithuania, the people adopted his works in numerous "folk" variations. In southwestern Lithuania, Father Antanas Tatare (1805-1889) published several widely read books of religious homilies and secular didactic stories during the 1840s and early 1850s. He glorified the bucolic enchantment of rural life and exhorted Lithuanian villagers to a moral life. Although unsophisticated by today's standards, these works were an improvement over the religious books and pamphlets of the eighteenth century that had been written in a Lithuanian so thoroughly Slavicized as to constitute a jargon all its own. Valancius once wrote that most of these old Lithuanian books contained such horrendously distorted language that some people "feared to take them into their hands." The Lithuanian books published in Lutheran East Prussia were of better quality, but their Gothic script made them difficult for Catholic peasants to read.

It was Bishop Valancius who singlehandedly did the most to develop Lithuanian letters before the end of the nineteenth century. In his desire to improve the lot and literature of the peasantry, he encouraged the publication of both religious and secular works; in fact, he wrote the best ones himself. The bishop published a series of religious and pro-temperance books for Lithuanian villagers, including a translation of Thomas à Kempis. Valancius supported the publishing efforts of Laurynas Ivinskis (1811-1881), a skilled popularizer of knowledge, whose *Kalendorius* (*Calendar*), a peasant almanac, combined practical farm advice, a survey of Lithuanian history, religious themes, and even poetry. And in a demonstration of his intellectual acumen, Valancius published the two-volume *Zemaijtiu wiskupiste* (*The Diocese of Samogitia*) in 1848, the first serious historical work in Lithuanian, a scholarly treatise still valued for its objectivity and use of sources. In later years, Valancius was to make his mark as a pioneer in Lithuanian fiction.

On the eve of the turbulent events of 1861-1864, Valancius dramatically emphasized the presence of the Church in the lives of the peasants. This was especially evident in his sponsorship of the temperance movement, one of the most interesting episodes in Lithuanian social history. The movement was a response to the plague of peasant drunkenness that by contemporary accounts had reached epidemic proportions during the nineteenth century. The temperance crusade originated in Ireland with Father Theobald Mathew's Total Abstinence Society in the 1830s. During the 1850s the abstinence drive had become popular in Lithuania and the Catholic Church took up the organization of peasant temperance fraternities. The clergy invited parishioners to join the movement and thousands of peasants responded. Their names were registered in the books of the "Golden Fraternity," and medals were issued to members. The temperance societies had a definite hierarchy led by the marshals of the parish chapters. This abstinence movement had a strong "revivalist" and emotional quality that occasionally led to some minor excesses: in some cases, heavy tipplers were forced to crawl around a church on their knees. Pastors occasionally locked up the boozers in church cellars, though in at least one instance this harsh method reportedly backfired: the confined drunkards raised such a din that they interrupted the Mass and had to be released.

While the temperance fraternities had their problematic moments and in the long run did not succeed in eliminating a serious social evil, the movement itself had a tremendous impact on the Lithuanian countryside. It encouraged the use of the national language among the peasantry, and the publication of Lithuanian antiliquor books and pamphlets stimulated the reading of popular Lithuanian literature. The response to the call for temperance also demonstrated the Church's power in organizing the peasant masses. In 1860 the total membership of the societies in Kaunas province approached seven hundred thousand. It is likely that the figure was at least a million for all of Lithuania. Such success brought on the opposition of those for whom the liquor monopoly provided an important and sometimes essential source of income: the tsarist government (tax receipts fell by more than half in the late 1850s) as well as the numerous innkeepers, especially the landowners and Jews. Most important, the very idea of an organized, militant peasantry was a challenge to the prevailing social and political order. Despite some obvious social benefits brought on by the militant teetotalers, such as a reduction in the crime rate, the tsarist regime banned the temperance fraternities in 1863.

It was no coincidence that the success of the temperance movement corresponded with the unrest that had been growing in the Lithuanian countryside and elsewhere in the Empire during the same period. Compounded by Russia's defeat in the Crimean War and the death of Nicholas I, peasant unrest waxed into a full-fledged agrarian crisis by the late 1850s. The major reason for the looming confrontation between village and estate was the peasantry's demand for an end to serfdom, particularly to the onerous manorial practice of exacting compulsory labor from the peasantry. By this time, the tsar himself recognized, even if some of his diehard nobles did not, that a major reform was necessary. In Poland and Lithuania, the crisis was amplified by the restlessness of the patriotic gentry, who began demanding freedom from Russian rule and precipitated the second of the century's violent uprisings, one that was to leave a decisive imprint on the Church and the Lithuanian nation.

The Crisis of 1861-1864 and Its Consequences

The revolutionary hopes that stirred Europe in 1848, the Russian defeat in the Crimean War, and the death of Nicholas I all helped dissipate the defeatism and apathy that had prevailed in Polish and Lithuanian society since the ill-fated venture of 1831. Initially, the new tsar, Alexander II, encouraged a kind of cautious liberalism. In Lithuania, this mood was represented by Vladimir Nazimov, the newly named governor-general, who presided over an easing of censorship and Russification. He also granted some concessions to the Catholic Church. The progressive gentry and intelligentsia now sought, as a minimum, the restoration of the pre-1831 situation, including the abolition of all restrictions on the Church.

However, as frequently happens in history, revolutionary impulses grew just as the situation seemed to improve. Dissatisfaction intensified when the tsar visited Vilnius in November of 1860 and informed the gentry that Lithuania would not receive administrative autonomy. For their part, the peasants were disappointed by the tsar's emancipation of the serfs (proclaimed in February 1861), which stipulated that the villagers on private estates were to continue performing compulsory labor for a transition period, after which they would have to purchase their land allotments through "redemption payments" over a forty-nine-year period. Agitators distributed leaflets among the peasants, informing them that the government aimed to destroy Catholicism. Priests harangued crowds of villagers on the obvious religious discrimination against Catholics. For the first time, a significant number of Jews also joined in the show of defiance against the tsar. As the anti-Russian mood grew, Lithuania and Poland experienced a period of constant disturbances. On February 27, 1861, five persons were killed when Russian troops opened fire on a crowd of demonstrators in Warsaw; another demonstration on April 8 resulted in the massacre of over a hundred Poles. Meanwhile in Lithuania, religious-patriotic demonstrations, often culminating in the singing of seditious hymns in Catholic churches, spread throughout the country. On August 18, 1861, between sixty and eighty people died in Vilnius when a gathering of some thirty thousand people was attacked by Cossacks.

Armed revolt broke out in Poland in January 1863 and the underground Lithuanian Committee declared itself the provisional government in Lithuania on February 1, 1863, calling upon the populace to rise up against the Russians. The rebels issued a decree providing land to the peasants without charge and granting them full citizenship. While the leaders of the insurrection were split into radical "Red" (mainly the petty gentry and the peasants) and moderate "White" (predominantly noble landowners) factions, they managed to coordinate military action. Encouraged by British and French diplomatic protests against Russian repression, the insurgents seized much of the country by the summer of 1863, confining the Russian Army to the cities and towns. The chief commander of the rebellion in Lithuania and Belorussia was Zygmunt Sierakowski (1827-1863), but its best-known heroes were Konstantin Kalinowski (1838-1864) and Father Antanas Mackevicius (Mackiewicz in Polish) (1828-1863), a Samogitian priest who organized bands of peasant guerrillas.

Despite widespread popular support from virtually all the social strata in Lithuania, the rebellion was eventually crushed by the Russians' superior numbers, equipment, and training, although fighting continued in parts of Samogitia until the fall of 1864. The arrival of the new governor-general, Michael Muraviev (popularly known as "The Hangman"), in May of 1863 signaled a wave of unprecedented repression. More than fifty villages were burned as "collective punishment," over a thousand gentry estates were confiscated, more than two hundred persons were publicly executed, and thousands were exiled to Siberia. In addition to military measures and his policy of terror, Muraviev also introduced a policy of intense Russification aimed at the Church and the Polonized nobility, the two forces that in his opinion had sparked the uprising. In 1864 Lithuanian books in the Latin alphabet were banned (an important measure discussed in more detail below). Among the additional steps taken against the Church were the closing of Catholic houses of worship: six churches and sixteen monasteries were liquidated in Samogitia alone. New restrictions concerning ecclesiastical administration and the appointment of priests were announced. The Polish language was banned from the school system and many Polish-speaking officials were dismissed. The entire Lithuanian Catholic primary school system was closed. At the same time, Muraviev tried to curry favor with the Lithuanian-speaking village by improving the economic conditions of the Emancipation, but these measures failed to gain much good will for the tsarist regime.

Muraviev believed that his policies would lead to the end of Catholic influence and "Polish" power in Lithuania. Once these twins of anti-Russian agitation were overcome, he assumed, Lithuania would become a Russian province in fact as well as in name, since the peasantry (whom he perceived as a collective intellectual tabula rasa) would easily absorb Russian culture and Orthodox religion. In retrospect, by provoking opposition among the peasantry, Muraviev's repressive policies actually promoted the growth of national consciousness. The insurgents had called upon the peasants to defend "their country and Christ's teachings." More than in 1831, rebel commanders, such as Mackevicius and Kalinowski, addressed their followers in Lithuanian and

Belorussian respectively, the languages of the peasantry. Mikalojus Akelaitis, a Lithuanian writer who was a rebel leader in southwestern Lithuania, published political propaganda aimed at gaining peasant support. Mackevicius, who was executed in 1863, wished to "awaken the Lithuanian nation," which could choose its own destiny in some kind of federation, preferably with a democratic Poland. Kalinowski believed in the right of Lithuanians and Belorussians to statehood and to their own national culture; on the eve of his execution in 1864, he warned the Russians that they underestimated the task of assimilating the Lithuanian peasantry. As a transitional figure, however, Kalinowski was still ethnically confused: he called himself a "Lithuanian," wrote to the peasants in Belorussian but actually hailed from the Polonized gentry. Men like Mackevicius and Kalinowski were not yet the modern nationalists of the next generation, but they understood that justice to the peasantry meant addressing the national issue, a fact now understood even by some Poles.

The crisis of 1861-1864 constituted a turning point in Lithuanian history, although in a different sense than that anticipated by Russian Slavophiles. Historian Manfred Hellmann perceptively wrote that the great insurrection of 1863 "saw, for the last time, Lithuanians fighting under Polish leadership for the restoration of a united Polish-Lithuanian political structure." This violent event also initiated the decline of the cultural and social influence of the Polonized nobility in Lithuania; conversely, it signaled the emergence of the Lithuanian-speaking peasantry as the new social and political force within the country. The peasantry had little interest in restoring the old commonwealth, that glorious "Gentry Republic" of the past. They sought a new identity. In this search, the Catholic Church played a most important role.

Catholicism and the Struggle for Lithuanian Culture

Bishop Motiejus Valancius had viewed the troubles of 1861-1864 with great apprehension. The situation placed him in a quandary. While he was an advocate of

134

reform, Valancius was no revolutionary and thus in late 1862 he appealed to the clergy to stay out of politics. In May of 1863, within days of Muraviev's arrival, Bishop Adam Krasinski of Vilnius was deported to Russia. Fearing further Russian retaliation against the Church and seeing no chance for the rebellion's success, Valancius favored the cessation of armed resistance. In September 1863 he issued a pastoral letter urging the insurgents to lay down their arms and submit to the tsar, promising the people mercy from their rulers. This action angered the rebels, who proclaimed Valancius a traitor, yet it did not result in smooth relations between the tsarist authorities and the Church. The Russians were deeply suspicious of the bishop; for his part, Valancius felt that the government's failure to grant amnesty to the rebels had undermined his prestige. In May of 1864 Valancius was ordered to transfer the seat of his diocese from the historic town of Varniai to Kaunas, an action that angered the Samogitian clergy and people. The closing of his cherished school system and the restrictions on the Church now led to confrontations between Valancius and the Russians. When the bishop ignored Russian restrictions, he was fined and harassed.

In the summer of 1864 Muraviev announced what seemed at the time a minor official regulation that was to have an enormous impact on the development of the Lithuanian national movement. Muraviev forbade the publication of Lithuanian books in the Latin alphabet; henceforth, only Lithuanian books published in the Russian Cyrillic script would be permitted. The prohibition was formalized into a comprehensive press ban on all Lithuanian publications in the Latin alphabet in September of 1865 by Governor-General C. P. Kaufman, Muraviev's successor, and was soon extended to the whole Russian Empire. In August 1865 the government established a commission for reviewing Lithuanian-language publications, which concluded that they were "filled with anti-Russian propaganda . . . and agitation against the dominant religion of the state — Orthodoxy." At first, Valancius did not oppose the press ban and even gave his reluctant imprimatur to the first Cyrillic Lithuanian book. However, very soon he changed his mind and in a dramatic turnabout condemned the use of the new alphabet. The bishop concluded that this Cyrillic "reform" was simply a means by which the Russians hoped to wean the peasants away from Catholic education and thereby undermine the Church.

The Russian attempt to introduce the Cyrillic alphabet failed miserably. Very few Lithuanian peasants could read the Russian letters. The strange, exotic shapes of the new script only provoked the villagers' fertile imaginations. Possibly encouraged by some local clergy, the peasants found that a few of the Cyrillic characters bore uncanny resemblance to icon candles, the steeples of Russian churches, or the Orthodox double cross. The Lithuanian Catholic peasant was deeply wary of anything that smacked of the religion of the "Muscovites" and this, more than anything, doomed the Russian government's Cyrillic reform. The "sacrilegious" books with their weird script were being thrown into the oven even before Bishop Valancius urged the people to do so.

Reluctantly, but with good reason, Valancius concluded that the government's ultimate goal was no less than the conversion of the Lithuanian peasantry to Orthodoxy. He now organized an active anti-Russian and anti-Orthodox campaign. Valancius began by writing a number of polemical brochures against the government's anti-Catholic policies, endeavoring to strengthen the Lithuanian peasants to resist Orthodox propaganda. The titles of his works published in the late 1860s are illustrative: *Brolej Katalikaj* (*Catholic Brothers*); *Perspieimas apej Szwenta Wiera* (*A Warning Concerning the Holy Faith*); *Szniakesis Katalika su nekataliku* (*A Dialogue of a Catholic and Non-Catholic*); *Wargai Bazniczios Kataliku Lietuwoj ir Zemajcziusi* (*The Woes of the Catholic Faith in Lithuania and Samogitia*). In these booklets Valancius gave the peasants detailed instructions on meeting the Russian challenge. He warned them that they could "lose their faith" by reading Cyrillic books and urged them to burn all Lithuanian texts that used the Russian alphabet. Valancius advised peasants to "protect their children from the Russian schools," which, he said, were intended to convert Catholic children to Orthodoxy. The people were told to teach pupils at home using old Lithuanian prayer books; in fact, for Lithuania this domestic "school of the spinning wheel" became a symbol of resistance to tsarism. Valancius also appealed to the peasants' sense of nationality. "How can the Russians demand that, at their pleasure, the people here learn Russian?" he wrote indignantly. "Let them learn Lithuanian."

Valancius also solved the practical problem of the press ban. He dipped into the episcopal treasury to finance the printing of his books across the border in Lithuanian East Prussia, mainly in Tilsit. The books were then smuggled into Russian Lithuania by either idealists or, more often, professional smugglers. This was the real beginning of the "book carrier" movement (*knygnesiai* in Lithuanian), which in later years became a well-organized network for the distribution of illegal literature. The *knygnesiai* became the heroes of the Lithuanian national movement in the nineteenth century; they were seen as its foot soldiers and martyrs by later generations. Some of the best-known book smugglers were priests. Father Martynas Sidaravicius (1829-1907), the pastor in the border town of Sudargas, was one of the most effective organizers of the illegal distribution network. Sidaravicius coordinated the printing of over thirty Lithuanian Catholic publications in tens of thousands of copies in Prussia, and in the early days he himself transported books into Lithuania, eluding the border patrol. The underground book-smuggling network established by Sidaravicius was later utilized for the distribution of nationalist and anti-Russian, rather than strictly religious, publications. Another zealous priest who helped launch the *knygnesiai* movement was Silvestras Gimzauskas (1844-1897), whose poetry of national reawakening provided an inspiration for young Lithuanian writers.

Valancius' abilities as a scholar have already been mentioned. He also made an enormous contribution to the development of modern Lithuanian literature, particularly the secular prose, most of which he wrote during the press ban. Valancius' works tended to be didactic in nature, portraying the virtues and vices of everyday life. The best of this genre is the delightful narrative *Palangos Juze* (*Juze of Palanga*), a collection of tales about the journeys of a village tailor, containing many colorful descriptions of the customs and mores of the people. This book went through many editions and was probably the most widely read work of fiction in nineteenth-century Lithuania. Valancius' *Vaiku knygele* (*The Little Book for Children*) and his *Paaugusiu zmoniu knygele* (*The Little Book for Older Folks*) were very popular as well. Valancius' literary style was extremely rich and varied but preserved an essentially folk character. His descriptions of village life became models for subsequent Lithuanian realist authors.

In the years between 1870 and 1875 Valancius represented the direction of the Lithuanian national movement. He tied the survival of Lithuanian cultural life to that of the Catholic Church, and for this reason the initial period of the national movement was strongly religious in character. But the Catholic hierarchy did not guide the movement for long. After Valancius' death in the spring of 1875, the bishop's office was occupied by men who were at best neutral toward Lithuanian national aspirations. The Samogitian rank-and-file clergy were drawn into the Lithuanian movement, but much of the Church hierarchy remained in the hands of men with a Polish orientation.

The Church and the Emergence of Modern Lithuanian Nationalism

A secular, nationally conscious Lithuanian intelligentsia emerged during Valancius' last years. This new elite consisted primarily of the student children of well-to-do peasants. The majority came from the prosperous regions of southwestern Lithuania, particularly from the area around Marijampole (present-day Kapsukas). The end of serfdom had given these peasant sons a chance at a higher education and most of them attended universities in St. Petersburg, Moscow, and Warsaw. As their numbers grew they formed student associations in which they discussed the political and ideological issues of the time.

In the beginning, this Lithuanian "peasant" intelligentsia faced a kind of identity crisis, a predicament arising out of nineteenth-century Lithuania's social and political milieu. The Polonized upper crust felt superior to these peasant upstarts, and for their part the village intelligentsia resented the traditionally privileged position of the Poles. Given the general climate, the Lithuanian students were unable to ally themselves with the Orthodox Russians, as no doubt the government would have preferred. There remained a third alternative for peasant students: to base their identity on the Lithuanian-speaking countryside. The emergence of an educated class that was not going to turn its back on the village was the real beginning of the modern Lithuanian nation.

The two foremost figures of the Lithuanian national movement were typical of this new intelligentsia. The most august and widely respected figure was Jonas Basanavicius (1851-1927), who was born into a prosperous peasant family in Suwalki province. Like thousands of other Lithuanian children, Basanavicius learned his letters at home from the village tutors, mostly organists, sacristans, or pious old women; prayer books and readers were his first textbooks. Typically, his devout parents saw a formal education as the road to the priesthood and with this in mind sent him to the secondary school in Marijampole, the educational and cultural center of the Uznemune region. However, Basanavicius soon developed a curiosity for secular rather than religious studies. His faith weakened when he read Polish translations of French agnostic writers. After graduation, he informed his parents that he lacked a vocation and proposed to attend the University of Moscow. Basanavicius' father swore that he would not contribute a kopeck to his son's education unless the latter enrolled in the seminary, while his mother wept through the long arguments between father and son that went on for days. However, young Basanavicius finally prevailed and departed for Moscow with a hundred rubles sown into his pocket.

This struggle of pious fathers and worldly sons is a powerful theme in Lithuanian life and literature. It can be grasped only if one understands the awe and respect that the Catholic clergy commanded as well as the temporal and spiritual power they exercised within the traditional Lithuanian village. One of the "secular sons," a well-known Lithuanian leftist, described this aura of the priest as well as anyone:

> He [the priest] had unchallenged power, not only in matters concerning the soul, but in temporal life as well. He was the light which, like the lantern in front of the church altar, shone in the parish day and night. He was the judge who could condemn a man through confession, scold him publicly from the pulpit . . . or privately while visiting the peasant home. . . . The priest was God's unassailable representative. The aureole that surrounded him spread from the altar to the rectory, and from there throughout the village. A part of the halo would be shared by the priest's parents and relatives. What, then, was a doctor, an engineer or even a lawyer before the priest?*

At Moscow Basanavicius took up history and philology but soon discovered that he could not abide the anti-Catholic prejudices of his conservative Russian professors. He transferred to the faculty of medicine but continued his extensive research in Lithuanian history and archaeology. Since the Russian authorities discouraged his return to Lithuania, Basanavicius obtained a position in newly independent Bulgaria where (except for a brief spell in Bohemia) he resided for the next twenty-five years. Despite the distance from his homeland, he

---

*Steponas Kairys, *Lietuva budo* (*Lithuania Awoke*) (New York, 1957), pp. 37-38.

gained his reputation as the dean of the Lithuanian national movement by inspiring the publication of the first Lithuanian secular newspaper for Russia's Lithuanians in 1883. It was appropriately called *Auszra (The Dawn)* and it gave its name to an entire generation of Lithuanian intelligentsia. Politically conservative, the new journal emphasized the need to preserve and develop the Lithuanian language and, equally important, it displayed none of the awe toward Polish culture that had characterized earlier generations of educated Lithuanians.

Auszra and the new intelligentsia were not without opposition. When Dr. Jonas Sliupas (1861-1944), an avowed liberal and freethinker, became its chief editor in 1884, the journal lost support among some of the Catholic clergy. For the most part, Lithuania's Polonized nobility viewed Lithuanian nationalism with a mixture of consternation and hostility; some hoped that the insistence of young, educated Lithuanians in speaking their own "village dialect" among themselves was a passing fad. Contrary to these expectations, which in fact simply revealed the nobility's isolation from social reality, the Lithuanian national movement achieved both maturity and diversity during the last decade of the nineteenth century. Under the leadership of Vincas Kudirka (1858-1899) and his liberal monthly *Varpas (The Bell)*, which appeared in 1889, it became more militant and political. Kudirka, the author and composer of Lithuania's national anthem, hailed from the same social class, region, and secondary school as Basanavicius. He experienced similar conflicts, emphatically rejecting Polish and Russian culture as well as his father's insistence on entering the priesthood. After graduating the University of Warsaw in medicine, Kudirka devoted most of his time to the national cause. His own brand of emotional nationalism was not based on the defense of the Catholic faith, as in the case of Bishop Valancius, or on the apolitical romanticism of Basanavicius: its driving force was a sense of national injustice and a militant defense of democratic values. Well known as a brilliant satirist, Kudirka attacked the press ban as barbaric, ridiculed the corrupt Russian bureaucracy, and urged Lithuanians to gain economic power by entering commercial and professional occupations, which until now had been the almost exclusive province of Lithuania's minorities: the Jews, Poles, Germans, and Russians. In short, he addressed most of Lithuania's economic and social problems of the day.

It would be wrong to view the secular intelligentsia as a replacement for the Church's role within the Lithuanian national movement. Rather, it expanded national life in new directions. The Church retained the loyalty of the vast majority of Lithuanians. Perhaps, for this reason, renewed attacks on the Catholic Church and intensified Russification characterized Lithuania during the 1880s and 1890s. These actions were part of the so-called tsarist policy of "bureaucratic nationalism" inspired by the influential archconservative Russian philosopher Konstantin Pobedonostsev (1827-1907), who advocated intense efforts to undermine Catholicism and proselytize Orthodoxy. The importance of Catholicism in Lithuanian national life and its confrontation with Russian rule was tragically revealed during a bloody incident in November of 1893, popularly known as the Kraziai Massacre, the most dramatic and violent in a series of repressions that were symptomatic of the growing rift between the tsarist regime and the Lithuanian people. No event of the nineteenth century so infuriated Catholic Lithuania.

The Kraziai story began in 1891 when I. S. Kakhanov, the governor-general of Vilnius, ordered the liquidation of the local Benedictine monastery and the parish church. The government could not have chosen a worse place for a showdown: the town of Kraziai had been a revered cultural and religious center in Samogitia since the fifteenth century. On November 9, 1893, Gen. N. Klingenberg, the governor of Kaunas province, arrived in Kraziai with a detachment of police and ordered the dispersal of crowds that had gathered to protect the threatened church. The people, displaying a cross and the portrait of the tsar, refused to obey. A melee ensued, the

142

police were overpowered, and the humiliated governor was pursued to the choir loft by an enraged mob of Lithuanian peasants. Klingenberg managed to hold off the crowd at gunpoint through the night until a punitive force of Cossacks arrived in the morning and stormed the church. After the people were subdued, the Cossacks went on a rampage; in addition to the usual looting, burning, and public floggings, scores were injured, women were raped, and at least nine persons were killed. Outrage was universal. In later years, even Marxist parties evoked the tragedy of Kraziai in their anti-tsarist propaganda. In *Varpas*, Kudirka compared Alexander II to Ivan the Terrible and Klingenberg to the infamous Muraviev. The trial of the fifty-five men and sixteen women accused of "rebellion" took place in the fall of 1894 and became a sensation. A team of sympathetic liberal Russian lawyers skillfully turned the tables and placed the regime itself on trial. In the end, the tsar amnestied most of the accused, but this did little to assuage the population's resentment.

As the national movement gained strength during the 1890s it began to reflect the prevailing political and ideological spectrum. On the left, the first tiny Marxist groups appeared and a Lithuanian Social Democratic Party was founded in 1896. On the right, dissatisfied with *Varpas*'s coolness toward Catholicism, Kazimieras Pakalniskis, a conservative and militant priest, established *Lietuvos ir Zemaiciu Apzvalga (The Lithuanian and Samogitian Review)* in 1891. The *Apzvalga* spent much of its time rebuffing the liberal *Varpas*, but it reserved its most scathing attacks for the Russians, who were dubbed the "servants of Lucifer." While popular with the peasants, this militant Catholic paper proved too anachronistic for much of the younger Lithuanian clergy, who desired cooperation with the secular nationalists. The young priests established the *Tevynes Sargas (Guardian of the Fatherland)*, which replaced *Apzvalga* and became the leading pre-independence Catholic periodical. The *Tevynes Sargas* became the seed of the future Lithuanian Christian Democratic Party.

The twofold Lithuanian national struggle against both Russian tsarism and the Polish nobility was mirrored by an emerging conflict within the Catholic Church itself. Some of the rank-and-file clergy were dissatisfied with the hierarchy's relatively passive response to the Kraziai incident and the other instances of Russian repression. Even more divisive was the clash of the young Lithuanian clergy with some of the conservative Polonized Church leadership over the issue of language and national culture. Here it is important to recall that the Catholic Church had pursued an ambiguous and contradictory course on the national issue: while throughout the nineteenth century some churchmen had fostered Lithuanian culture, powerful Polish elements of the hierarchy had simultaneously pressed a policy of Polonization. For example, Pawel Straszynski, the bishop of Sejny between 1837 and 1847, publicly insulted Lithuanian as a "language of sheep" and abolished Lithuanian-language services in many parishes. While such militancy was certainly not the norm, it occurred frequently enough to create tensions between Poles and Lithuanians. Among the clergy, the battle was sharpest within the seminaries, particularly those of Kaunas and Sejny, where young students became increasingly attracted to the Lithuanian national movement, often against the wishes of their conservative professors. The struggle of young Lithuanian curates and their Polonized pastors, the "battle in the rectories," became a favorite theme in modern Lithuanian literature. In real life, the ambiguities and inner conflicts of the Polish-Lithuanian conundrum were played out within the person of Antanas Baranauskas (1835-1902), one of the most popular lyrical poets in the Lithuanian language and bishop of Sejny from 1897 to 1902. Initially an enthusiastic supporter of Lithuanian national culture and much admired as a writer, he became a political anachronism in his later years when he denounced the national movement for its anti-Polish separatism and endorsed a Polish-Lithuanian union. Perhaps appropriately, his classic poem *Anyksciu silelis (The Pine Grove of Anyksciai)* is still a favorite recitation for schoolchildren, but paradoxically Baranauskas's mausoleum in Sejny bears his Polish name of Antoni Baranowski.

Gradually, the majority of the younger clergy adopted the values of the nineteenth-century Lithuanian national movement, including its democratic peasant orientation, and in fact provided it with some of its greatest writers and leaders. Canon Jonas Maciulis-Maironis (1862-1932) became the master of lyric poetry in modern standard Lithuanian and is still revered today as the bard of the national renaissance, best known for his popular collection of poems, *Pavasario balsai* (*Voices of Spring*). Another priest, Juozas Tumas-Vaizgantas (1869-1932), was the greatest Lithuanian prose writer of his generation, unparalleled in his vivid descriptions of village life. His novel *Pragiedruliai* (*Sunrays*) was the first and, some say, best novel about the national movement. He also became known as a commentator and public figure of unusual tolerance and vision. Both Maironis and Vaizgantas played important roles in the modernization of Lithuanian culture. The newly assertive Lithuanian clergy became interested in social issues as well, inspired by the progressive ideas in the encyclicals of Leo XIII and by the general revival of Catholic learning that followed the reign of the conservative Pius IX.

The disagreements of the Polish and Lithuanian clergy were naturally confined to disputations in Lithuania's seminaries, rectories, and ecclesiastical offices. Unfortunately, the conflicts of Catholic laymen were expressed in more ferocious terms. In one of the darker pages of Church history, the issue of language in church services turned violent in dozens of the mixed Polish-Lithuanian parishes at the turn of the century, particularly in the dioceses of Vilnius and Sejny. Some churches were closed as partisans of the different languages resorted to bricks and bats in settling the issue of which language was best for prayer. This was proof, if any were needed, that since the Church was not an island, it could hardly escape unscathed from the social and national changes that had seized nineteenth-century Lithuania.

Despite its problems and growing pains, the national movement proceeded apace. By the end of the century, the number of illegal Lithuanian publications circulating throughout Lithuania increased, including dozens of new periodicals distributed by a well-organized secret network. About a third of the illegal press now came from the United States, where thousands of Lithuanians had emigrated by the turn of the century. Even the Russian bureaucracy came to acknowledge the futility of the press ban, the most glaring symbol of national oppression. Clearly, the ban antagonized the Lithuanians without retarding the development of their national consciousness. In 1903 Governor-General P. D. Sviatopolk-Mirsky reported that during the previous dozen years nearly two hundred thousand items of illegal Lithuanian literature had been confiscated at the German-Russian border. Assuming that the majority of the publications evaded capture, it can be estimated that despite the efforts of the authorities more than a million pieces of literature had reached Lithuania during the forty years of the press ban. In any event, the Russo-Japanese War and the need for internal unity persuaded the tsar to lift the ban on Lithuanian publications in the Latin alphabet in April 1904.

The Lithuanian Nation at the Turn of the Century

Before turning to the events preceding the First World War, it might be useful to briefly review the state of Lithuania and its people after a century of change. At the beginning of the twentieth century, the Lithuanians were a vastly different people from what they had been when the Polish-Lithuanian Commonwealth ended in 1795. In economic and social terms, the most important change was the end of serfdom. It is almost symbolic that Lithuania's first railroad became operational in April 1861, only a month after the tsar announced the emancipation. During the last quarter of the century Lithuania saw the beginnings of industrialization that were, however, modest even by the standards of the backward Russian Empire. On the other hand, Lithua-

146

nian agriculture developed more quickly, with the result that Lithuania had a somewhat higher standard of living than much of the rest of the Empire (despite the fact that it was industrially less developed). Characteristically, when the pace of industrialization quickened during the 1890s, food processing still made up the largest single industrial sector.

Although Lithuania remained predominantly agricultural, the cities grew. Vilnius tripled in size from a population of just under forty-seven thousand in 1823 to over one hundred fifty thousand in 1897. During the same period the population of Kaunas increased tenfold while the smaller towns grew less quickly. The commercial and professional urban classes were still primarily represented by the Jews and Poles, whereas the Russians and Germans made up a significant minority. More than half of urban workers were Jews and about a quarter were Poles. Only about ten percent of the small industrial working class were Lithuanians. The formation of an urban Lithuanian middle class was still in its infancy at the turn of the century; according to the census of 1897, Lithuanians managed less than four percent of urban commerce and about twelve percent of the rural trade. The number of Lithuanians in the cities grew somewhat more quickly after the turn of the century; when the First World War broke out, they constituted almost a quarter of Kaunas's population, the second largest national group after the Jews. According to the Russian census of 1897 ethnic Lithuanians made up only two percent of the inhabitants in Vilnius, the historic capital. The vast majority of Lithuanian-speaking people in 1900 were still peasants. However, unlike a century before, the majority of villagers owned land, and a large minority could be classed as well-to-do. By the standards of the Russian Empire, the Lithuanian peasantry enjoyed a relatively high literacy rate of about fifty percent, a remarkable feat considering the press ban and the enforced absence of native-language schools.

The population of the ethnographically Lithuanian lands grew steadily during the nineteenth century: from an estimated 2,100,000 in 1846 to 2,350,000 in 1861, and about 3,300,000 in 1897 (including Lithuanian East Prussia). Population density more than doubled during the same period. Lithuanian speakers made up roughly seventy percent of ethnographic Lithuania in 1861 or about 1,650,000 of the total population. Yet, while the population on the whole increased, the percentage of ethnic Lithuanians actually declined during the century, a phenomenon caused by two demographic factors. One was the progressive Slavicization of eastern Lithuania, where many villagers assimilated into the Polish or Belorussian-speaking communities. The second was emigration, a process that gained momentum during the 1880s and achieved massive scale during the decade preceding the Great War, as the First World War was called. Emigration created an enormous diaspora, mainly in America. At least a quarter million Lithuanians arrived in the United States between 1899 and 1914 while additional thousands emigrated to Britain, Canada, and other destinations. As a rule, the lot of the emigrants, so aptly portrayed in Upton Sinclair's *Jungle*, was not an easy one, and understandably the majority came from the land-hungry peasantry. Within the Russian Empire, many thousands flocked to the major industrial centers; by 1913 there were over forty thousand Lithuanians in St. Petersburg, an estimated thirty-five thousand in Riga, and at least seven thousand in Odessa.

Emigration and assimilation thus made it certain that the Lithuanian-speaking population experienced little growth during the second half of the nineteenth century. At the same time, Lithuania as a whole, and the Lithuanian nation in particular, underwent enormous change. The economy seemingly still preserved many of the characteristics of 1795: a weakly developed industrial structure, an aristocratic minority with large landholdings, and an overwhelmingly rural population. Yet appearances were deceptive, for, below the surface, life had been altered drastically. The nobility had lost most of its prestige and influence, whereas the prosperous landed peasantry along with a budding middle and working class had transformed the real balance of social power in Lithuania. As we have seen, the Lithuanian intelligentsia, which emerged from the increasingly assertive village, rejected both the government's Russification and the nobility's Polish heritage. The basis for modern Lithuanian culture was created.

The spirit of the Lithuanian national movement slowly penetrated the Church, the towns, and to a limited extent the gentry's salons. From the latter, a small but growing number of women entered the mainstream of the Lithuanian intelligentsia as "refugees" from the Polonized gentry. (In general, formal education was closed to peasant daughters.) Julia Zymantas (1845-1921), writing under the pen name Zemaite (Lithuanian for "The Samogitian Woman"), was an author of leftist views who sometimes inclined toward anticlerical themes. By contrast, Marija Peckauskas (1878-1930), better known as Satrijos Ragana ("The Witch of Satrija"), became one of the country's prominent Catholic writers, chronicling the social and moral demise of Lithuania's gentry. As Lithuanian national life became more diverse and complex it escaped the village milieu in a process of modernization that transformed not only Lithuania's society and economy but its cultural life as well.

Revolution and War (1905-1915)

The population had little time to consider the consequences and opportunities presented by the legalization of the Lithuanian press in 1904 (limited, of course, to non-subversive publications). The initial defeats suffered by the Russian Empire at the hands of the Japanese helped provoke the Revolution of 1905. In Lithuania, the revolution manifested itself in different ways, reflecting the country's ethnic and economic diversity. The strikes and demonstrations of the country's small industrial working class did not reflect Lithuanian national aspirations; within this group, ethnic Lithuanians were the minority. On the other hand, the spontaneous rural disturbances that engulfed Lithuania between 1905 and 1907 revolved around the issue of national and religious rights. Armed bands of Lithuanian peasants attacked government rural schools, expelling hundreds of Russian teachers. Unlike the Russian peasantry, Lithuanian villagers had little faith in the myth of a "good tsar" deceived by evil advisers; in many places the portraits of Nicholas and Alexandra were vandalized or destroyed. In numerous petitions and declarations, the peasants expressed specific grievances and demands: an end to the privileged position of the Orthodox Church; the introduction of primary and secondary education in the Lithuanian language; the appointment of Catholics to local government positions; the conducting of official business in the native language. In many of their rallies, the Lithuanian villagers demanded national rights for the Jews and Belorussians as well.

For the Lithuanians, the events of 1905 culminated in what has become known as the Great Assembly of Vilnius (Didysis Vilniaus Seimas in Lithuanian), the first modern Lithuanian political convention, which opened under the chairmanship of Jonas Basanavicius on December 4, 1905, and was attended by over two thousand delegates. A slight majority were peasants and there were over a hundred Catholic clergy. The Vilnius assembly represented virtually the entire Lithuanian political spectrum, ranging from the rightists and Catholics to the liberals and Social Democrats. After a few days of deliberations, the assembly issued a resolution demanding an autonomous, democratic Lithuania with full national rights for all of its ethnic groups; it described reactionary tsarism as the "irreconcilable enemy" of the Lithuanian people and counseled passive resistance until the objectives of the assembly were met.

Anxiously conciliatory at first, the government seized upon repressive measures as the revolution weakened and the army remained loyal. During 1906 and 1907 the regime of Prime Minister Peter Stolypin sent out punitive expeditions to the Lithuanian countryside. They included units of the notorious "Black Hundreds," rightist goon squads that terrorized the non-Russian populace. To instill terror, the Black Hundreds actually shelled some towns and villages with artillery. By 1907 the revolutionary disturbances in Lithuania had died down, and during the years of the Stolypin regime (1906-1911) the policies of Russification and political repression were revived.

However, the Russian government found it impossible to return entirely to the arbitrary autocracy of the past. As a result of promises made by the tsar, the Duma (Russia's first modern parliament) was created. A genuine opposition and legal political parties now made their appearance in Lithuania. Martynas Ycas, a member of the moderate Constitutional Democratic (Cadet) Party, became Lithuania's best-known politician in the Duma. Although a Lutheran, Ycas ably defended Catholic causes. Another deputy was Father Juozas Laukaitis, a conservative priest from the Suwalki region. In general, the elections to the various Dumas stimulated the development of political maturity among the Lithuanians. In some elections the peasants' deputies joined forces with the Jews to offset the bias of the electoral laws that were tilted toward the landowners. Lithuanian politicians managed to present the "Lithuanian Question" before Russian society as more than just an ethnographic curiosity, explaining the national and social aspirations of their constituents. The political process also resulted in the continued development of Lithuanian political parties that reflected the emergence of various Lithuanian social classes and interests. The most extreme of the Social Democrats turned toward Bolshevism, whereas the moderates retained faith in representative democracy. The middle-class parties developed liberal and conservative wings that went beyond the old ideology of Kudirka's *Varpas*: a new organization of Populists confronted peasant issues. The Lithuanian Christian Democratic Union was formed for Catholics. In 1907 they began the publication of *Draugija (Association)*, a monthly that emphasized a moderate political program designed to appeal to nationally conscious Lithuanians. All the parties favored, at the very least, a political program of wide-ranging autonomy for Lithuania, including the demand for some kind of parliament in Vilnius.

The outbreak of the Great War in August of 1914 did not initially affect Lithuanian attitudes toward the Russian Empire. Some of the Lithuanian leadership, while dissatisfied with the Russian response to their demands, formally supported the tsarist government, hoping that the Russians would unite the Lithuanian lands in East Prussia with those in Russian Lithuania. However, the early Russian military successes were soon reversed and in the spring of 1915 the German Army entered Lithuania. The Russians were driven out by the end of the year and the tsar's army was never to return. For Lithuania, this was to mean the beginning of a new era, fraught with both possibilities and perils.

CHAPTER 7

Catholics in the Republic of Lithuania

This chapter deals with the Church and Lithuania during the two decades of the country's independence, a period marked by political, social, and economic changes more rapid than any in Lithuania's previous history. The political shifts are outlined below in three general areas: (1) the initial battle for independence; (2) the period of multiparty democracy; and (3) the years of the authoritarian regime of Antanas Smetona. The place of the Church in Lithuanian society will be examined against the backdrop of the country's overall internal development. Finally, there is a brief overview of the international political crisis as it affected Lithuania in the final years of the republic's independence.

The Great War and the Struggle for Independence

The Russian retreat of 1915 and the subsequent German occupation of Lithuania caused destruction and dislocation on a scale that the country had not seen since the wars and famine of the late seventeenth and early eighteenth centuries. It is estimated that as the Russians withdrew, about a half million of Lithuania's inhabitants, including some three hundred thousand ethnic Lithuanians, either fled or were forcibly evacuated to the Russian interior. In November of 1914 the Central Committee for Assistance to Victims of the War was established in Vilnius. Following the German occupation of Vilnius in September of 1915, a part of the war-relief committee was transferred to Petrograd. Despite wartime conditions, the committee not only dispensed relief but managed to create Lithuanian public and educational institutions to look after the displaced Lithuanians. It established hundreds of Lithuanian primary schools and several fine secondary institutions, particularly in the central Russian city of Voronezh, which became an important Lithuanian cultural and religious center during the war. In the absence of any other viable organizations, this war-relief committee became, in effect, a government-in-exile for Russia's dispossessed Lithuanians.

The part of the committee based in Lithuania itself had the unenviable task of dealing with the German occupation. Between 1915 and 1918 Lithuania was governed by a German military administration that ruthlessly exploited Lithuania's economy for the war effort, especially through agricultural requisitions and forced labor. Initially confident of victory, the Germans planned to annex Lithuania and other adjacent territories, envisioning grandiose plans of conquest in the East disturbingly reminiscent of later Nazi fantasies. However, a series of complex and interrelated events, beginning with the outbreak of the Russian revolution in 1917 and culminating with the defeat of the Kaiser's armies in the West, forced the Germans to reluctantly accommodate Lithuanian political aspirations. The March revolution of 1917 in Russia, which dethroned the tsar, gave Lithuanians an opportunity to voice their demands concerning the future of the country. In May 1917, despite bitter divisions between socialist and conservative forces, a Lithuanian convention in Petrograd passed a resolution demanding an independent Lithuanian state. The October Bolshevik revolution effectively put an end to organized Lithuanian activity in Russia itself, including the organization of ethnic Lithuanian military units.

In German-occupied Lithuania, the military administration had driven the population to the brink of famine, but the initially bleak political situation gradually improved. On December 11, 1917, the recently created Lithuanian council, known as the Taryba, issued a resolution declaring Lithuania's independence from Russia. However, under German pressure, it proclaimed the establishment of a Lithuanian state that fostered close military and economic ties with Germany amounting to the creation of a protectorate. This situation failed to satisfy many Lithuanians; thus on February 16, 1918, the Taryba issued a declaration of independence, which, much to German displeasure, proclaimed the establishment of an independent, democratic Lithuanian state with no mention of any special relationship with Germany. The failure of the German offensive in the West during the spring of 1918 and the armistice of November 11 gave the Lithuanians more leeway. In addition, Lithuanians abroad, particularly in the United States, contributed to the independence movement with money and propaganda while a small but effective group of Lithuanian intelligentsia in Switzerland proselytized for independence in Western Europe.

The infant republic was beset by foes. In December 1918 the Bolsheviks invaded Lithuania and in early January they occupied Vilnius, proclaiming a short-lived Soviet state. A combination of German assistance and volunteer enthusiasm enabled the tiny and ill-equipped Lithuanian Army to drive out the Bolsheviks who were also hard-pressed by Latvian and Polish forces. On July 12, 1920, the Russian government signed a peace treaty with Lithuania, renouncing in perpetuity any Russian claims to the country. Aside from the Bolsheviks, Lithuania faced other enemies. In July 1919 a large and well-trained force of German and Russian volunteers led by an eccentric White Russian officer, Col. Paul Bermondt-Avalov, invaded Lithuania. These so-called Bermondtists, who were in league with German officers hoping to perpetuate Germany's power in the Baltic, overran much of western Lithuania, ravaging the countryside and its people. Fortunately, the Bermondtists suffered a defeat at the hands of the Lithuanian Army in November 1919, and they were driven out of the remainder of the Baltic area by Estonian and Latvian forces assisted by the British Navy.

Of all the hostile powers facing Lithuania, it was Poland that became the country's most implacable and bitter enemy during the period of independence. Some of the hostility between Poles and Lithuanians arose because of Polish hopes of reestablishing the old Polish-Lithuanian Commonwealth, a dream long since abandoned by most Lithuanians. After the Great War, the most explosive bone of contention between the two nations was the problem of Vilnius. To Lithuanians, it was the country's natural political center and historic capital: they could no more imagine Lithuania without Vilnius, than Americans could think of the United States without Washington, or the Jews imagine Israel without Jerusalem. In fact, Vilnius is the single issue that unites virtually all Lithuanians, regardless of political persuasion. To Poles, Vilnius was an important Polish cultural center and the hub of their influence in the historically Polonized and predominantly Catholic lands of eastern Lithuania and western Belorussia. To complicate this painful dilemma, the city itself had a clear Polish and Jewish majority with only a small ethnically Lithuanian population. By contrast, the surrounding countryside contained a substantial Lithuanian population, the majority of which clearly preferred inclusion within the Republic of Lithuania.

After the withdrawal of the Germans in January 1919, Vilnius changed hands a number of times among the Bolsheviks, Poles, and Lithuanians. In July 1920, Lithuanian forces entered the city with the approval of the Allied powers and without any official objections from the Poles. On October 7 the latter signed an agreement with the Lithuanians at Suwalki, drawing a temporary line of demarcation that left Vilnius under Lithuanian administration. However, on the following day, Gen. Lucjan Zeligowski, with the connivance of the Polish government, launched a thinly disguised "rebellion" by an army of "volunteers" that initially overwhelmed the Lithuanian Army and threatened the occupation of the entire country. Lithuanian forces eventually halted the Polish invasion and defeated Zeligowski's troops, but they were unable to retake Vilnius itself, and the city remained under Polish control until 1939.

Dismayed by what they saw as Polish treachery, the Lithuanians never gave up their claim to Vilnius as their legitimate capital even when the administration of the country was moved to the "temporary capital" in Kaunas. A formal state of war existed between Lithuania and Poland until 1927. The national trauma over the loss of Vilnius remained Lithuania's foremost obsession in foreign policy; it was also a major factor in obstructing attempts at Baltic regional cooperation in the interwar period. The animosity and national hatred generated by this issue poisoned relations between Poles and Lithuanians for decades; the effects are felt to this day.

The cessation of Polish-Lithuanian armed hostilities in late 1920 basically ended Lithuania's wars of independence. Bitterness over the lost capital continued, but the country now embarked on a period of reconstruction and development. The Catholic Church was an active participant in this process during Lithuania's years of struggle and reconstruction.

The Church and Society in a Troubled Democracy (1920-1926)

As we have seen, much if not most of Lithuania's Catholic Church, particularly its younger clergy, had come to support Lithuanian national aspirations on the eve of the Great War (1914-1918). Under Pranciskus Karevicius (1861-1945), the last bishop of Samogitia appointed in 1914, the Church acquired a clear Lithuanian identity even among the hierarchy and the influential pastors in the parishes. For the first time, Lithuanian became the language of formal Church communications and was adopted as the medium of instruction at the Kaunas theological seminary. Bishop Karevicius publicly supported Lithuanian aspirations at home and abroad. Among the signatories of the declaration of independence were such prominent clergymen as Father Justinas Staugaitis, Canon Kazimieras Saulys, and Father Vladas Mironas as well as prominent Catholic laymen like Pranas Dovydaitis and Aleksandras Stulginskis. During the war, the clergy were particularly active in the war-relief committee, and during the first years of independence the Church established numerous educational institutions. In addition to the support for Lithuania's independence, which now irrevocably identified the Lithuanian Catholic Church with the Lithuanian majority rather than with the country's vanishing Polonized elite, the Church acquired an active social role, particularly in welfare and education. This was a natural continuation of the important part played by the clergy in the Lithuanian national movement of the nineteenth century and of the social prestige of the priests, particularly on the local parish level. Inevitably, the activities of the Church involved it in the country's turbulent political life.

The first years of independence saw Lithuanian politics marked by radical tendencies. Virtually all Lithuanian political factions sought the social and economic restructuring of a country long dominated by a Polonized nobility and an alien bureaucracy. In the parliamentary democracy that existed during the years 1920 through 1926, three major groups emerged: (1) the Social Democrats, representing the most radical democratic party; (2) the Populists, a left-of-center formation that drew strength from small landholders; and (3) the Catholic Bloc, of which the main element consisted of the Christian Democrats, a party that depended heavily on the clergy and had a large following among nationalist and Catholic Lithuanians. The constituent assembly elected in 1920 gave the Catholic Bloc a majority of fifty-nine out of one hundred twelve seats. In addition to these groups, there were smaller parties ranging from the tiny Communist Party on the extreme left to the Nationalists on the right.

While the Christian Democrats were the most moderate of the three major parties mentioned above and vigorously defended the rights of the Church, they were not conservatives as the term is presently understood in America, particularly on social and economic issues. It was Father (later Monsignor) Mykolas Krupavicius (1885-1970) who coauthored the legislation for the radical land reform of 1922, which distributed hundreds of thousands of hectares to the peasantry. As minister of agriculture, Krupavicius supervised the law's implementation that marked, as it were, the formal end of the old estate system. Other clergymen also figured prominently in the government and the Seimas, Lithuania's parliament. Father Justinas Staugaitis served as president of the Seimas while the future archbishop of Vilnius, Mecislovas Reinys (1884-1953), became foreign minister in 1926 and negotiated an important nonagression pact with the Soviet Union. In 1922 the Catholic Bloc, supported by the ethnic minorities, was instrumental in shaping Lithuania's new constitution, which mandated a parliamentary democracy based on proportionate representation. The Church approved the participation of the clergy in politics, pointing out that priests were citizens and that there was a need to defend the rights of the Church.

The most striking figure in Lithuanian Catholicism during the independence wars and the 1920s was Blessed Jurgis Matulaitis-Matulevicius (1871-1927), a man of remarkable character and intellectual gifts who was beatified by Pope John Paul II on June 28, 1987. Before his appointment as bishop of Vilnius in December of 1918, Matulaitis had established a reputation as a professor at the theological academy in St. Petersburg and became renowned as the renovator of the Marian Order in Lithuania. In addition to his profound spirituality, he was widely respected for his attempts to integrate new teachings and scientific disciplines, such as sociology, into a Catholic philosophy of social action. A Lithuanian with a masterful command of the Polish language and an appreciation for Polish culture, Matulaitis was the logical choice to be named bishop of the troubled diocese of Vilnius, a region beset by national antagonisms and foreign invasions. The turbulent years of Matulaitis's episcopate are reflected in the bishop's diary, a remarkable historical document detailing the problems confronting the diocese, particularly during the 1919-1921 period. In short order Matulaitis confronted: (1) a four-month period of Bolshevik rule; (2) several Polish occupations of the city; (3) anti-Semitic pogroms initiated by invading troops; and (4) political intrigues and national conflicts, primarily between the Poles on one side, and the Jews, Lithuanians, and Belorussians on the other. Finally, there was nationalist opposition to his episcopate, particularly from among some of the Polish clergy who had come under the influence of chauvinistic National Democrats. The latter desired the Church to continue its historic role as the propagator of Polish culture in the eastern borderlands of the former Polish-Lithuanian Commonwealth (the so-called *kresy*); they were profoundly upset that Bishop Matulaitis did not consider this function a proper role for the Catholic Church. On the contrary, Matulaitis, who had studied at Fribourg, admired the Swiss Church as a model of ethnic and linguistic tolerance.

Throughout his ordeal, Bishop Matulaitis consistently defended the Church as a supranational institution, attempting to steer clear of partisan politics while preaching national and religious tolerance. He interceded for the Jews and was particularly solicitous of the Belorussians who suffered discrimination at the hands of nationalist Polish priests claiming that a Belorussian nation never actually existed. Matulaitis hoped that the Poles and Lithuanians would come to an understanding over the Vilnius issue. Unfortunately, the Zeligowski coup made a Polish-Lithuanian compromise impossible. Many Lithuanians, Jews, and Belorussians boycotted the subsequent elections to the local parliament that led to the formal incorporation of the area into Poland in March 1922. Bishop Matulaitis's position became increasingly difficult as Polish politicians, particularly the National Democrats and some of the diocese's clergy, pressed him to take a stand on political issues. During the early 1920s, attacks against the bishop in the Polish press escalated. Following disturbances at the bilingual Polish-Lithuanian parish of Rodune in 1922 and 1923, Poland's foreign ministry alleged that Bishop Matulaitis was attempting to deny the Poles their language rights. In later years, Polish sources admitted that the allegations against Bishop Matulaitis lacked merit and were for the most part the result of the exaggerated nationalism then current in the *kresy* regions.

A further complication arose when plans were made to raise Vilnius to the rank of an archdiocese; it was certain that the Polish government would oppose Matulaitis's elevation to archbishop. Under these conditions, Matulaitis concluded that he could no longer serve the Church adequately in Vilnius. On June 27, 1925, he wrote Pope Pius XI asking to be relieved of his position as bishop of Vilnius, frankly expressing the problems he faced as a Lithuanian bishop in a Polish-dominated diocese. A few weeks later, the Holy See reluctantly agreed to Matulaitis's resignation and, in a slap at his opposition, made him titular archbishop of Aduli in September 1925. After a brief stay in Rome, where he busied himself with the affairs of the Marian Congregation, Archbishop Matulaitis was named apostolic visitator to Lithuania on December 7, 1925.

The Lithuanians who lived under Polish rule during the period between 1920 and 1939 were subject to the administration of the Polonized hierarchy of Vilnius. In this sense, the Lithuanian experience here was not significantly different from that of past centuries. The resignation of Matulaitis ended a brief period during which attempts were made to make the Church responsive to the national aspirations of all of the Catholic nations inhabiting the Vilnius region: the Poles, Lithuanians, and Belorussians. The story of the Church in the Republic of Lithuania, with its capital in Kaunas, was vastly different. Here the Lithuanian Catholic Church tackled a number of different problems: the restructuring of ecclesiastical administration; the creation of a new basis for relations between Church and State; the question of participation in politics; and the establishment of Catholic social, cultural, and economic organizations.

One of the problems facing the Church during the 1920s was administrative reorganization in the face of the new domestic and international realities that emerged after independence. Little was accomplished in this regard until the appointment of Archbishop Matulaitis as apostolic visitator to Lithuania. Together with the other Lithuanian bishops, Matulaitis prepared a proposal creating a Lithuanian ecclesiastical province consisting of five subdivisions. The archdiocese of Kaunas and the dioceses of Telsiai and Panevezys were carved out of the former diocese of Samogitia. The part of the former diocese of Vilnius that had remained under Lithuanian rule after 1920 was included in the diocese of Kaisiadorys, whereas the Lithuanian areas of the Sejny region in the southwest became the diocese of Vilkaviskis. In 1926 Pius XI formally approved the new province, which consisted of "territories now within the bundaries of the Republic of Lithuania," and named Juozas Skvireckas (1873-1959), the archbishop of Kaunas, as the metropolitan (or head) of the Catholic Church in Lithuania.

The establishment of the new ecclesiastical province went a long way toward modernizing Church administration, but it did not establish harmonious relations between Church and State. There were several bones of contention, but for the sake of convenience they can be broken down into two areas of conflict: (1) the Lithuanian government's strained relations with the Vatican and (2) the domestic conflict between the Catholic Bloc and its opponents on both the right and left. The government's problems with the Vatican, like most of its other foreign-policy dilemmas, lay in the Polish-Lithuanian territorial conflict, which made the old diocesan boundaries unviable. The Vatican's attempts to organize new units of ecclesiastical administration within the newly emerged national states encountered this unresolved conflict over Vilnius. In February 1925 the Holy See signed a concordat with Poland, accepting its sovereignty over Vilnius. This action outraged Lithuanians who had expected the pope to support their country's goals regarding the disputed territory. Anti-Vatican demonstrations erupted in Lithuania and feelings became so intense that the government expelled the papal envoy Monsignor Antonino Zecchini.

Thus the proposal for the organization of the new

Church province was submitted to Rome during a politically volatile period. Pius XI's approval of the plan came on the eve of the 1926 elections to the Seimas, which brought to power a left-of-center coalition of Populists and Social Democrats. The new government refused to approve the changes in administration and engaged in political maneuvering against the Church, particularly in the field of education. In fact, the concordat with the Vatican was signed only after the military coup of December 17, 1926, which enthroned the Nationalist regime of Antanas Smetona. This event initiated a new stage in Lithuanian political development and profoundly affected the Catholic Church.

The Church in the Authoritarian Republic (1926-1940)

During the first years of parliamentary democracy in Lithuania, the Christian Democrats and their allies had dominated the government, successful in maintaining at least a slight majority in the country's legislature. However, the elections of May 1926 were a setback to the Catholic Bloc: the control of the government went to the Social Democrats and Populists. Despite a vigorous campaign by the Christian Democrats, the controversy over Lithuanian-Vatican relations, corruption in the government, and economic troubles contributed to defeat at the polls. The leftist government was headed by two of Lithuania's most able and respected statesmen: Populist Prime Minister Mykolas Slezevicius (1882-1939) and Populist President Kazys Grinius (1866-1950). Virtually from its inception, this government faced strong opposition. Nationalist Lithuanians were dismayed by the government's favoring (or, according to opponents, "coddling") of the minorities, particularly the Poles. Many were worried that the leftist regime, committed to civil liberties, was overly tolerant of Communist activities. The Church was disturbed by what it perceived as the leftists' intention to secularize society, particularly education. Thoughtful moderates were disturbed by the decline in the spirit of compromise and the increasingly acrid factional strife; religious and ideological differences were made worse by strident rhetoric from all sides.

Some of the criticism leveled at the Slezevicius government was unfair, but it provided the requisite ammunition for the military coup carried out by rightist officers on December 17, 1926, and shortsightedly supported by the Christian Democrats. Antanas Smetona, the leader of the small Nationalist Union, was installed as president. The Seimas was dismissed and Smetona proceeded to construct an authoritarian regime, eventually banning all political parties except for his Lithuanian Nationalist Union. In general, Smetona's Nationalist regime sought to establish a unified national state: it claimed to reject the extremes of both "limitless democracy" and outright fascism as "un-Lithuanian." Its ideology was a mixture of agrarian populism, the personality cult of Smetona as "Leader of the Nation," a stress on national unity, and some superficial borrowings from Italian Fascism. On the other hand, Smetona explicitly rejected racism. His government, unlike the neighboring totalitarian regimes in Russia and Germany, tolerated a substantial degree of ethnic, cultural, and religious pluralism. The Nationalist regime repressed political opposition and exercised limited censorship, but it reserved its harshest methods for use against the political extremes: the Communists and, to a lesser degree, right-wing extremists — particularly those associated with Smetona's charismatic rival, Professor Augustinas Voldemaras (1883-1942).

The history of the Catholic Church during the years of the Nationalist regime entails a paradox: it flourished, developed, and grew at a time when Catholicism suffered a certain amount of political repression. As mentioned above, the Christian Democrats at first welcomed the coup, which was actively supported by Catholic youth organizations. The Catholic Bloc fell out with the Nationalists only when it became clear that the latter intended to rule the country alone. Aside from the political conflicts, tensions between the government and the Church arose over the implementation of the concordat signed with the Vatican on September 27, 1927. This agreement gave the Church considerable control over education, approved religious instruction in state schools, provided for state salaries to the clergy, guaranteed the autonomy of Catholic Action organizations, and granted financial aid to theological seminaries. On the other hand, the state required an oath of loyalty from the clergy and a hand in the appointment of priests.

It soon became clear that the Smetona regime intended to curtail certain Catholic activities as a way of undermining the Christian Democratic establishment. In 1930 Smetona banned the secondary school chapters of the Ateitis Catholic Federation, which will be described in detail later on in this chapter. (Ateitis means "the future" in Lithuanian.) In violation of the concordat, the government interfered with the theological-philosophical faculty of the University of Kaunas, the country's leading Catholic institution of higher learning. Some Catholic intellectuals (including Pranas Dovydaitis, a signatory of Lithuania's declaration of independence) were arrested and briefly imprisoned. The abolition of political parties and censorship, which affected the Catholic press, were other divisive issues. The suppression of Catholic Action groups embroiled the Lithuanian government in conflict with the Vatican. In 1931 the regime expelled the papal envoy Monsignor Riccardo Bartaloni, although a formal break in relations with the Holy See was avoided. The bishops were anxious to speak out against Smetona's dictatorship, but they were restrained by Lithuania's metropolitan, Archbishop Juozas Skvireckas, a withdrawn scholar and translator of the Bible who tended to accommodate political authority.

The government's conflict with Lithuania's churchmen and the Vatican eased only on the eve of World War II. The series of crises that shook Lithuania, beginning with the Polish ultimatum of March 1938, revealed the weakness of the Nationalist regime. The new prime minister, Vladas Mironas, himself a Catholic priest, hoped to restore Catholic support for Smetona and normalized relations with the Holy See. Still, the government continued to drag its feet on Catholic participation in politics until the German seizure of Klaipeda (Memel in German) in March 1939 plunged the country into another political crisis. The Christian Democrats and Populists were quickly brought into a "government of national unity."

As part of its mutual assistance pact with the Soviet Union, Lithuania regained Vilnius in October 1939. This led to a serious conflict with the Catholic hierarchy there, since Romuald Jalbrzykowski, the Polish archbishop, proved hostile to Lithuanian interests. The government initially demanded the archbishop's removal but relented when this position endangered the recently normalized relations with the Vatican. Polish-Lithuanian relations in the archdiocese of Vilnius remained tense as the Lithuanians pressed for more influence in the episcopal administration and for church services in their language; for its part, the Polish hierarchy resisted change, attempting to grant only minimum concessions, and accepting the new situation with obvious reluctance.

During two decades of politics in independent Lithuania, the Church underwent several stages of development. In the first, it played a dominant role, primarily through the Christian Democratic Party. After the consolidation of the Nationalist regime in 1927, the Catholics were excluded from politics as a group, but the Lithuanian Church maintained most of the Catholic Action organizations. The spiritual vigor and intellectual diversity of Lithuanian Catholicism actually grew during the repressive period of Nationalist rule when the Catholics constituted, as it were, much of the political and moral opposition to the government. Finally, on the eve of the war, the Church regained some of the political influence it had enjoyed during the period of parliamentary democracy.

Religion, Society, and Culture in an Independent State

Before examining the place of Catholicism in Lithuanian society, it would perhaps be useful to place it, in briefest outline, within the framework of the economy, society, and culture of the interwar period. While Lithuania was a predominantly agrarian country with a Roman Catholic and ethnic Lithuanian majority, its society was more complex and diverse than it might have appeared to the superficial observer.

The population census of 1923 and the survey of the Klaipeda Territory in 1925 registered independent Lithuania's population at about 2,250,000 (excluding the disputed Vilnius region). Over eighty percent of this populace were ethnic Lithuanians. The national minorities included the Jews (7.6 percent), Germans (about 4 percent), Poles (3.2 percent), Russians (2.5 percent), and others. In the early 1920s some eighty-four percent of Lithuania's citizens lived in villages; by 1939 about a fourth resided in cities and towns. The majority of the Lithuanians were landed peasants, whereas the largest minority, the Jews, tended to occupy positions in petty trade, business, and the professions. The loss of Klaipeda to Germany in March 1939 was demographically more than compensated by the recovery of Vilnius later in the year; as a result, Lithuania's population increased to over three million. The addition of the Vilnius region also substantially raised the percentage of the Jewish, Polish, and Belorussian minorities within the general population. Even so, ethnic Lithuanians constituted almost three-fourths of the country's inhabitants in 1940.

At least eighty percent of Lithuania's population considered itself Catholic, representing primarily the ethnic Lithuanians and the Polish minority. The Protestants made up about nine percent of the republic's population in the 1920s; nearly half of them were Germans and Latvians, concentrated mainly in the Klaipeda Territory, Birzai, and Kedainiai. Most were Lutherans; but, in addition, there were about twenty-five thousand members of the Evangelical Reformed Church as well as a few thousand Baptists and Methodists. Virtually all of Lithuania's Eastern Orthodox and Old Believers were ethnic Russians. The Jews were by far the most numerous non-Christian group, the majority professing the Orthodox brand of Judaism. Rounding out Lithuania's ethnic and religious mosaic were about a thousand Muslims, mostly descendants of the Tatars, who maintained several houses of prayer, including a mosque in Kaunas. Lithuania's Christian and non-Christian religious communities were subsidized by the government. The state contributed to the salaries of priests, ministers, and rabbis. Understandably, the Catholic Church received the lion's share of the total budget devoted to religious subsidies; however, in terms of per capita expenditures, there was no discrimination.

Throughout the independence period, Lithuania remained primarily an exporter of agricultural products and an importer of manufactured goods. Until the early 1930s when, as a result of Hitler's rise to power, German-Lithuanian relations deteriorated badly, Germany absorbed the major part of Lithuanian agricultural exports; later, Britain became the major customer. Naturally, the worldwide economic crisis of the 1930s depressed agricultural prices and set back economic development. Industrialization proceeded slowly, but there was a considerable advance in light industry, particularly food-processing. Lithuania's economic development lagged behind countries of similar size in Western Europe as well as neighboring Latvia and Estonia. On the other hand, Lithuania's standard of living was higher than in some other parts of Eastern Europe, for example, the rural regions of eastern Poland and the Balkans, and far ahead of that in the Soviet Union.

The most remarkable legacy of the independence period was the progress made in education and culture. From the tsars Lithuania inherited an illiteracy rate of forty-four percent; by 1940 this had been reduced to less than fifteen percent. The number of primary-school students more than quadrupled between 1920 and 1938. The secondary-school system of state and private gymnasiums was expanded, and a modern university was established in Kaunas; later, another university in Vilnius was restored to academic life. Opera, ballet, theater, and contemporary music were integrated into the national culture. Despite some official censorship, the number and variety of Lithuanian-language publications rose rapidly; they included many scholarly and literary journals that exposed the growing number of educated readers to the ideas current in Western Europe and America.

The Catholic Church influenced the course of change in Lithuanian society during the twenties and thirties; conversely, it was itself deeply affected by the development of the Lithuanian nation. As we have seen, until 1927 Catholics had played a decisive role in Lithuania's politics; however, even after the advent of the Smetona regime, the Church's position in society remained pivotal. Catholic religious education, subsidized by the government, reached virtually all Lithuanian-language schools. The Church remained, as it were, the country's record keeper. Civil registry had not yet been introduced by 1940, and thus all births and marriages among Catholics were handled by the Church (religious leaders of non-Catholic communities did the same for their members). This led some Lithuanians to question such a situation: in 1940 Lithuania remained the only European state that did not yet have civil registry for marriage. On this matter, the Lithuanian bishops took a conservative approach: in April 1940 they condemned civil marriage and demanded that in Catholic marriages only the jurisdiction of ecclesiastical courts be recognized. Therefore, despite conflicts with the government, in some respects Catholicism, while not quite a state religion, enjoyed some prerogatives similar to those in Spain and Italy until recent times (with the difference that inasmuch as they received subsidies all religions had official status in Lithuania).

In 1940 the Lithuanian Church contained six dioceses (Vilnius, Kaunas, Panevezys, Telsiai, Kaisiadorys, and Vilkaviskis). There were over fourteen hundred secular and monastic clergy, about four hundred seminarians, and more than seven hundred churches. These figures represented solid growth: between 1914 and 1940 the number of priests rose by forty percent and the number of seminarians grew fourfold. The religious congregations contained nine hundred sisters and about five hundred brothers. These communities performed various spiritual and social tasks: they led retreats, operated orphanages and other charitable institutions, worked with juvenile delinquents, and provided the teaching staff for educational institutions ranging from secondary schools to kindergartens. Since Catholic religious congregations had all been either banned or restricted by the tsarist government, their revival was impressive.

The Jesuits returned to Lithuania in 1923 after an absence of some one hundred fifty years. In 1924 they established a highly regarded secondary school in Kaunas. By 1940 they numbered seventeen priests, thirty-nine seminarians, and forty-six brothers, a modest group considering the Jesuits' prominence in the eighteenth century. The Franciscans were revived by Father Antanas Bizauskas, and by 1938 there were some fifty-three monks in Lithuania. Their lay affiliate, the Franciscans' Third Order, counted three hundred forty chapters with nearly fifty thousand members. One of the most dramatic revivals was that of the Marian Order, which had practically ceased to exist in Lithuania before World War I. Restored by Blessed Jurgis Matulaitis in 1909, the Marian Order came to include some of Lithuania's most respected Catholic minds, among them historian Dr. Jonas Totoraitis, Archbishop Pranciskus Bucys, and Archbishop Pranciskus Karevicius. There were also other male congregations — for example, the Salesians, Dominicans, and Capuchins.

Of the women's religious communities in Lithuania, the Sisters of St. Casimir were founded in the United States in 1907. Five nuns arrived in Lithuania from Chicago in 1920 and established a convent near Kaunas, where they renovated and restored the beautiful baroque monastery in Pazaislis, one of the country's outstanding architectural monuments. The Casimirites also established the popular Saule girls' secondary school in Kaunas. By 1940 there were about one hundred fifty sisters in Lithuania. Another popular community was that of the Sisters of the Immaculate Conception, founded by Blessed Jurgis Matulaitis in 1918. Like the other women religious, the Immaculate Conception community performed educational and charitable work, but its members were also known for their work in the distribution and publication of Catholic books and periodicals. The Sisters of St. Catherine abolished strict cloister in 1923 and introduced Lithuanian as the language of the community; thus modernized, their Lithuanian province grew to over a hundred nuns, respected for their charitable work among the disadvantaged youth and handicapped. Other significant communities included the Benedictines, the Sisters of St. Francis, and the Sisters of the Sacred Heart. It must be remembered that Lithuania's women religious contributed numerous social services to the young, the orphans, the elderly, and the handicapped at a time when the state welfare system was, as yet, only weakly developed.

In addition to its institutions and religious communities, the Church maintained a myriad of lay organizations, specialized to meet the needs of professionals, peasants, students, women, and labor, thus enabling Catholicism to exercise a powerful influence in virtually every aspect of Lithuanian life. Excluded from politics and led by Metropolitan Juozas Skvireckas, who avoided confrontation with the Smetona government, the policy of the Church hierarchy was to promote the educational and cultural development of lay people. The Ateitis Catholic Federation represented the intelligentsia and the students. The secondary-school chapters of Ateitis were banned by the Ministry of Education in 1930; nonetheless, Ateitis had about ten thousand members in the secondary schools by 1940. The graduate component of the organization (the so-called *sendraugiai*, literally "old friends") included Lithuania's most prominent Catholic intelligentsia. For rural youth, there was the Catholic organization Pavasaris (The Spring). Between 1922 and 1928 it was ably led by Juozas Eretas, a Lithuanian citizen of Swiss extraction, who introduced West European planning methods, began organizing mass conventions, and attracted many students. As a result, Pavasaris attained a membership of almost one hundred thousand by 1940. In addition to promoting Catholic devotion,

Pavasaris organized numerous concerts, theaters, and sporting events, and maintained museums and libraries, thus trying to bridge the cultural gap between town and village.

On the eve of World War II, well over one hundred thousand women were included in the Union of Catholic Women's Organizations. The national Catholic children's organization, Angelaiciai (The Angels), counted some fifty-five thousand members by 1940. Rytas (The Morning) and the Association of St. Casimir were two unique organizations whose combined membership was in the tens of thousands. Both operated schools and libraries among the Lithuanians of the Polish-ruled Vilnius region, providing them with education and cultural activities in the native language. These organizations were banned in 1937 during one of the Polish government's periodic crackdowns against the Lithuanian population of the area.

The Farmers' Union, a small pro-Catholic peasant party, had been one of the members of the parliamentary Catholic Bloc, but it was suspended in 1928. The Catholic Federation of Labor, the other part of the Catholic Bloc (aside from the proscribed Christian Democratic Party), had been founded in 1919. It played an important part in pressuring the government for improvements in the social conditions of the working class, advocating minimum wages, calling for restrictions on the length of the working day, and proposing the introduction of compulsory health insurance. Since the Federation of Labor constituted an anti-Communist force among a group potentially susceptible to left-wing propaganda, it was tolerated by the Nationalist government on the condition that it withdraw from politics. As a result, in 1934 the federation was renamed the Association of Christian Workers of Lithuania and devoted its activities to social and cultural issues. In 1940 it had an estimated membership of some ten thousand workingmen.

There were numerous other more specialized groups, such as the Lithuanian Catholic Abstinence Society, the Lithuanian branch of the St. Vincent de Paul Society, and the like. Of Lithuania's over two million Catholics in 1940, at least half were probably involved in some lay organization. Virtually everyone in the populace was in some way affected by the activity of the various educational, charitable, and social Catholic organizations. Organized lay Catholicism was coordinated through the Catholic Action Center in Kaunas; half of its executive board was appointed by the bishops, while the other half were elected by Catholic organizations.

Although it is difficult to quantify, the impact of Catholicism on Lithuania's intellectual development during the 1920s and 1930s was perhaps even more important than its organizational power. Catholic organizations and congregations published numerous periodicals for their members, but the most significant Catholic newspapers and journals were those that reached out to the intelligentsia of various ideological persuasions. Lithuania's foremost Catholic newspaper — the widely read daily *XX Amzius* (*The Twentieth Century*), published between 1936 and 1940 — had a large following outside strictly "Catholic" circles because, despite censorship, it maintained an urbane and progressive tone, espousing democratization and criticizing social inequities. The monthly journal *Zidinys* (*The Hearth*), published between 1924 and 1940, became the leading non-Nationalist scholarly and literary periodical; while it emphasized a Catholic and democratic world view, it was open to contributors of varying ideological shades. One of the most original and lively prewar publications was the illustrated cultural weekly *Naujoji Romuva* (*New Romuva*), edited by Juozas Keliuotis. It emphasized the creation of a national culture, inveighed against a mechanical acceptance of foreign influences, and supported the idea of an "organic state" with a "true Lithuanian spirit." However, unlike the Nationalist government, this weekly also advocated such things as political tolerance and modern art.

Since religious instruction was carried out in public schools at the government's expense, Lithuania did not develop a system of parochial education like that of the

United States, although the religious orders operated some fine Catholic secondary schools. Higher education and research were a different matter. The most important center of Catholic thought was the theological-philosophical faculty of the University of Kaunas. In effect, the faculty was a Catholic college (equivalent to a university school in America) and included the study of history and literature as well as philosophy and theology. The faculty's best-known academic periodical, *Athenaeum*, which covered history, literature, and geography, was aimed at professional academicians and intellectuals. The Lithuanian Catholic Academy of Sciences established by Bishop Pranciscus Karevicius in 1922 served as the Catholic "think tank." The academy organized conferences and published works in the various scientific and scholarly disciplines.

As the clergy were, with few exceptions, barred from politics after 1927, the secular Catholic intelligentsia gradually assumed the political and intellectual leadership of Lithuania's Catholic community. Sometimes this led Catholic intellectuals into conflicts with the more conservative hierarchy (for example, some Catholic activists favored the legalization of civil marriage). However, the younger clergy were more in tune with the times. The typical Catholic intellectual of the 1930s was a nationalist with a firm grounding in contemporary Western European Catholic thought as a basis for the renovation of the Church and the reform of society. Most saw Lithuania's future in developing a national culture based on Western Christian ideas (for instance, *Naujoji Romuva* had a high regard for French Catholic culture). Many of the academicians with advanced degrees had studied at Western European Catholic universities, such as the Louvain and Fribourg. Independent Lithuania's most prominent Catholic philosopher was Stasys Salkauskis (1886-1941), the one-time rector of the University of Kaunas and the guiding light of the Ateitis movement. Salkauskis proposed the democratization of public life and called on Lithuanians to create a unique synthesis of Eastern and Western cultures based on Catholic principles. Another intellectual, Monsignor Aleksandras Dambrauskas (1860-1938), better known by his pseudonym Adomas Jakstas, sought to combine rationalism and modern science with Catholic dogma. In general, Catholic thought in Lithuania was diverse: at different times, Catholic thinkers advocated democracy, authoritarianism, nationalism, and pluralism. Such diversity was not unhealthy, as the conflict of different viewpoints was indicative of growth and vitality.

Jonas Maciulis-Maironis and Juozas Tumas-Vaizgantas, the two Catholic giants of Lithuanian literature, still dominated the cultural scene during the earlier independence period. However, literature, like the rest of Lithuanian life, sought new directions. Some talented writers, like the poets Bernardas Brazdzionis (born 1907) and Jonas Kossu-Aleksandravicius (or Aistis) (1904-1973), developed new genres while remaining clearly within the Catholic fold. Others went through a more tortuous course; among them was Salomeja Neris (1904-1945), who published in both Catholic and leftist journals, winning the State Prize for Literature in 1938. Perhaps the most dramatic writer of the thirties was the gifted poet and novelist Vincas Mykolaitis-Putinas (1893-1967), whose sensational novel *Altoriu sesely* (*In the Shadow of the Altars*) depicted a tormented priest's love for a woman and his estrangement from the Church. In fact, the novel was descriptive of Putinas's own situation: in 1935 he left the priesthood to marry and consequently suffered excommunication (which was lifted by the Holy See in 1966 when he reconciled with the Church). The tragic personal situation of one of Lithuania's most beloved writers pointed up the fact that while Catholicism was a dominant culture and social force in Lithuania, it existed in an increasingly secular milieu.

The whole institutional and spiritual complex of the Church, which included the Catholic community, was profoundly affected by the economic and social changes that stirred Lithuania and indeed all of Europe between the wars. The Church did not always smoothly adjust to the transformation of Lithuania from a traditional agrarian society to a modernizing one, and some of the conflicts among Catholics, such as the issue of the Church's landed property and the problem of civil marriage, were normal problems within such a modernizing society. To some extent, Catholics simply reflected the diversity of the society: there were conservatives and radicals, nationalists and internationalists, authoritarians and democrats.

Finally, it must be remembered that the role of the Church, sometimes in cooperation with opposition groups such as the Populists, was vital in maintaining an "opposition" culture and society independent of the regime. The fact that the Smetona government never descended into outright Fascism or extremism was due not only to the relative moderation of the president-leader but also to the opposition of the Church and its advocacy of limited government. The maintenance of a vigorous, independent, and organized Catholicism played a part in preserving within the society a political culture imbued with democratic ideals and an acceptance of pluralism even while the country was under authoritarian rule. In this, and in its commitment to the West as a cultural model, Lithuania (as well as some other East European states) was vastly different from Soviet Russia and Nazi Germany: neither Communism nor Nazism had any use for the Western Christian tradition and democratic values that occupied an important place in Lithuanian society.

The End of Independence

Like the other Eastern European peoples who had achieved their independence after the Great War, the Lithuanians were acutely aware that they lived in a particularly exposed and dangerous part of the world, flanked from the east and west by their powerful Russian and German neighbors. Lithuania's own position was further complicated by its bitter struggle with Poland over Vilnius. During the twenties and thirties, the East European states sought to develop collective security either through alliances, or an "eastern version" of the Locarno agreement, referring to the 1925 treaty that had provided international guarantees for Germany's western borders. Unfortunately, the Western Powers, particularly Britain, were more interested in restraining German revisionism in the west rather than in the east, accepting the delusion that Eastern and Central Europe, or the "far-away people of whom we know little," as Neville Chamberlain put it, were not vital to their security. (It was forgotten that these "far-away" people were only hours by plane from London.) In hindsight, it seems clear that the Versailles Treaty and its territorial arrangements, which for all their faults were vastly superior and more just than the order that had existed in 1914, made little sense if the smaller East European states were not guaranteed against German and Russian imperialism. Too late, Britain and France grasped that the peace of Europe could not be maintained if Germany were allowed to unilaterally redraw its eastern boundaries, and if Russia and Germany were permitted to conspire against the independence of the countries that represented some one hundred million Europeans living between the Adriatic and the Baltic.

Lithuania was cut off from a direct border with the Soviet Union by the Polish-ruled Vilnius region and, in any case, its relations with the Soviets (who supported Lithuanian claims against Poland) ranged from adequate to friendly. The Lithuanian republic's first serious security problem arose with the emergence of the Nazi regime in Germany, which made no secret of its dissatisfaction with the status of the Klaipeda Territory, called Memel by the Germans. This area constituted an autonomous region on the Prussian border inhabited by Lithuanians and Germans, which had been detached from Germany by the Treaty of Versailles and assigned to Lithuania by the Conference of Ambassadors in March 1923. German-Lithuanian relations were severely strained when in 1934 the Lithuanian government responded to conspiracy among the Nazi-led Klaipeda Germans to overthrow Lithuanian rule. The government arrested and tried the local Nazi leaders and banned the pro-Nazi parties of the German minority. Lithuania was one of the first European countries to put Nazis on trial. Hitler's regime responded with a trade embargo on Lithuania, causing severe economic hardship and a reorientation of foreign trade and relations toward closer ties with Britain.

The prelude to the collapse of independent Lithuania was marked by the "period of the three ultimatums" during 1938-1940. In March 1938, while Europe's attention was drawn to the German takeover of Austria, Poland presented Lithuania with an ultimatum demanding the establishment of diplomatic relations, threatening military action in case of refusal. Without foreign support, Lithuania accepted this humiliation. An even more severe shock was the second ultimatum: Germany's abrupt demand in March 1939 that Lithuania cede the Klaipeda Territory. Advised by Britain and France that there was no alternative, the Smetona government abandoned Lithuania's only major port to the Reich, setting off a domestic political crisis for a regime that had always sworn to defend the country's territorial integrity, whatever the odds or consequences. The infamous Nazi-Soviet Pact of August 23, 1939, negotiated by Vyacheslav Molotov and Joachim von Ribbentrop, was another shock to a terrified Europe. This agreement, whose secret protocols amounted to a fourth partition of Poland and the division of much of Eastern Europe into "spheres of influence" between Hitler and Stalin, stands as a monument to hypocrisy and cynicism. As part of this de facto Soviet-German alliance, the Baltic States (Estonia, Latvia, and Lithuania) were placed in the Soviet "sphere." The pact's immediate effect was to make war inevitable. On September 1, 1939, German armies invaded Poland; sixteen days later, Soviet troops attacked Poland from the east.

Despite German pressure to join in the offensive against Poland as well as some popular sentiment to use this opportunity to regain the virtually undefended city of Vilnius from a detested foe, Lithuania clung to a policy of neutrality, hoping that such a stance would preserve the country's now precarious independence until the Western

Allies prevailed. However, in late September 1939 Stalin demanded that the Baltic States sign mutual assistance pacts with the Soviet Union that would allow the Red Army to maintain bases in the three countries while solemnly proclaiming noninterference in their internal affairs. The Lithuanian-Soviet mutual assistance treaty signed on October 10, 1939, included the return of Vilnius and its environs to the Republic of Lithuania. The recovery of Lithuania's capital, along with the fact that the Soviets made no initially obvious attempts to interfere in the country's internal affairs, made the pill easier to swallow and lulled some of the population into a false sense of security, only partially jarred by the Soviet assault on Finland on November 30, 1939.

The third and final ultimatum, which sealed independent Lithuania's fate, came eight months after the mutual assistance pact with the Soviets. As the Western Alliance reeled from the German offensive in France the Soviet government accused the Republic of Lithuania of abducting Soviet soldiers and conspiring to create an anti-Soviet military alliance together with Latvia and Estonia. On June 14, 1940, on the same day the Germans entered Paris, the Soviets presented an ultimatum to the Lithuanian government demanding, among other things, the admission of the Red Army into the country's population centers. In effect, this meant a military occupation. The president and a few cabinet members showed great personal courage in counseling armed resistance, but when the majority of the cabinet disagreed, Smetona left the country. Soviet troops occupied Kaunas on June 15. The fear of bloodshed and the illusory hope that the entry of still more Russian soldiers would curtail but not end Lithuania's independence discouraged organized resistance to the invaders.

Even the most optimistically inclined soon realized that Soviet occupation meant more than the end of the Smetona regime and the establishment of a pro-Soviet Lithuanian government. The transitional People's Government headed by leftist journalist Justas Paleckis (1899-1980) and including some respected Lithuanian democrats had no real power. Lithuania's affairs were directed by Vladimir Dekanozov, Moscow's plenipotentiary in Kaunas. In mid-July the Communist-controlled security forces carried out the first mass arrests: several thousand prominent non-Communist Lithuanians were detained and many were deported. Non-Communist public activity was restricted and virtually all political, social, ideological, and cultural groups that could not be included in Communist front organizations were banned. Given Lithuanian conditions, it was the Catholics who naturally suffered the most. Lithuania's tiny Communist Party of less than two thousand was legalized, but it was widely unpopular and its power was based primarily on the Red Army and the NKVD, or the National Commissariat for Internal Affairs, the Soviet secret police and precursor of the KGB. It appealed to a relatively small section of the total society: part of the radicalized urban workers, some poor peasants, a segment of the leftist intelligentsia, and elements among the Jewish and Russian minorities, especially the youth. Elections to the People's Diet in July 1940 constituted a cynical charade so thoroughly marked by fraud and intimidation that even many Communists did not believe the official claim that 99.5 percent of the electorate had cast 99.2 percent of its votes for the Communist-controlled and hastily organized Working People's League (it is estimated that no more than a third of eligible voters actually cast ballots).

The People's Diet quickly ended any lingering illusions about maintaining at least a formally independent state. On July 21, 1940, the ruling diet declared a Soviet Socialist form of government and chose a delegation to proceed to Moscow and "apply" for membership in the USSR, a request granted on August 3, 1940, with the admission of the Lithuanian SSR into the Soviet Union. Only the Communists and those who hoped to benefit by Soviet rule actively supported the new system. Abroad, most governments refused to recognize this blatant seizure of territory by force and continued to accredit Baltic diplomats. At home, the silent majority seethed with resentment. One did not have to be much of a "nationalist'' to mourn the loss of statehood or to see that Sovietization was nothing other than foreign occupation. However, even the doomsayers could not have predicted the horrors that Stalinism and Nazism were to visit on Lithuania over the next decade.

CHAPTER 8

The Catholic Church Under Siege (1940-1972)

The Soviet Occupation of 1940-1941

Like the majority of Lithuanians, Catholic leaders responded to foreign occupation in the summer of 1940 with a combination of adaptation and resistance. To many people, the initial situation, while difficult and painful, did not appear hopeless. The country had survived foreign rule before and, in any case, the unpredictable course of war and international diplomacy convinced many Lithuanians at home and abroad, correctly as it turned out, that this Soviet occupation would be short-lived. In addition, the first months of Soviet rule, aside from the arrests in July and the banning of most organized non-Communist public activity, did not exhibit the full ferocity of which Stalinism was capable. That was to come later.

Lithuania was the first Roman Catholic country to come under Soviet domination. Within days of the Soviet invasion, the new government announced its intention to carry out secularization measures, including the abolition of religious instruction in public schools and the end of government support for religious institutions. Since many Lithuanians, including some Catholics, had favored the separation of Church and State and a limited secularization of society, these intentions were not altogether ominous. At first, the government ridiculed any suggestion that it would restrict the practice of religion or the freedom of religious institutions. However, as the regime came under increasingly direct Communist control, and as the Soviets saw less reason to mollify the Catholic masses, the campaign to drive Catholicism from public life escalated. By the end of June, the People's Government had abolished religious instruction in the schools and outlawed religious symbols in public buildings. On July 5 the government formally denounced the concordat with the Vatican and the papal nuncio was ordered to leave the country. For all practical purposes, the independent Catholic press ceased to exist by the middle of July: the popular daily *XX Amzius* was closed on August 1. The process of stripping the Church of its public functions accelerated with Lithuania's formal Sovietization in early August. On August 15 the regime instituted civil marriage, denied church weddings any legal validity, legalized divorce, and transferred registration of births and deaths to civil authority. Religious holidays were abolished.

Steadily, the Communists went beyond the secularization of Lithuanian society, undertaking measures clearly aimed at destroying organized Catholicism or restricting it to the practice of a cult without any meaningful social role. The government confiscated Church lands, including those held by monastic orders. The educational institutions operated by the Catholics and Jews were nationalized in late August. More ominously, police measures against the clergy intensified after Lithuania's incorporation into the Soviet Union. The Commissariat of Internal Affairs began to recruit clergymen and Catholic lay people in an attempt to penetrate the Church with agents working for the NKVD. The secret police undertook to gather detailed information on all religious denominations in Lithuania. Captured Soviet documents later revealed that the commissar, Aleksandras Guzevicius, was acting on orders from Moscow, where the Communists were planning "active measures" against religious communities in Lithuania, particularly the Catholic Church. Stalinist paranoia was evident in the elaborate precautions taken by the regime to ensure (unsuccessfully) that the All Souls and Christmas celebrations in late 1940 did not provide occasions for "hostile anti-Soviet propaganda." As a result of the Soviet occupation of 1940-1941, hundreds of priests were interrogated, scores disappeared after being arrested, and at least twenty were killed.

For their part, Catholics viewed the Communist regime with suspicion. However, at least during the first months of Soviet rule, the Catholic Church avoided public confrontation with the new regime, despite the obvious ideological rifts between Catholicism and Marxism. Some of the Catholic intelligentsia who favored social reform and had opposed the Smetona regime argued that Soviet occupation was less dangerous to Lithuania than German rule, since the Russians were supposedly on a lower cultural level; others thought that Communism had changed since the Great Terror of the 1930s and that there would be no repetition of the destructive campaign against Church and society that the Soviets had launched elsewhere — for example, in the Ukraine. Among the clergy, there were voices urging that the disagreements between "Catholics and commissars" be confined to the realm of ideas. The most conspicuous attempt at peaceful coexistence between Church and State was the controversial memorandum of Father Mykolas Krupavicius, the well-known architect of the 1922 land reform. In his statement, which was approved by the Lithuanian bishops and the papal nuncio, Krupavicius tried to show that the Church in fact shared goals of social reform with the socialist government, emphasizing the need to allow freedom for Catholic pastoral work.

Bishop Vincentas Brizgys, the recently installed thirty-seven-year-old auxiliary archbishop of Kaunas, took over much of the Church's administrative and managerial work from Juozas Skvireckas, the aging metropolitan archbishop. Despite the fact that some of his relatives, including his own brother, had been arrested by the Soviets, Brizgys sought to gain what he could by patient dialogue and debate with the Communists. On August 24, 1940, he wrote a conciliatory note to the Ministry of Education, arguing that permitting enlightened and rational religious instruction within a secular framework could only help society's progress, pointing to the American experience where public and parochial education were separate but complementary. In short, Brizgys hoped to avoid any and all provocations that would give the Soviets an excuse to crack down even harder on religious practices.

The realization that only an unconscionable capitulation of the Catholic Church to Soviet dictates could end the regime's hostility occurred primarily as a result of growing repression, which contradicted the public assurances of Chairman of the Commissars Mecislovas Gedvilas regarding freedom of religion. There was a perceptible increase in anti-Catholic activity following a Baltic Communist meeting with Stalin in early September 1940 in which the latter demanded "firmness" in dealing with the population of the Baltic Republics. The nationalization of Church lands was now followed by the confiscation of episcopal offices and residences, particularly in the provinces: bishops and priests were literally thrown out of their homes. The seminaries in Telsiai, Vilkaviskis, and Vilnius were seized. The aggressive anti-Catholic attitude was evident in the fate of the Kaunas theological seminary, the country's lone Catholic college after the closing of the university's faculty of theology and philosophy. In August 1940 a group of Jews petitioned the Ministry of Health for permission to occupy the seminary and utilize the complex as additional quarters for the Kaunas Jewish hospital. At the time, even the Lithuanian Communists quickly rejected the idea as an inane provocation in a predominantly Catholic country, but they later announced that the seminary complex would be transferred to the Red Army, which was in fact accomplished in January 1941. Thus the mood was changing; there were no longer any possibilities of a modus vivendi between the Communist state and the Catholic Church. In April 1941 the Lithuanian bishops met to discuss the escalating repression of religious activity that could no longer be dismissed as a misunderstanding or the work of overzealous local Communists. Consequently, the bishops presented the Soviet regime with a detailed memorandum, outlining the violations of Catholics' rights and demanding that the situation be rectified. The Communists simply dismissed the letter.

The spring of 1941 was marked by an overall deterioration in the political situation and the mood of the country; by then at least twelve thousand persons had been arrested or deported for political reasons. Tensions between those collaborating with the Soviets and opponents of the regime grew as rumors of an approaching Russo-German conflict proliferated. Underground opposition to the Soviets, partly encouraged by the Germans, became more organized. Unbeknownst to the country, Stalin's regime was planning a massive operation against "unreliable elements" of the population in the Baltic Republics. In the early hours of June 14, 1941, NKVD troops, assisted by local Party and Komsomol activists, struck in a surprise move: within three days some thirty-five thousand men, women, and children (ranging from infants to the aged) were loaded into cattle cars in stifling heat and deported to destinations east. Families were broken up and many died from starvation and ill-treatment along the way. The majority were the families of so-called "anti-Soviet" and "antisocial" elements, a definition that according to captured NKVD documents included people whose only crime was studying Esperanto or collecting foreign postage stamps. While this attack was primarily aimed at the Lithuanian intelligentsia and former officialdom in an apparent attempt to "decapitate" the society, virtually every social class, profession, and ethnic group was represented among the deportees. It is not clear how many would have been deported had the German-Soviet war not intervened; one Communist defector with knowledge of the operation estimated that the intended number of deportees may have been as high as seven hundred thousand, a fourth of the entire population.

In terms of scale, the deportations of June 1941 were later dwarfed by the Holocaust and the postwar Soviet "pacification" of Lithuania, but the shock of the June deportations on the psyche of the generation that experienced it should not be underestimated. Carried out with stunning swiftness and surprise, this was undoubtedly the greatest single disaster that had struck the Lithuanian nation in over two centuries. The operation, in full view of the populace, plunged many Lithuanians into a state of emotional turmoil. Since no one understood the specific criteria for deportation (even relatives of powerful Communist officials were caught in the net), everyone felt insecure. In desperation normally peace-loving people later admitted praying for war if it meant the departure of the Russians. Others swore that they would do all in their power to eradicate Soviet rule and everything it represented. Few imagined that the worst was yet to come.

The Nazi Occupation

In the early morning hours of Sunday, June 22, 1941, the German war machine attacked the Soviet Union all along its western border. The Nazi advance was rapid. The majority of the local population greeted the war, which was widely understood as marking the end of Stalinist terror, with a contradictory mixture of joy, relief, anxiety, and anticipation. Except for some Communists and their supporters, virtually no Lithuanians offered any resistance to the invaders, hardly a surprising situation given the traumatic deportations of a few days earlier. Lithuanian Red Army men, seeing no reason to die for Stalin, deserted by the thousands. Soviet forces were quickly overwhelmed and in many areas the retreat turned into a rout. The demoralized Russian troops were also confronted by an anti-Soviet uprising.

On June 23, 1941, an insurrection led by the Lithuanian Activist Front, a national anti-Soviet underground coalition, engulfed the city of Kaunas. On the same day, the rebels captured the radio station and announced a provisional government under Acting Prime Minister Juozas Ambrazevicius (1903-1974), a Catholic literary scholar. The uprising soon spread to the rest of the country, exposing the Red Army to vengeful partisans. Tens of thousands participated in the rebellion, and several thousand are estimated to have died in combat against the Russians. The destruction inflicted during the first days of the fighting was made immeasurably worse by the excesses against various groups of civilians. In addition to the looting and rape perpetrated by some of the Russian troops (units of the retreating Red Army), the NKVD and some Communist activists massacred nearly two thousand Lithuanians, some of them in particularly gruesome group murders — for example, in the Rainiai woods near Telsiai. Nazi special squads murdered Jews in the border areas and in the cities. In some instances, German troops attacked Lithuanian civilians. In yet other incidents of the early days, armed men of dubious allegiances took advantage of the disorder to commit acts of violence and settle personal scores under various pretexts. Some real as well as suspected Communists perished in the first phase of the invasion in an atmosphere of vengeance and revulsion against Stalinism.

It was against this background that the provisional government declared the restoration of Lithuanian independence and a willingness to fight Bolshevism. However, the Germans had no intention of allowing any independent authority in the Baltic States. The provisional government was thus caught in a peculiar bind: it possessed popularity and legitimacy in the eyes of most Lithuanians but had no real power to affect the fate of the country or to force the Germans to grant the country its independence. In mid-July Gen. Stasys Rastikis, the provisional government's minister of defense, expressed his concern at the killings of the Jews to the German high command but was dismissed by the Wehrmacht. On August 5, the provisional government resigned in protest against the inauguration of a Nazi civilian occupational administration, and Ambrazevicius in his closing speech declared that his government was denied transport and the requisite communications by the Germans and was therefore not in a position to halt the "excesses" against the Jews. Most of the government's members refused to join the German-sponsored council headed by Gen. Petras Kubiliunas (1894-1946), a pro-German officer.

The Nazis heeded no one: they had their own preplanned agenda of destruction. During the late summer and early fall of 1941, in operations of unprecedented savagery, well-organized Nazi killer squads known collectively as the *Einsatzgruppen* unleashed a campaign of systematic mass murder against Lithuania's Jews, slaughtering over one hundred thousand men, women, and children in little more than two months. In most cases, the killings were conducted out of public view, but their extent soon became apparent to a terrified populace.

While many if not most Lithuanians had welcomed the Germans as the force that drove out the Soviets, this positive feeling faded as Nazi aims and policy in the East unfolded. Initially, the Church hierarchy had welcomed the departure of the Communists, urging the people to remain calm and carry on under the new administration. After the Soviet retreat, the Church managed to partly retrieve its pastoral rights and some of the properties seized by the Communists; however, this situation depended on the skill of pro-Catholic Lithuanian officials in "looking out" for Church interests. In terms of pastoral work, the Church was able to continue with somewhat less obstruction than under the Communists. Despite German suspicions and displeasure, formerly closed seminaries were reopened. The hierarchy made efforts, with limited success, to provide Lithuanian priests for the thousands of young people deported to the Reich for labor service under difficult conditions. Religious instructors to the schools were appointed with the assistance of the counselor for education. While the Nazis showed little interest in obliterating religion as such, the situation of the Church was anything but easy. In March 1942 the Germans deported Archbishop Romuald Jalbrzykowski of Vilnius as well as a number of Polish religious to the provinces while some nuns were taken to Germany for forced labor. Archbishop Mecislovas Reinys took charge of the archdiocese; once again, just as in the 1920s, the Polish-Lithuanian conflict escalated.

The inhuman policies of the Nazis posed a moral challenge. To their credit, a number of priests angrily condemned the killers and those who had looted the property of the victims. In July 1941 the archdiocese of Kaunas requested the German and Lithuanian military commandants in Kaunas to intercede on behalf of the Jews. Monsignor Kazimieras Saulys, the general vicar of the archdiocese, was the most persistent petitioner, but he was unable to achieve any positive results. In early August, the Lithuanian bishops' conference proposed to address German authorities on the Nazis' actions against the Jews and other pressing matters; but Adrian von Renteln, the new German general commissar for Lithuania, would not receive Bishops Vincentas Brizgys and Teofilis Matulionis, the hierarchy's representatives. At the same time, Gen. Petras Kubiliunas refused to consider any intercession for the Jews, telling the bishops and other concerned officials that such problems were explicitly within German jurisdiction. Another request from the hierarchy for a meeting with the general commissar in early October was also rejected.

German-Lithuanian relations steadily deteriorated after the summer of 1941. In the fall of 1942 the Nazis arrested three prominent former Lithuanian statesmen — Father Mykolas Krupavicius, former Agriculture Minister Jonas Aleksa, and former President Kazys Grinius — for publicly expressing their opposition to Nazi atrocities and protesting the deportation and resettlement of Lithuania's Polish farmers to the east. The bishops also opposed the resettlement scheme in the form of a sermon given by Bishop Brizgys in October 1942, the contents of which were broadcast a few days later by the BBC. In addition, there were spontaneous individual efforts of resistance to the Germans. One example was the campaign of numerous persons to save the Jews. Thousands of Lithuanians, many of them Catholic laymen and religious, assisted the persecuted Jews in various ways. Among the priests who were active in helping Jews were Father Alfonsas Lipniunas (who died soon after his release from the Stutthof concentration camp), Father Jonas Borevicius in Siauliai, Canon A. Zelvys in Kaunas, and Father Bronius Paukstys. The work was dangerous and difficult: while one perpetrator could kill dozens of people within minutes, it often took the efforts of scores of dedicated souls over a long period to save a single Jew. In the end, only several thousand Jews survived in Lithuania. On another front, in 1943 the bishops successfully opposed the proposed genocide of the handicapped and mentally impaired.

Could more have been done to oppose the Nazi schemes of murder and repression? Every occupied country contained those who sought to survive by taking no risks: an understandable though hardly Christian position. It is difficult to do justice to the complex history of the Catholic Church, the Holocaust, and German-Lithuanian relations in a short work. Yet in constructing a balanced view, two oft-forgotten points should be brought out. First, whatever the reasons some Lithuanians may have had in supporting the German war effort against Russia, ideological affinity for Nazism was the least important; fear of a Soviet return was the major factor. Second, while the relationship of the Christian churches to the Jews has been critically discussed in recent historical literature, even among Catholic theologians sensitized by the Holocaust, it is clear from the accounts of survivors themselves that many of those who risked their lives to save Jews were motivated by a desire to do what they perceived as their Christian duty.

Even as their disenchantment with the Germans grew, the majority of Lithuanians eschewed armed struggle. Most were distrustful of the anti-German Soviet or Polish partisans concentrated in eastern Lithuania, since these groups were hostile to Lithuanian national aspirations and they themselves often utilized terror and intimidation against civilians. To most people, it was axiomatic that nothing should be done to assist the return of the Russians. Encouraged by the stand taken by the provisional government, the non-Communist resistance grew after the fall of 1941. In the main, it took the form of passive (that is, unarmed) resistance such as the obstruction and sabotage of Nazi economic and cultural policies; for instance, numerous fictitious student ID's were passed out by university administrators to gain young people exemptions from the Reich's noxious labor service. During the second and third year of the German occupation, Lithuanian anti-Nazi groups developed increased coordination and a strategy of resistance. After negotiations to paper over differences between antagonistic "Catholic" and "Leftist-Laicist" factions reflecting prewar divisions, a compromise coalition, the Supreme Committee for the Liberation of Lithuania (better known by its Lithuanian acronym VLIK), was founded on November 25, 1943. The aim of the resistance was to establish an independent Lithuania but to do nothing that would hasten the return of Stalin's army. Most Lithuanians pinned their hopes on the idealistic provisions of the Altantic Charter in the belief that the Western democracies would never allow the Soviet Union control of territories it had acquired during the period of Stalin's cooperation with Hitler between 1939 and 1941. This attitude also explains the pronouncements of some prominent Church and secular leaders in 1943 and 1944 urging the Lithuanians to work hard for the defeat of Bolshevism and the preservation of freedom, at the same time studiously avoiding any mention of support for Nazism or statements critical of the Western Powers.

The growth of resistance was a reaction to German repressions in the wake of the population's universal refusal to enlist in a Nazi-organized Lithuanian SS Legion in March 1943. As a result, the Nazis closed the Universities of Vilnius and Kaunas, and arrested forty-six prominent officials and intelligentsia, including well-known Catholic activists, confining them in the Stutthof concentration camp as hostages. The uncooperative native administration also suffered: dozens of unreliable or resistant Lithuanian police officers were arrested and some were executed. In a desperate search for provisions and manpower, the Nazis resorted to increasing violence, executing uncooperative peasants and invading churches in search of young people for labor service in Germany, considered a particularly outrageous practice by Catholics. One widely reported incident of the time involved

Monsignor Bernardas Suziedelis, the pastor of Ziezmariai, who was arrested after he protested against the Germans' seizure of young people during Mass at his church.

As the Eastern Front approached Lithuania the desperate Germans promised the Lithuanians that they would sponsor autonomous Lithuanian military units whose sole purpose was to defend the country against the Russians. Since this was quite a different matter from the earlier attempt at creating a Lithuanian SS Legion, tens of thousands of volunteers responded to the call of Gen. Povilas Plechavicius and joined the so-called Local Force during the spring of 1944 in the hope that such a Lithuanian army could stave off the Russian threat until the British and Americans saved the day. However, in May 1944 the Germans, realizing that the Lithuanians intended to use the new army for their own national ends rather than the defense of the Reich, abruptly arrested the Local Force's senior officers and executed about a score of its soldiers to intimidate the rest. The Germans then interned those recruits they could find. Thousands, warned by their officers, evaded Nazi capture by dispersing or fleeing into the forests. The Germans also arrested a number of resistance operatives after uncovering a large part of the underground network. These events were a fitting background to the German-Lithuanian relationship at the end of the war and a prime example of the Nazis' political stupidity: through their own savagery and arrogance they had failed to take advantage of the enormous ground swell of anti-Soviet feeling that they had first encountered three years before.

In early July Soviet troops entered Vilnius and on August 1 the Germans abandoned Kaunas. Except for Klaipeda, Lithuania had been cleared of Germans by October of 1944. The three years of Nazi rule had decimated the country. Nearly a quarter of a million people, the majority Jews, had been systematically slaughtered. Thousands of ethnic Lithuanians had also been arrested and killed by the Nazis. About seventy-five thousand young people had been deported to the Reich for labor under harsh conditions. Obviously, the damage to the economic and cultural infrastructure of the country was immense.

Like the majority of the population, the Catholic bishops viewed the return of the Soviets with alarm. Archbishop Juozas Skvireckas, Bishop Vincentas Brizgys, and Bishop Vincentas Padolskis (1904-1960) were evacuated by the Germans; hundreds of priests and nuns fled to the West. In all, over a hundred thousand Lithuanian civilians attempted an escape westward and more than sixty thousand succeeded in making their way into Germany ahead of the advancing Soviets. That number would certainly have been higher had not many people been convinced that the Soviet presence would be a brief one, given the faith in the impressive power of the Western democracies. There was a widespread belief that the British and Americans would never allow this "war against tyranny" to end by acquiescing in a Soviet occupation of countries that the West publicly recognized as independent states. Many recalled recent history and hoped for a repeat of World War I: a Russian reversal followed by Germany's defeat at the hands of the West.

This attitude may seem strange, indeed bizarre, to Americans weaned on a history of World War II that comfortably divides the belligerents into heroes and villains. The view of many East Europeans is not so difficult to understand, and in fact becomes entirely logical if one remembers the incomparably more brutal political and human realities of the Eastern Front when compared to the war in the West. These realities induced radically conflicting perspectives among those undergoing "liberation." In short, to the nations of Western Europe, the coming of American and British troops meant the restoration of genuine national independence and the destruction of totalitarian rule. To Jews and Gypsies everywhere, the arrival of Allied troops (whether Soviet or Western) meant deliverance from death; to the local Communists, the Red Army was an instrument of their power. But for millions of East Europeans, and for a majority of the suffering population in the Baltic States and the Ukraine, the surrender of Nazi Germany and the advent of Soviet power brought no peace, security, freedom, or national independence; in fact, in some districts of Lithuania, the cruel irony was that more Lithuanians met a violent death in the five years following the German surrender than during the entire duration of the Second World War.

Postwar Communism: The Violent Years

Chaos and violence were the norm in Lithuania during the eight years that followed the end of World War II. As the front passed through the country there was an outbreak of looting and rape accompanied by several mass executions; but, in general, Soviet behavior during the first months stopped short of mass terror. Overall policy seems to have been aimed at conciliating an unfriendly population while the war with Germany was still in progress. There was also a severe shortage of native administrative personnel: during the immediate postwar years only about a fourth of all Communist Party members in Lithuania were ethnic Lithuanians.

Some people were relieved at the failure of their worst expectations to materialize immediately. However, once the war had ended and it became clear that the Western Allies would not seriously challenge Soviet prerogatives in the Baltic, the situation in Lithuania grew worse. In August and September 1945 over sixty thousand civilians were exiled to points east. Between 1946 and 1950, at least a quarter million more of Lithuania's inhabitants were deported, mainly to the Far North, Siberia, and Kazakhstan. As in 1941, the exceptionally harsh conditions of the deportations and the difficult situation of the deportees at their destinations meant a high death rate among the victims. The deportations were in large part motivated by the Soviet desire to break resistance to the collectivization of Lithuanian agriculture, a process that was completed by the early fifties. The collectivization and other aspects of Lithuania's postwar Sovietization were supervised by Mikhail Suslov (1902-1982), who was later to become the major Soviet ideologue under Khrushchev and Brezhnev.

Perhaps the most violent and traumatic aspect of postwar life was the anti-Soviet guerrilla war that raged in Lithuania during the mid- and late forties. By early 1945 there were some thirty thousand armed men in the country's forests, although during the eight years of intense warfare (1944-1952) as many as one hundred thousand people may have participated in the anti-Soviet resistance in one way or another. The partisans' ranks were swelled by indiscriminate Soviet repression that made nearly every non-Communist a potential target. At the height of the armed campaign in 1946-1948, the Soviets employed security forces numbering over one hundred thousand men. For a small country, the cost of this "war that followed the war" was frightful: the lowest estimate is that some twenty thousand resistance fighters were killed with at least an equal number of casualties among the occupation forces. An undetermined but large number of Lithuanian civilians were victims of atrocities carried out by the various Russian and local security units. In addition, thousands of Communist activists and alleged or real pro-Soviet collaborators were assassinated, ambushed, or executed by the partisans. Although out of sight of Western news cameras, the human toll of this conflict was probably greater than the violence that plagued El Salvador during the 1970s and 1980s; more than likely it equaled the agony of Lebanon during the same period. In the end, the lack of any substantive outside assistance and an erosion of popular support due primarily to collectivization ended the main armed rebellion by 1952, although isolated bands of armed men were still reported by the Soviet press in the 1960s.

The fate of the Catholic Church in Lithuania very closely mirrored that of the society at large. At the onset of the second Soviet occupation in 1944 the Communists, still embroiled in war with Germany, adopted a conciliatory attitude toward the Catholic Church. During the war atheist propaganda was virtually nonexistent. It is interesting to note that in November 1944 Nikita Khrushchev, then Ukrainian Communist Party chief, attended the funeral of the popular Archbishop Andrew Sheptytsky (Szeptycki in Polish) of Lvov, the metropolitan of the Uniate Catholic Church, despite the latter's known support for the establishment of an independent Ukrainian state. The Lithuanian Catholic Church also carried out its work with relatively little obstruction during the 1944-1945 period, although the Catholic press, religious education, and the Church social institutions were not permitted to revive. There was little antireligious propaganda, religious instruction in the parishes was permitted, and three diocesan seminaries with hundreds of students continued their studies.

The relations between the Communists and the Church worsened after the formal end of hostilities in Europe. Beginning in December of 1945 the Catholic Church was burdened with huge taxes for its buildings and, soon after, monasteries and convents were closed. One of the central problems involved religious education: the terror that intensified throughout the country during 1946 made religious instruction in the churches very difficult, and in 1948 the government banned such activity outright. The most outspoken opponent of the Soviet regime was Teofilis Matulionis (1873-1962), bishop of Kaisiadorys, a veteran of Soviet prison camps in the twenties and thirties when he had tried to work among Catholics in Russia. Matulionis protested the arbitrary policies of the regime, announcing that an accommodation was possible only if the Communists did not attempt to make the Church an instrument of the government. Another member of the hierarchy who took a clear stand in defense of Catholic rights was Mecislovas Reinys, the archbishop of Vilnius, who argued eloquently that Soviet law, the UN Charter, and even the Nuremberg Trials (by condemning Nazi suppression of Church schools) granted the Church social and educational rights.

The Soviets were angered by the refusal of some bishops to fully endorse the regime's calls for the guerrilla resistance to lay down its arms. With very few exceptions, the clergy naturally opposed violence, even though they may have sympathized with the goals of the underground; on the other hand, since most guerrillas were Catholics, contact with them was inevitable. Archbishop Reinys condemned all indiscriminate violence, thus angering the Communists. Bishop Matulionis was blunt: the Soviet government, he said, was responsible for creating the severe conditions that led to armed rebellion. In early 1946, under pressure from the regime, the bishops issued an appeal for an end to the violence, which, however, was denounced as unsatisfactory by the Communists. In addition to the clash over this issue, the regime's restrictions on Catholic activities continued. Two of Lithuania's seminaries were closed and the remaining one in Kaunas was ordered to reduce its size by half. Finally, the Soviet regime sought to destroy the autonomy of the Church, particularly its hierarchical structure, thus contradicting the officially stated policy of noninterference in the internal affairs of Catholic believers. The authorities attempted to introduce a system of small religious communities responsible to government committees, a transparent attempt to subvert the traditional Catholic parish system and exclude the clergy from leadership of the faithful. The government hoped that in this way Church organization would fall into the hands of the Communist Party. Finally, in 1948 the regime nationalized all Church properties: the buildings were now leased to religious communities.

Unable to force the Catholic hierarchy and the majority of the clergy to accept the new changes, the Soviet regime intensified its offensive against the Church. The Kremlin's policy in Lithuania was foreshadowed by the arrest in April 1945 of Joseph Slipyj (the metropolitan of the Uniates) and the official "abolition" of the Ukrainian Catholic Church. In February 1946 the authorities arrested Bishop Vincentas Borisevicius (1887-1946) of Telsiai, a well-known opponent of both Nazism and Communism, who was sentenced to death and executed soon after. His auxiliary, Bishop Pranas Ramanauskas (1893-1959), was exiled to Siberia later in the same year. The same fate befell Bishop Matulionis of Kaisiadorys and his replacement, the diocesan administrator Monsignor Bernardas Suziedelis. Archbishop Reinys of Vilnius was arrested in June 1947 and died in Vladimir prison in 1953. By the middle of 1947 Lithuania's only active bishop was Kazimieras Paltarokas (1875-1958), the bishop of Panevezys, who became the administrator of the archdiocese of Vilnius in 1949. The Soviet authorities also struck at the clergy at large, particularly the middle-level administration of the Church, the superiors of monasteries and convents, and the more prominent pastors; in all, about a third of Lithuania's Catholic clergy were deported during the late forties.

The attack on the clergy was followed by a dramatic rise in atheistic and anticlerical propaganda. An endless supply of brochures, pamphlets, newspaper articles, and books depicted the Church as a "handmaiden of fascism," an organizer of the nationalist underground, and an agent of Western intelligence services. In 1949 the authorities founded the Lithuanian Society for the Dissemination of Political and Scientific Information, an important source of anticlerical and antireligious propaganda. There were attempts to undermine the Lithuanian Church's ties with the Vatican and induce Lithuanian priests to denounce Pius XII, especially after the pontiff's statement of 1949 threatening excommunication of Italian Catholics who belonged to Communist organizations. The regime then sought to persuade the clergy to set up a Lithuanian Church independent of Rome. None of these measures brought any success, although the Communists did intimidate a few clerics into participating in conferences that "defended peace," denounced American imperialism in Korea, and otherwise supported Soviet domestic and foreign policy aims. It is doubtful that these Cold War charades had any credibility among a Lithuanian population with such recent experiences of close ties to the West.

The years of Stalin's rule in Lithuania constituted a terrifying and trying time for the Catholic Church. The country's anguish was expressed in the letter of the "Roman Catholics of the Republic of Lithuania" to Pius XII, dated September 20, 1947, and brought to the West by

Lithuanian partisan leader Juozas Luksa-Daumantas in early 1948. It was delivered to the pope in October 1948. The letter detailed the attacks on the clergy, the pressure on everyone to cooperate with the NKVD, and the general state of terror. In one poignant passage the authors summed up the general condition of Catholic Lithuania:

> Oppression, fear, bloodshed and suffering exist everywhere. More than 100,000 have died from torture or from the cold and hunger in Siberia. New victims are found every day. There is no home in which tears have not been shed. Only one free bishop remains in all of Lithuania. The curia is suppressed, the seminary is barely functioning, the convents and monasteries destroyed or scattered. No one knows when the police may come.

This period of Stalinist rule represented a nadir in the modern history of the Lithuanian people. The spiritual oppression was compounded by huge population and economic losses as well as society's violent integration into a totalitarian system alien to the traditions and political culture of the country. Even the Communists have recognized the national trauma of the period. The bloody nature of the decade that followed the end of World War II is a favorite theme in Soviet-Lithuanian literature, albeit with a different interpretation. The bleak outlook of the early fifties must have convinced many an observer that Lithuania's Catholic and Western-oriented value system was irretrievably lost.

Postwar Communism: Destalinization and Struggle

The death of Stalin on March 5, 1953, is considered to have initiated a new period in Soviet history: the so-called "thaw." Stalin's eventual successor, Nikita Khrushchev, startled the religious community when he stated in November 1954 that there had been excesses in the campaign against the Church. Khrushchev's announcement coincided with a limited relaxation of the Stalinist dictatorship. Thousands of surviving Lithuanian deportees were released from camps or their places of exile; however, only some were allowed to return to their country. About a third of the deported priests and two bishops, Matulionis and Ramanauskas, also returned to Lithuania, although the last-named were not allowed to resume their episcopal duties.

The Communist Party made other changes. For several years following Stalin's death antireligious propaganda declined. There was even official criticism of primitive and strident atheist indoctrination. In April 1954 *L'Osservatore Romano* reported a radio speech by Bishop Paltarokas outlining some aspects of religious oppression between 1944 and 1953. In general, the amount of information concerning the situation in Lithuania increased considerably, partly as a result of the fact that regular correspondence was now permitted between Lithuanians at home and their relatives who had fled to the West in 1944. In 1955 two new bishops, Petras Mazelis (1894-1966) and Julijonas Steponavicius (born 1911), were consecrated and assigned to Telsiai and Vilnius respectively. The new bishops were allowed to visit parishes and administer confirmation, activities that had been restricted for many years.

The tenuous relaxation of tensions between the regime and the Church was also accompanied by a resurgence of faith and confidence among Lithuanian believers. In 1956 the Catholic Church announced that it had received permission to build a new church in the rapidly growing port city of Klaipeda, utilizing donations of the faithful, the first time the Soviet government had authorized such construction. For the first time in over a decade, limited official contact with the Holy See was permitted. In the late fifties, some Lithuanian priests visited Rome and several Church officials were allowed to attend the Second Vatican Council (1962-1965). Beginning with the late fifties, the regime allowed the publication of a limited quantity of religious literature, mostly liturgical texts and calendars. Compounding the spirit of relaxation and hope was a new and relatively daring assertion of national prerogatives among the secular Lithuanian cultural elite and even among some Party members. Some people in and outside the political establishment had long resented the intense Russification of the Stalin years and now lobbied with some success to restore the Lithuanian language to greater use in public life.

The "thaw" of destalinization and its implications frightened the Party's leaders. After a time, they sought to reverse the trends of liberalization in religious policy, the arts, and national culture by a series of repressive actions without, however, reverting to the mass terror of the Stalin years. In Lithuania, the rector of Vilnius University and other high Party officials were dismissed for "nationalist deviations" while cultural workers were warned to adhere to Communist principles. In 1961 Khrushchev personally denounced Lithuanian Communists for permitting the restoration of Trakai, the medieval castle complex revered as the birthplace of Grand Duke Vytautas. A renewed hostility toward the Church also became evident. In 1957 the aging Bishop Matulionis consecrated Vincentas Sladkevicius (born 1920) as his successor in Kaisiadorys without awaiting government approval. The following year the authorities exiled both bishops from the diocese. In 1960 the Soviets seized the just-completed Queen of Peace church in Klaipeda, tore down the tower, and converted the building into a concert hall; the pastor and assistant were arrested in 1962 and tried on charges of black marketeering. In 1961 Bishop Steponavicius, the administrator of the archdiocese of Vilnius, was exiled to the northern border town of Zagare. The authorities appointed Father Ceslovas Krivaitis, who was to gain a reputation for compliance with the regime, to administer the archdiocese. The number of seminarians allowed to study at the Kaunas theological seminary was reduced from eighty in 1959 to less than thirty in 1964.

The various restrictions on Catholic life in Lithuania were accompanied by a renewed emphasis on atheist indoctrination and a resurgence of Soviet propaganda concerning alleged Catholic and "bourgeois nationalist" participation in Nazi war crimes, including attacks on

Lithuanian clerics living in the West. There was also a spate of scholarly and pseudoscholarly works portending to show that during the years of independence the Lithuanian Catholic Church had normally taken the most reactionary positions on social, cultural, and political issues. Antireligious propaganda ranged from relatively sophisticated sociological analyses of the Church to crude and even laughable propaganda tracts, such as one in 1962 that included the publication of excerpts from an obviously fictitious letter allegedly written by Pope Pius XII in 1941 urging Archbishop Skvireckas to support the German war effort. There were heavy-handed efforts to actually erase some of Catholic Lithuania's physical landscape. In 1965 the largest city in southwestern Lithuania, Marijampole (The City of Mary), was renamed Kapsukas in honor of the famous Lithuanian Communist leader. Zemaiciu Kalvarija (The Calvary of Samogitia) was now termed Varduva. In an arrogant display of callous disregard for people's feelings, Soviet troops bulldozed the famous Hill of Crosses in 1961, a popular pilgrimage site that contained thousands of crosses erected by the faithful in memory of the deceased or to commemorate various events in their lives, including deeply personal experiences.

At the same time, the Soviet government initiated official contacts with the Vatican and thus attempted to "normalize" relations, a process that culminated in 1967 with Soviet President Nikolai Podgorny's visit to the Vatican. The Church also sought an "opening to the East" during the 1960s in the hope of easing the situation of Catholics in Eastern Europe. The Soviet strategy of dealing with the Catholic Church emerged with greater clarity during the 1960s: enforcement of restrictions on religious activity, particularly religious education, while trying to maintain control over the Church administration by allowing the appointment of what the regime hoped would be cooperative bishops and pastors. In Lithuania, this program of the 1960s was manifest in the campaign against religious instruction, especially the catechization of children, and interference in virtually all aspects of pastoral work, explicitly mandated by Soviet legislation enacted in 1966. On the other hand, the regime approved the consecration of several new bishops. Juozas Matulaitis-Labukas (1894-1979) was consecrated in Rome in 1965 and was appointed apostolic administrator of the archdiocese of Kaunas. Bishop Juozas Pletkus (1895-1975) was assigned on the same basis to the diocese of Telsiai in 1968, and in the following year Liudvikas Povilonis was designated for Vilkaviskis. Romualdas Kriksciunas was consecrated bishop and appointed apostolic administrator for Panevezys. A council of bishops, headed by Matulaitis-Labukas, was formally acknowledged as the governing body of the Lithuanian Catholic Church.

Believers were understandably relieved at the disappearance of the Stalinist terror and massive repression. Contrary to Soviet expectations, however, the Church and Lithuania's Catholic believers did not gratefully await their fate in the new atmosphere. One did not have to be extraordinarily perceptive to grasp that according to this policy the Church was to be, in effect, spiritually emasculated, internally divided, separated from meaningful social and pastoral functions, and transformed into an officially approved administrator of a meaningless "cult." Resistance to the authorities' anti-Catholic campaign mounted during the 1960s amidst increasing signs that for many Lithuanians the Catholic faith was an important, even central, aspect of their lives. These indications were later confirmed by the emergence in the seventies of an organized Catholic dissident movement (which will be described in more detail below). In 1959 the West received a unique document of religious faith, a prayer book entitled *Marija, Gelbek Mus* (*Mary, Save Us*), which was smuggled out of the Soviet Union. It contained the original prayers and thoughts of four young Lithuanian girls who had been deported to Siberia. The poignant text, remarkable for its simple lyric beauty and lack of bitterness, depicted the attempt of Siberian deportees to maintain their faith, humanity, and dignity under murderously harsh and degrading conditions. It was translated into a dozen languages and given great publicity. During the early 1960s Catholic laymen and the clergy began to complain about anti-Catholic discrimination to Communist newspapers and especially to the government's commissioner for religious affairs. Part of the reason for the growth of dissent at this time may lie in the fact that in contrast to the fifties the hopes for an improvement in the conditions of the faithful declined as the Party's policy toward the Church became increasingly reactionary.

Despite such manifestations of faith and dissatisfaction, an organized Catholic movement did not emerge until 1968 when the more activist clergy began to present formal petitions to both Soviet authorities and the bishops. They protested anti-Catholic discrimination, the regime's campaign against religious instruction, and even the Catholic hierarchy's passivity in the face of the attack on the Church. The regime reacted harshly to the activist clergy's calls for religious freedom, particularly for the freedom of Catholic instruction: between September 1970 and January 1972 four major show trials were held resulting in the imprisonment of clergy and lay persons. The priests included Fathers Juozas Seskevicius, Juozas Zdebskis, and Prosperas Bubnys. The usual response of Soviet authorities to human rights petitions in those years was twofold: official refusal to even acknowledge the appeals, followed by KGB harassment of people sponsoring or signing the petitions.

In December 1971 Lithuania's Catholics began an organized petition drive directed to Party Secretary Leonid Brezhnev. In late March 1972 the memorandum signed by seventeen thousand believers, and intended for transmission to the Soviet leader, reached Kurt Waldheim's office at the UN. There was no official response, but the petition made news in the United States. The appeal outlined the various abuses Catholics had suffered at the hands of Soviet authorities describing them as a violation of freedoms guaranteed under the Universal Declaration of Human Rights. During the following year, Klaipeda's Catholics presented their own petition with over five thousand signatures pleading for the return of the Queen of Peace church that the parishioners had constructed with their own funds. The theme of most such mass petitions was that the Soviet regime should abide by its own constitution and the international obligations it had formally undertaken, such as the Universal Declaration of Human Rights.

While petitions are a routine method of political action in the West, their presentation to the government of a totalitarian state that controls the citizens' access to such necessities as housing, education, and employment is a moral and political act requiring considerable courage. Soviet authorities responded quickly to the unwanted publicity of the Brezhnev-Waldheim memorandum in the West and the other appeals of the Catholic community. They browbeat the Lithuanian episcopate into a public disavowal of the memorandum to the UN only two weeks after it was published in the West. However, many priests simply ignored the government's demand that they read the bishops' pastoral letter in their churches. Increasingly, the Catholic protest movement began to take on the themes of human rights, giving them a specific national and religious character appropriate to the Lithuanian context.

CHAPTER 9

Faith and Human Rights: The Church Since 1972

The Growth of Dissent and the 'Chronicle'

Two significant events, one violent and the other quite peaceful, marked 1972 as a unique year in the postwar history of Lithuania. The first occurred exactly a year after the much-publicized trial in Vilnius of Simas Kudirka, the Lithuanian sailor who had caused an uproar in the U.S. when he was forcibly returned by Coast Guard officers to his Soviet vessel at Martha's Vineyard after seeking asylum aboard the American ship *Vigilant*. On May 14, 1972, Romas Kalanta, a nineteen-year-old son of a college lecturer, sat down in a Kaunas park, poured gasoline over his body, and by his own statement immolated himself in protest against the Soviet occupation of Lithuania. It may be that this act of defiance was planned to coincide with President Nixon's visit to Moscow. On the following day, people began to gather at the park, and a sizable pile of flowers had accumulated at the site of the suicide. Kalanta's funeral was scheduled for the afternoon of May 18, but his body was secretly buried before the appointed hour. This subterfuge enraged a crowd of young people who had gathered for the funeral and resulted in two days of rioting that was widely reported in the Western press and clumsily acknowledged by Soviet authorities. There were conflicting reports of injuries and numbers arrested (reportedly in the hundreds), but one fact could not be denied: there was a definite national and anti-Russian motivation behind the disturbances. There were several other reported self-immolations within a few days. The antiestablishment mood was also reflected at an international handball tournament in Vilnius the following month. Young people refused to stand for the Soviet anthem, jeered the Soviet team, and openly rooted for the "foreigners." In the local press, the government complained of "hooliganism." The Kaunas demonstrations have not been forgotten: it is reported that to this day flowers appear at Kalanta's grave and the site of his death. Travelers say that both places are under obvious police surveillance.

In contrast to the disturbances described above, the appearance of the samizdat, or self-published, journal *Lietuvos Kataliku Baznycios Kronika (Chronicle of the Lithuanian Catholic Church*, henceforth to be cited simply as the *Chronicle)* in March 1972 was scarcely noticed at first. The very first issue of the *Chronicle* reported on the trials of the aforementioned Fathers Zdebskis (1928-1986), Bubnys, and Seskevicius; but, unlike the Party press, it also described the reaction of the congregations who supported the men during their ordeal. In addition to reporting on the trials of Catholic dissidents, the *Chronicle* has since its inception addressed virtually every issue that faces the Catholic community in Lithuania. The goal of this new Catholic journal, which is at least in part modeled on the Russian dissidents' *Chronicle of Current Events*, is to report incidents of discrimination against the faithful in Lithuania. It recounts court proceedings against believers and clergy, conflicts within the Church and among the hierarchy, and presents a survey of events concerning religious and Lithuanian national issues. One of the *Chronicle*'s most attractive features is its philosophy of journalism. It reports only concrete instances of discrimination against believers, avoids excessive rhetoric, acknowledges factual errors on the occasions when they occur, and cautions the contributors to provide only credible data. The journal itself is reproduced in limited editions, laboriously retyped or photocopied, then passed from hand to hand until it is smuggled out of the country. However, it is extensively quoted in radio broadcasts to Lithuania, such as those transmitted by Vatican Radio, the Voice of America, and Radio Free Europe-Radio Liberty; thus the *Chronicle* reaches a greater number of people in Lithuania than would be possible via print alone.

Not surprisingly, one of the major problems described in the *Chronicle* has also been the most persistent source of conflict between the Catholic Church and the Communist state since 1940: the issue of religious education. At its most basic level the battle has centered on the right of priests and parents to instruct minors in the Catholic faith. Government statutes promulgated in 1966 allowed only parents to provide religious instruction to their children (today even that is forbidden). This means a prohibition on systematic catechization of Catholic youth, the core of Catholic religious education.

The *Chronicle* provided details concerning the arrest of Father Bubnys as described in the parishioners' petition to the authorities. Lacking religious textbooks, the parents had requested their pastor to assist them in instructing the children. According to the parents, representatives of the Raseiniai Party Executive Committee then "broke into the church and, finding the children waiting for the pastor [Father Bubnys], raised a ruckus." Bitterly, the parents described the effect on their children: "The officials hunted down the frightened youngsters and dragged them through the town to the fire station; there they locked them up, demanding that the children write statements implicating the pastor." In their petition, the parishioners described how the weeping children, some of whom later literally became sick with fear, wrote their depositions unaware of legal distinctions between organized "teaching" and private "examining" of religious concepts, thus paving the way for Bubnys's one-year prison sentence. He had allegedly violated the Soviet legal code against "organized religious instruction" (see the *Chronicle*, 1972, No. 1). The human side of the Bubnys story as presented in the *Chronicle* is instructive: even in the absence of mass Stalinist terror, it illustrates the psychological and social stress on the Catholic faithful, the price paid as a result of activities considered routine in a normal, democratic society.

Since the trials of 1971 and 1972, Soviet authorities have partially relaxed the campaign against religious education, although throughout the 1970s and 1980s administrative penalties, especially fines, have been leveled against the clergy for allegedly violating the law against conducting religious instruction of minors.

The other side of the coin relating to the issue of religious education concerns the problem of atheist instruction in schools that (at least according to numerous incidents described in the *Chronicle*) frequently degenerates into harassment of youth from Catholic homes. It should be made clear that the teaching of atheism is not simply a matter of attacking religion as an ideological system or the Church as an institution. Ideally, the Soviet educational system seeks to create an individual imbued with the values of "Communist morality" consisting of a comprehensive code of ethical and social behavior founded on what is ironically termed "spiritual values." This means adherence to a philosophy of what is called scientific materialism to explain the objective world, and a strong commitment to the Party. Thus Soviet atheism should not be confused with the philosophies of the atheists, free thinkers, or agnostics of bourgeois persuasion found in prewar Lithuania or the contemporary West — that is, democratic atheism or agnosticism in its various forms that presupposes society's right to actively propagate contradicting views.

In their struggle against the "remnants" of religion, Soviet thinkers as well as the regime have often switched tactics. The approach has ranged from crude violence to a recognition by some sophisticated Lithuanian Marxist philosophers that since religion has deep psychological roots and may not inherently contradict science, Catholicism will not be destroyed by simply cutting its social roots. There has also been grudging admission that Communism itself is susceptible to degeneration into something approaching a dogmatic pseudoreligious cult, a fact readily apparent to any agnostic visiting Lenin's tomb. At its most open-minded, the regime has admitted that crude attacks on Catholic beliefs and practices result in the alienation of people from atheistic indoctrination. In any case, whatever the swing of the pendulum regarding official attitudes, it is clear that the practice of anti-religious proselytizing involves considerable coercion on the local level.

The most painful and controversial area of atheist pressure is in the schools. According to persistent reports in the *Chronicle* and from other sources, school administrators and teachers are encouraged to fulfill an atheistic "plan" of indoctrination. This leads to unfortunate cases of zeal in harassing religious primary- and secondary-school students as well as their parents, sometimes in the most personal areas of their lives. The *Chronicle* reported that in April 1975 a middle-school student in the northern Lithuanian town of Debeikiai was killed in a highway accident; the youth's widowed mother then made plans for a Catholic funeral. The local Party secretary, a teacher, threatened to disrupt the funeral if it were held in church and, finally, in a rage tore up the wreath ribbons in full view of students who had gathered for the viewing of the body. In the end, the mother was intimidated into accepting an areligious funeral (*Chronicle*, 1975, No. 17). In March 1976 the parents in Veisiejai charged that a fourteen-year-old boy had attempted suicide after being beaten by a police interrogator. The incident grew out of the fact that a group of youths had attended religious services on February 16, Lithuania's Independence Day, the commemoration of which is, of course, now banned by Soviet authorities (*Chronicle*, 1976, No. 22).

Over the years the *Chronicle* has reported literally hundreds of incidents in which school personnel, police, and Party activists have harassed students over the issue of religious practice. There is evidence that the regime has become sensitive to public revelation of such incidents. In August 1975 a Party official who had just returned from a visit to the West told a teachers' conference in Sakiai to avoid "tactless" behavior, since such mistakes would be reported in "the journal . . . without exaggeration, publishing our surnames, the time and school." This, in the Party's view, served the cause of anti-Soviet propaganda in the West (*Chronicle*, 1975, No. 20). Yet these admonitions do not seem to have had much effect on the behavior of atheist activists. The *Chronicle* (1978, No. 32) reported that in 1977 and 1978 the KGB displayed increased interest in the students in Telsiai, conducting interrogations and seeking to recruit informers. The authorities' concern about the "proper" attitude of the youth is amplified by the persistence of national loyalties: in 1980 two brothers were questioned at the Prienai KGB station in connection with the raising of the prewar Lithuanian flag during the February 16 anniversary (*Chronicle*, 1980, No. 44). In 1984 a group of students in Kybartai signed a petition defending one of their Catholic classmates when the latter was questioned by the security police for allegedly raising the independence flag on the eve of the anniversary and writing anti-Soviet slogans on the walls of the city hall (*Chronicle*, 1984, No. 63).

It does not seem likely that the atmosphere in the schools can change much within a totalitarian system in which intolerance and dogmatism are integral parts of the political culture. Perhaps, at its most vulgar, it is illustrated by the following classroom exchange reported to have taken place in the town of Saukenai after the teacher had explained that the world originated from matter (*Chronicle*, 1978, No. 34):

> [Student]: Madam Teacher, if the world originated from matter, then where did the matter come from?
> [Teacher]: That's none of your business.
> [Student]: So who can explain that to me?
> [Teacher]: Sit down, stupid!
> [Student]: If I'm an idiot, please let me go to a doctor.
> [Teacher]: Get out!

There is another and even more controversial level at which the struggle for religious education is played out in Lithuania. This concerns the training of priests at the

Kaunas theological seminary, the country's only official-ly permitted Catholic school. The entire process of educating new clergy has become critical in the face of the gradual disappearance of the clerical generation or-dained in the independence period or during the war. There are still numerous priests who have received their education in the pluralistic society of independent Lith-uania. For these men, Western values form the basis of their cultural and social philosophy. Clearly, however, most of them will be gone within the next decade. The is-sue of the character and education of new clergy has be-come inflamed by two factors: the role of the regime in selecting seminary candidates and the accusation by some Catholics that the Lithuanian Church hierarchy has remained passive in the face of Soviet attempts to debase theological education and infiltrate those training for the priesthood.

From the point of view of those seriously concerned with the survival of Catholicism in Lithuania, the Kaunas theological seminary presents a dilemma. On the one hand, the number of seminarians has risen dramatically: from scarcely two dozen theological students during the crackdown of the mid-1960s to seventy-two students in 1979. A secret government report leaked by the *Chron-icle* (1985, No. 66) reported one hundred four semi-narians as of January 1, 1984. Many Catholics were pleased with the ordination of eighteen priests in June 1982, the largest number ordained at one time in twenty years. On the other hand, there has been widespread ap-prehension about the conditions of instruction and the suitability of some of the new candidates. According to virtually all sources, the regime interferes openly in the seminary's admission process and there is evidence that the KGB constantly seeks to pressure young men with vocations to become informers and regime col-laborators. It can be assumed that some of the semi-narians are police agents. The Catholic protest move-ment has been highly critical of the rector, Father Viktoras Butkus, whom it perceives as subservient to the regime's interests.

The issue of the seminary has opened wounds among the Catholic clergy in Lithuania. A number of priests, particularly in the hierarchy, have counseled accommodation with the authorities as the only way for the Church to survive. They see activism as useless in the face of the Soviet police. The episcopate is particularly vulnerable to threats and manipulation, since bishops fear that their disappearance would leave the Church leaderless. For their part, activist priests have decried accommodation, arguing that such a policy is equivalent to allowing a Trojan horse into the Catholic community. The divisions among the clergy were brought to the surface in the affair of a young seminarian dismissed from the seminary in 1977 for drinking and womanizing. Some activist priests were outraged when the aforesaid young man was later ordained a deacon and assigned to a parish, charging that this was done under pressure and in connivance with Communist authorities. In addition to protesting the admission and ordination of unsuitable candidates, there have been voices against the dismissal of devout seminarians at the insistence of the authorities.

The problem of control over religious education goes to the heart of the canonical and spiritual issue of Church-State relations in Communist Lithuania where, in contrast to Poland, the independence of the Church is not formally recognized. Several years ago, the *Chronicle* (1984, No. 64) presented its point of view bluntly:

The Apostolic See has condemned the efforts of atheists to divide the Church in Nicaragua. The atheists have tried to do the same thing in Lithuania for a long time: they keep trying in every way to place in key positions of the ecclesiastical hierarchy, priests who have betrayed the Church. It is almost exclusively such clergy that officials allow to inform the Vatican.

Today priests who have sold out to the government are still in the minority, so the KGB is making great efforts to see that in the future such priests should constitute a majority . . . the recruiting of collaborators with the KGB among the young men entering the Kaunas Seminary has intensified. The KGB, as usual, has been threatening almost every applicant that, unless he promises in writing to be an agent of the KGB, he will never set foot in the seminary. They have pressured the young men, saying that many of the other candidates have already signed.

In addition to the issues of religious education, which are so important for the continuation of Catholicism, the *Chronicle* has described a wide variety of other problems confronting believers in Lithuania. There is the issue of social and economic discrimination faced by acknowledged Catholics in a society where, at the very least, public indifference to religion is a prerequisite for any prospect of professional advancement. The *Chronicle* (1975, No. 16) has reported a number of such problems of discrimination. One case involved an agronomist fired from his job and unable to find work because of his public religiosity. Another was the example of a music teacher in a Vilnius school who was dismissed after twenty-five years of officially acknowledged meritorious service: the director simply alleged that the teacher was "religious" (*Chronicle*, 1975, No. 17). A recent issue of the *Chronicle* (1986, No. 71) revealed that in March 1986 a young woman was released from a school of medicine in Kaunas: she was reportedly told that "medicine and religion are two incompatible things."

One of the cruder aspects of the regime's anti-religious policy is the destruction of local religious monuments. It is true that the state has expended highly publicized sums of money in restoring some of the more famous churches as "architectural monuments of the Republic," such as St. John's in Vilnius and the Pazaislis monastery near Kaunas. However, it should be remembered that these buildings no longer function as places of worship and that the policy of preservation does not extend to lesser-known locales. The closing of dozens of historic churches to the faithful in the cities has been well documented. Yet the less publicized elimination of what can be called the "Catholic landscape" continues apace in more remote areas. Catholics are particularly galled at the destruction of the hundreds of traditional wayside crosses, shrines, and chapels that served not only as places of worship but also were considered important cultural, historical, and commemorative artifacts, some of great value as objects of folk art. The *Chronicle* reported that in October 1975 crosses were destroyed at the famous Hill of Crosses near Siauliai for the third time since the war. Even so, the crosses are being constantly replaced by believers. In July 1975 an old man in Lazdijai district complained to the local authorities that drunken officials had torn down a cross he had erected in his front yard. He was told that "structures" could be erected solely with the permission of the "district's architectural inspector" (*Chronicle*, 1975, No. 18).

Reporting on the difficulties facing Catholic believers in Lithuania is an important function of the religious protest movement. Clearly, the publication of the *Chronicle* requires some organization among committed persons willing to risk a confrontation with authorities. There are also other aspects to the organized Catholic movement in Lithuania. One of the more interesting developments has been the emergence of an unofficial "catacomb" Church largely bypassing the formal hierarchy. The appearance of an incipient underground Church was admitted by a regime spokesman in 1972. Neither the *Chronicle* nor the government has denied the existence of a "catacomb" Church, but, given its nature, specific information about it is scarce. Party officials suggested in 1976 that there were about fifteen hundred secret nuns in Lithuania. The *Chronicle* (1979, No. 37) reported that in November 1978 Father Virgilijus Jaugelis, who had been denied entry into the Kaunas theological seminary but had been ordained "in underground conditions," publicly held Mass in the town of Kybartai. The phenomenon of the unofficial priests has prompted the Soviets to seek ways to "legalize" the extension-course clergy. In the *Chronicle*'s opinion, the Church was fully justified in applying Canon 235 II, which provides for the education of clerics outside the seminary (*Chronicle*, 1984, No. 64). A Soviet government report of 1984 listed ten such "priest-illegals" by name but implied there were more. According to the *Chronicle* (1985, No. 66), the report stated:

> Some priest-illegals have been tried for various crimes against the state, and most of them are extremist-oriented. The illegals are prepared for the priesthood by dissident clergy of the Catholic Church, with the purpose of using religion and the church as a cover to carry on disruptive work and to arouse dissatisfaction among believers concerning state policy regarding religion and the Church. Such "priests," if they are working, must be brought to justice according to their place of residence, as parasites, since they do not have certificates of registration. Recommendations from heads of religious headquarters, bishops or administrators, submitted by them at the time of registration are invalid, since the church is separated from the state.

The last sentence of the above passage is instructive: it clearly distinguishes the Communist interpretation of the separation of Church and State (that is, State control of the Church) from that in the West (separation of Church-State functions).

One of the most active Catholic bodies in opposition to the Soviet regime was the Catholic Committee for the Defense of the Rights of Believers, which was inaugurated and announced at a press conference in Moscow in November 1978. The committee explained its four goals as the following: (1) to present to Soviet authorities instances of discrimination against believers; (2) to inform the Church hierarchy and society about the situation of believers in Lithuania and other Soviet Republics; (3) to ensure that Soviet laws regarding the Church do not interfere with international obligations undertaken by the Soviet Union; and (4) to explain their rights to believers and the clergy and to help defend them when necessary. The committee eschewed political goals and proclaimed it would act publicly. For a while, the Soviet government tolerated the committee's activities; but when it became clear that much of the Lithuanian clergy supported its efforts, a crackdown was ordered in the early eighties and two of the clergy, Father Alfonsas Svarinskas and the young priest Sigitas Tamkevicius, were arrested. (This will be covered in detail later on in this chapter.)

Other currents of Catholic dissent became evident during the seventies. In 1975 there appeared *Ausra* (*The Dawn*), an underground journal consciously named after the nineteenth-century Lithuanian periodical of the same name. *Ausra* espoused a kind of Catholic nationalism, counseling moral opposition to Russification, stressing Catholic and democratic values as a means of preserving national identity. Another publication, entitled *Dievas ir Tevyne* (*God and Fatherland*), has adopted a more stridently militant tone toward non-Catholic Lithuanians. There has also been *Rupintojelis* (*Wayside Shrine*) and *Tiesos Kelias* (*The Road of Truth*). All these publications have different and sometimes conflicting viewpoints; in any case, the *Chronicle* remains the most credible and best known. This is not to suggest that the *Chronicle* is infallible. It has made factual errors, some of which it has retracted, and, of course, it has its own bias and point of view. In a closed society no publication, official or unofficial, can be subjected to the kind of close and independent journalistic scrutiny possible in the West. Yet the *Chronicle*'s integrity has never been seriously challenged and it has remained Catholic Lithuania's most credible voice.

Although the Lithuanian Catholic movement has its own programs and purpose, these are closely related to the general struggle for human rights within the totalitarian systems of Eastern Europe. In November 1976 the Committee for Monitoring the Helsinki Agreement was established in Lithuania. It contained one Jesuit, a Catholic layman, an agnostic poet, and a Jewish activist. In Lithuania, the rights of Catholics were an important issue for the Helsinki committee, which managed to publicize a series of documents dealing with freedom of conscience. The Helsinki committee was quickly suppressed and by 1980 only two members remained at large. This committee's fate is a monument to the hypocrisy of the totalitarian mentality: a government arresting its own citizens for exercising rights it had solemnly proclaimed in an international treaty. Lithuania's contacts with dissidents elsewhere in the Soviet Union were revealed in the case of Sergei Kovaliev, a Russian scientist and founder of the first Amnesty International group in Moscow. He was arrested and brought to Vilnius in 1974 for possession of the *Chronicle* and was tried in December 1975, a trial noteworthy for the presence of Andrei Sakharov who came to support his friend. According to the *Chronicle* (1976, No. 21), "the sacrifices of Russian dissidents have helped Lithuanians see the Russian nation in a new light."

Of course, it is impossible to ascertain precisely the degree of support for the *Chronicle* and the dissidents in general. It is likely that the Lithuanian Catholic protest movement combines a hard core of dedicated workers moving among larger groups who are in passive sympathy. Actually, the numbers are not that significant. The ability of devout Catholics and nonreligious persons like Kovaliev and Sakharov to agree on common goals of human rights is encouraging. It means that in Eastern Europe the Church has the opportunity to forge a progressive identity by allying itself to ideals of tolerance and democracy that are accepted in open societies. This has already happened in Poland. It may yet be one of the greatest ironies of history that "revolutionary" Marxism — at least in Eastern Europe — will come to represent a militarized and ossified "old order" jealously defending the privileges of an elite class against a revitalized Catholicism advocating change and progress for the benefit of society at large.

The Soviet Regime Against Catholic Dissent

It is stating the obvious to be reminded that although the tactics, emphasis, and administrative methods of Soviet repression have varied during the last four decades, ranging from mass terror to wrist-slapping fines, the basic aim of Communist control in Lithuania has remained constant: the elimination of those religious, national, and cultural factors that hamper the "Sovietization" of the country. The latter concept is not easy to describe, but, for our purposes, it is sufficient to say that Sovietization in Lithuania includes a campaign against Catholic and Western values that have survived Soviet rule. Like all stories of repression and dissent, the history of Soviet tactics in response to the Lithuanian Catholic protest movement during the 1970s and 1980s has its own built-in "vicious cycle." Protest is, of course, a reaction to repression, and in turn the latter sometimes varies in relation to the intensity of dissent. Hence it is difficult to determine cause and effect in describing Soviet tactics regarding the repression of dissent.

One of the ways the regime seeks to eliminate the "remnants" of what it terms religious fanaticism (or genuine religious devotion) and bourgeois nationalism (that is, the propagation of national values outside the Soviet context) is to discourage any incipient attempts to revive national and religious life where it is already threatened. One example is the regime's obstruction to contacts with the thousands of Lithuanian villagers living outside Lithuania, primarily in Belorussia, where, despite the Slavicization of much of the Lithuanian population during the last hundred years, isolated pockets of Lithuanian speakers have survived assimilation. It has been persistently reported that local Belorussian Party officials, obviously complying with directives from above, have banned the use of Lithuanian in public and church functions. One report described how a local official fined Lithuanians in Polese (Belorussia) for daring to speak Lithuanian on state property, in this case, the collective farm (*Chronicle*, 1976, No. 21). Conservative in speech and custom because of their relative isolation from changes that have affected the rest of the Lithuanian nation, these "islands" of Lithuanian speech have attracted some interest among ethnographers and students; however, this is actively discouraged by local authorities, and visitors have reported harassment. In one of the more ludicrous aspects of nationalities policy, Lithuanians in Belorussia reportedly have been prohibited from subscribing to Soviet Lithuanian periodicals published a few miles away. Lithuanian-speaking Catholics in Belorussia have had extreme difficulty in obtaining priests for services in their native language. Obviously, the regime is promoting the elimination of the national and religious traditions of the Lithuanian communities in Belorussia.

The authorities have also cracked down on cultural activities that foster interest in the pre-Soviet period. It is dogma that only the Party is capable of interpreting the "bourgeois" past. During the 1970s and 1980s the KGB virtually ended the popular ethnographic expeditions of high-school and university groups when the young people began to show an unhealthy interest in local religious and cultural shrines that reflected the period of independence and postwar struggle. Lithuanian ethnography and study groups were told to direct their work toward the examination of the country's "revolutionary" past and wartime Soviet heroics, such as visiting monuments to the Red Army.

The consistent Soviet campaign against Lithuanian national values in culture, science, and the arts as well as the specific Russification policy of the government is an important concern of the Catholic protest movement. Within the USSR the later Brezhnev years witnessed an intensification of the campaign for "internationalism," widely understood as the code word for cultural Russification and antinationalist Party vigilance in the non-Russian republics. The Tashkent conference of 1975, which mandated a greatly expanded program of teaching Russian in non-Russian Soviet schools, aroused concern for the future of the national languages. A particularly humiliating blow in Lithuania was the decision, handed down from Moscow, to accept all doctoral dissertations, even those dealing with Lithuanian studies, only in the Russian language. There is no doubt that the long-range goals of the regime include the relegation of Lithuanian to a subsidiary role, particularly in economic and administrative matters.

The linguistic problems of doctoral dissertations and school curricula may seem trivial to people in the West, but, no matter how subtle, they are life-and-death issues for threatened cultures. There seems little prospect that the Soviet regime would resort to the tsar's crude "ban-the-alphabet" campaign of the last century, or that the Lithuanian language will soon disappear. Yet, despite the official rhetoric, it is obvious that the Party is no more a fan of national diversity than it is a supporter of any other kind of pluralism. And inasmuch as the Catholic movement invariably supports traditional values, its suppression serves the cause of weakening the Lithuanian national movement.

At present, it should be said that under Gorbachev, the atmosphere regarding Russification has changed in some parts of the Soviet Union. In August 1986, writing in the Soviet Union's largest literary perodical, the internationally acclaimed Kirghiz writer Chingiz Aitmatov openly criticized the practice of slavishly worshiping the Russian language and ridiculed the idea of creating an ethnically amorphous "Soviet nation," which had been Party dogma during the Brezhnev years. By contrast, the conservative Lithuanian Party leadership, well known for its subservience on national matters, has recently reemphasized the need for greater efforts in promoting "internationalism."

This official campaign has encountered a rising tide of protest against Russification and vocal support for the Lithuanian national movement. Under the umbrella of *glasnost*, much of the intelligentsia have spoken out openly, revealing their long-disguised rage at the Soviet assault on national values, such as the destruction of religious art and the crude distortions of Lithuania's past. In August 1987 a large Lithuanian national demonstration on the anniversary of the August 1939 Nazi-Soviet Pact attracted wide attention in the Soviet and Western press. Later in the year, thousands gathered at the cathedral in Kaunas to commemorate the one hundred twenty-fifth anniversary of the beloved national poet Jonas Maciulis-Maironis, turning the event into a patriotic and religious demonstration that included many young people. The regime required police measures to prevent street demonstrations during the seventieth anniversary of Lithuanian independence in February 1988; tens of thousands commemorated the event by attending church. In May of 1988 demonstrations were held to remember victims of the Stalinist deportations of 1948. On June 14 a gathering of about six thousand people assembled at the old cathedral in Vilnius to honor those who were deported in 1941. On June 24, 1988, an enormous crowd, perhaps as many as fifty thousand, massed in Vilnius at the behest of the new Movement for the Support of Perestroika to send off delegates to the extraordinary Communist Party conference in Moscow; many in the crowd waved the prewar Lithuanian flag and chanted for restoration of the country's sovereignty. According to the Soviet news agency Tass, on July 9 one hundred thousand gathered in Vilnius's Vingis Park to support the process of change in Lithuania. The Catholic Church is reported to have quietly encouraged the Lithuanian Movement for Perestroika, which has raised demands for democracy, religious liberty, cultural freedom, protection of the environment, and strengthening Lithuania's historic ties to the West. According to *The New York Times* of July 23, 1988, Lithuania's Russians fear that the new Lithuanian movement's ultimate goal is independence. The mood of genuine and massive political activism that has emerged in Lithuania is both unprecedented and unpredictable. However, one thing is clear: growing numbers of Lithuanians support change, since they see the current situation in their country as both undesirable and untenable.

It must be discouraging to Party leaders to realize the powerful attraction exerted by religious faith, national values, and the tradition of Lithuanian independence — all despite more than four decades of intense effort to Sovietize the country. The specific future forms of nationalities policy in Lithuania are impossible to predict, but it is certain that in large part they will depend on developments elsewhere in the Soviet union. There has been widespread unrest in Estonia and Latvia; in February and March 1988 national problems exploded into violence in Armenia and Azerbaijan. In a speech to the Central Committee in February 1988 Party Secretary Mikhail Gorbachev termed the nationalities problem the most fundamental issue facing Soviet society. Thus Western society has been exposed to a fundamental problem in the Soviet Bloc that it has long neglected and whose critical importance it is only now beginning to grasp.

In Lithuanian reality, Catholic and national dissent are closely tied. Like the tsars, the regime knows that by weakening one, it will diminish the other. This is why the Church, as the only remaining non-Soviet national institution, has come under such heavy pressure. Since the Catholic Church is certain to exist in Lithuania for a long time, part of the Soviet strategy has been to undermine its independence and make it a tool of the state. The divisions within the clergy alluded to earlier are, of course, primarily a result of the Soviet presence. This is to say that while each side has accused the other of "destroying the unity of the Church," the sharp differences of opinion between "loyal" clergy and dissident priests have arisen only because of the fact of Soviet rule in Lithuania. (When we say "loyal" clergy, we are referring to those who may sincerely believe that extensive collaboration with the regime is better for the future of Catholicism, following Vatican "Ostpolitik" under John XXIII and Paul VI.) The divisions within the Lithuanian Church cannot be compared to the normal differences of opinion and policy within the Catholic community in other countries where the authorities are not actively engaged in fostering conflict within the Church. In general, it can be said that Bishops Julijonas Steponavicius and Vincentas Sladkevicius, who have remained popular with the faithful, have been associated with a more determined defense of Catholic rights (reminiscent of Vatican policy under Pius XII), while Bishop Liudvikas Povilonis and Monsignor Ceslovas Krivaitis, the former administrator of the archdiocese of Vilnius, have adopted "loyal" positions. The newest bishop, Antanas Vaicius of Telsiai, consecrated in the summer of 1982, is widely respected for his pastoral work and personal integrity, reflecting the mood and policies of Pope John Paul II.

More sinister than the direct and indirect fostering of divisions within the ranks of the clergy has been the Soviet policy of recruiting police informers among priests and especially seminarians. Instances of such recruitment have been revealed in the *Chronicle*, but their exact extent and effectiveness, given the nature of the activity, are difficult to gauge. However, few people familiar with the workings of the KGB within the Soviet state can doubt that attempts to infiltrate the Catholic Church with persons whose primary loyalty is to the regime will continue. Some Catholic dissidents have gone so far as to suggest that ninety percent of the student body at the Kaunas seminary has been infiltrated and that the Church would be better served if the school were closed.

Of course, the most dramatic and public forms of Soviet repression have been the arrests, trials, and imprisonment of both secular and clerical Catholic activists during the seventies and eighties. In a few cases, there has been suspicion that persons have been done in by the KGB for their dissident activities. The trials of Fathers Juozas Zdebskis, Prosperas Bubnys, and Juozas Seskevicius in 1970-1972 (as related in Chapter 9) were only the beginning. The next wave of arrests and trials was closely related to the publication of the *Chronicle* and the founding of the human rights' groups. The new campaign against national and religious values was signaled by the KGB's arrest in March 1973 of about a hundred activists of ethnographic study groups in Lithuania and Latvia. Most of the detainees were soon released, some were later harassed, but five were put on trial in Lithuania for antistate activities.

In December 1973 the Soviet authorities tried Antanas Terleckas, a Lithuanian economist, on trumped-up charges of stealing state property, although the real nature of the attack on him was revealed by his rearrest in

225

1977 because of his work with the Lithuanian Helsinki monitoring group and alleged ties to the Catholic *Chronicle*. Terleckas's life is instructive of the difficult path endured by some of Lithuania's dissidents. In an open letter to KGB head Yuri Andropov in 1975, Terleckas described his story. Hailing from an impoverished peasant family in eastern Lithuania, he had, as a thirteen-year-old, witnessed the deportation of his (ironically pro-Soviet) uncle's entire family in June 1941 by the Russians, an ordeal that killed the parents.

"That night," remembered Terleckas, "an indelible hatred of Stalin was born in my soul." During the German occupation, Terleckas smuggled food to starving Russian POW's, recalling that he "detested fascism and terror." Nonetheless, he was arrested and beaten by the NKVD after the Soviets returned in 1944. Although Terleckas joined the Komsomol as a member of the proper social class in 1949, he never did fit into the Communist scheme of things and was constantly harassed, interrogated for "nationalist deviations," and finally arrested and sentenced in 1958, serving a four-year term. Then Terleckas's trial in 1973 began a new phase in his life of opposition. In 1987 Terleckas returned from exile in Magadan.

Numerous searches and arrests were carried out in 1973 and 1974. Between September 1974 and December 1975 a number of fairly well-reported trials were held in Vilnius. One of the defendants, Juozas Grazys, was of the older generation who, like Terleckas, had served prison terms. Others, like Nijole Sadunaite (born 1938), Virgilijus Jaugelis (born 1948), and Petras Plumpa-Pliuira (born 1948), had grown up during the Soviet period. Except for Sadunaite, whose father was a professor, the defendants came from poor peasant or working class backgrounds. The interest in the cause of the Catholic dissidents was heightened by the trial of Sergei Kovaliev, the agnostic Russian friend of Sakharov who supported the Lithuanians on human rights grounds. Another event that attracted attention was the apparent suicide death in November 1975 of the much-harassed Mindaugas Tamonis, an architect who had been given corrective "psychiatric treatment" as a result of his advocacy of a democratic socialist system. One of the most appealing victims of this set of arrests in the mid-seventies was Ms. Sadunaite, who eschewed obvious political motifs and, in her court speech of June 1975, based her entire defense on the principles of Christian charity and support for freedom of expression. She returned from exile in July 1980 but has become even more active than before in defense of religious and national causes.

The *Chronicle* continued to appear, and by the middle of the 1970s new dissenters — the Helsinki group (the Committee for Monitoring the Helsinki Agreement) and the Catholic defense committee (the Catholic Committee for the Defense of the Rights of Believers) — had appeared. There were new arrests. In July 1977 three lay people — Ona Pranskunaite, Vladas Lapienis, and Jonas Matulionis — were sentenced for possession of illegal literature. In 1978 Balys Gajauskas (born 1926), who had finished a twenty-five-year sentence for anti-Soviet activities in 1973, was sentenced to another fifteen-year term for "possession of anti-Soviet literature." At about the same time Helsinki group member Viktoras Petkus, active in Catholic circles, was sentenced to a ten-year term for "participation in an anti-Soviet organization." Dr. Algirdas Statkevicius, another member of the Helsinki group, was sentenced to compulsory psychiatric treatment in August 1980 but was permitted to come to the United States in 1988. Vytautas Skuodis, an American-born professor of geology at the University of Vilnius who was active in human rights causes and well known for his Catholic beliefs, received a twelve-year sentence in December of 1980 but was released and allowed to come to the United States in 1987. In June 1981 Vytautas Vaiciunas was sentenced to a two-year prison term for organizing a pilgrimage of believers.

Among Catholics, the cases that aroused the greatest reaction were the trials of Fathers Sigitas Tamkevicius and Alfonsas Svarinskas, the most active members of the Catholic defense committee. In May 1983 Svarinskas was sentenced to seven years in prison for preparing "slanderous materials" against the Soviet state; he was released in July of 1988. According to the *Chronicle* (1983, No. 57), thousands of Catholics signed petitions to free the priest. Tamkevicius was arrested at Svarinskas's trial and is presently serving a sentence. In January 1985 Father Jonas Matulionis and a young Catholic by the name of Romas Zemaitis were sentenced for organizing religious processions (*Chronicle*, 1985, No. 66).

The above list by no means exhausts the tribulations of Lithuania's Catholic protest movement in its confrontation with Soviet authorities. Still others have been arrested, detained, "informally" harassed, and threatened. As a result of Gorbachev's "restructuring" campaign, some people have been released and have returned to Lithuania. It is impossible to say how the Soviet authorities will now respond to the Catholic and national movements under the Gorbachev regime. Discouraging signs were reported from Moscow where the Lithuanian Communist Party has been criticized as too lenient toward believers. There has been a crackdown on parental teaching on religion, a previously tolerated practice. The organizers of the Vilnius demonstration commemorating the Molotov-Ribbentrop Pact (that is, the Soviet-Nazi Pact of 1939) in August 1987 have been physically assaulted and intimidated. No doubt, human rights groups and the press will closely watch the activities of the KGB and its cohorts, particularly Lithuanian officials in charge of the repression such as Jurgis Bakucionis, a chief Soviet prosecutor in Lithuanian political cases during the seventies and eighties. In any case, one can predict that the Soviets' struggle with religion will continue, whatever new methods they may undertake.

Society and Religion Today: An Overview

During the 1970s and 1980s Lithuanian society underwent some demographic and economic changes without, however, altering the basic structures of the last twenty years. Demographically, Lithuania has continued its historic tradition of ethnic and linguistic diversity. In 1988 the population stood at about 3.7 million within the present area of the Lithuanian SSR of 65,200 square kilometers, or 25,174 square miles (slightly smaller but more densely populated than the Republic of Ireland). Of this number, nearly three million, or about eighty percent of the populace, regard Lithuanian as their mother tongue, most of them ethnic Lithuanians. The largest single national minority are the Russians: about nine percent (or roughly three hundred thirty thousand) of the total, the vast majority of whom have arrived since the end of World War II and live primarily in the larger cities. There are still about a quarter million Poles concentrated in Vilnius and eastern Lithuania, making up a little over seven percent of the populace. There are nearly a hundred thousand Belorussians and Ukrainians. Fewer than fifteen thousand Jews remain of a once thriving community. Of the other groups, there are a few thousand each of Latvians, Germans, Tatars, and Gypsies. The smallest of the historically established groups are the few hundred Karaites, an originally Turkic-speaking Judaic sect. Except for the postwar Russians and Ukrainians, Lithuania's different national communities have centuries-old historical ties to the country.

Lithuanian remains the mother tongue of all but a fraction of the republic's ethnic Lithuanians. A small but growing minority of other nationalities, particularly the youth, speak Lithuanian as a second language. In the 1979 census, fifty-two percent of Lithuanians revealed that they are fluent in Russian. It is no secret that ethnic tensions persist and sometimes ugly incidents are reluctantly acknowledged by the regime. The major conflict seems to be between Lithuanians and the postwar Russian arrivals. Lithuanian natives, like the other Baltic peoples, have often told Western visitors that they see these Russians as foreign colonizers. On the positive side, some of the other historical animosities have diminished, such as the one between Lithuanians and Poles.

The population is becoming increasingly urbanized. In 1982 nearly sixty-five percent of the total population (but only fifty-seven percent of Lithuanians) were classified as urban. The countryside is still predominantly Lithuanian and Roman Catholic. Vilnius, the capital, now has some five hundred fifty thousand inhabitants; Kaunas, the most ethnically Lithuanian city, has over four hundred thousand. Other large cities are the seaport Klaipeda with almost two hundred thousand and Siauliai with about one hundred forty thousand. The regime estimates that over fifty-six percent of the population are working class and twenty-three percent are of white-collar background. Only about twenty percent of the population are now classified as collective farmers.

Industrialization has continued apace; however, it has slowed somewhat during the last decade and it is still too early to access the impact of Gorbachev's efforts at "decentralization" of the economy. As a result of slower growth, environmental problems, and an aging labor pool, there has been considerable talk of economic reorganization. While there is no doubt that the standard of living in Lithuania has risen compared to the difficult period of the forties and early fifties, recent years have seen economic stagnation, even decline. The Party, of course, is routinely given sole credit for masterminding economic progress, sometimes giving the impression that no economic development would have been possible under a "bourgeois" Lithuanian government. In science and high technology, Lithuania has achieved a fine reputation internationally in mathematics, computer science, and electronics.

Education has been greatly expanded and Lithuanian remains the language of instruction in the majority of the republic's primary, secondary, and higher schools. In recent years, however, Russification of the curriculum has been encouraged. By the mid-eighties, the University of Vilnius enrolled seventeen thousand students. Cultural life — or, more specifically, the canons of socialist realism — has been relaxed and modernized during the seventies and eighties. Censorship, of course, remains an everyday reality of life and, judging from recent pronouncements of the Party elite, constant vigilance regarding ideological deviations is emphasized. This and other factors indicate that the Lithuanian intelligentsia have continued in their fascination for Western ideas and their interest in Lithuania's past. In the past few years intellectual life has been marked by increased openness and diversity, which has at times elicited nervous criticism from Party leaders.

Television has entered the homes of the majority of Lithuanians and there has been considerable success in developing a Lithuanian film industry. In some specific areas of cultural life, Lithuania has achieved distinction. Photography and the graphic arts have become especially popular in Lithuania and have achieved international recognition. In terms of mass entertainment, basketball (which has been the national sport since the 1930s) has now become a national mania: Zalgiris of Kaunas has consistently won the USSR basketball championship since 1985 and is now recognized as one of the top amateur clubs in the world.

The modernization and urbanization of Lithuanian society has brought with it the usual problems. The birth rate has fallen while the divorce rate, negligent in the early fifties, is now approaching the American norm. Lithuania's abortion rate has skyrocketed and this is one of the prime concerns of the Christian community, often reiterated by the country's Catholic hierarchy. As in the West, the population is aging. The crime rate has grown and there are now reports of drug addiction among the youth. Environmental concerns about the now obvious costs of industrial growth have become a prime and somewhat controversial topic, especially among the intelligentsia, a concern greatly amplified by a disastrous oil spill off the Lithuanian coast in 1983. The idea of slowing industrialization to protect natural phenomena does not come easily to Soviet industrial managers who have for years literally worshiped rapid growth of heavy industry as the key to human progress.

In the face of this changing secular society, what briefly is the state of religion in Lithuania today? The 1987 edition of the *Catholic Directory of Lithuania* lists six hundred thirty Roman Catholic parishes divided among two archdioceses (Kaunas and Vilnius) and four dioceses (Kaisiadorys, Panevezys, Telsiai, and Vilkaviskis). In view of the abnormal political situation, all of the dioceses are ruled by "apostolic administrators." Roman Catholic canon law provides that each bishop, apostolic administrator, or capitular vicar is directly responsible to the Holy See. However, in the spirit of collegiality revived by the Second Vatican Council, the Lithuanian Catholic Bishops' Conference was established in 1981 as the coordinating body for Catholic believers. The conference is officially subject to the Soviet government's Office of Religious Affairs.

In 1984 councils of priests were established in the dioceses and archdioceses as advisory bodies, not without a struggle with the government over their makeup. The aged and ailing Archbishop Liudvikas Povilonis, the apostolic administrator of both the archdiocese of Kaunas and the diocese of Vilkaviskis, is the president of the bishops' conference. He has two auxiliary bishops: Juozas Preiksas and Vladas Michelevicius. Bishop Vincentas Sladkevicius and Bishop Antanas Vaicius are the apostolic administrators of Kaisiadorys and Telsiai respectively. Monsignor Kazimieras Dulksnys is currently administering the diocese of Panevezys, replacing Bishop Romualdas Kriksciunas who has resigned because of ill health. The archdiocese of Vilnius is headed by its administrator, Capitular Vicar Monsignor Algirdas Gutauskas, in lieu of the exiled Bishop Julijonas Steponavicius. Perhaps the most significant event for Lithuania's hierarchy has been the appointment of Vincentas Sladkevicius to the College of Cardinals. The elevation of Cardinal Sladkevicius, which took place in Rome on June 28, 1988, has brought considerable joy among Catholics in Lithuania and has even been given some prominence in the Soviet Lithuanian press. Some speculate that Julijonas Steponavicius has been named cardinal in pectore.

Lithuania's priests are now considerably older and fewer in number. In 1974 there were a total of seven hundred seventy-two Catholic clergymen in Lithuania, nearly half of them over the age of sixty and only seventy below the age of forty. This was only about half of the total that had existed in 1940. By 1982 there were less than seven hundred priests. The 1987 *Catholic Directory* listed six hundred sixty-five priests of whom nearly a hundred are retired, semiretired, or invalids. As a consequence, an increasing number of churches (one hundred fifty-six in 1987) are being left without resident pastors. A serious long-term problem for the Catholic community has been Lithuania's urbanization: as the population moves to the towns, new churches are not being opened in the cities. Thus rural churches will soon have "excess capacity." Of the other Western churches the regime acknowledges twenty-five Evangelical Lutheran congregations in Lithuania and five Evangelical Reformed parishes. There are several officially approved congregations of Baptists and possibly hundreds of believers who are "unregistered" Baptists and Pentecostals. The government also counts forty-one Russian Orthodox congregations in Lithuania. Of the non-Christian religions, the Jews maintain functioning synagogues in Vilnius and Kaunas. There are three communities of Muslims and a small group of Karaites.

It is not easy to determine with any precision the number of Catholic believers in Lithuania and even more difficult to estimate the extent of religious practice. In 1969 an East German "progressive" Catholic newspaper reported that as many as three-fourths of Lithuania's people still identified themselves as Catholics. In an official 1986 publication the Soviets stated that "the majority of the population of the Lithuanian SSR are non-believers." However, this statement refers to Lithuania's total population; the picture is certainly different if one considers only the Poles and Lithuanians, the country's historically Catholic peoples. Based on questionnaires, some Communist sources have maintained that a majority of youth are "active atheists"; then again, a Party official in 1974 complained about the rise of religious "fanaticism" among young people. Other surveys of the early 1970s showed that only a minority of students thought religion was harmful. Another study concluded that in the late seventies the parents in about half of the families were religious. In terms of raw numbers, the Soviet government estimated that in 1983 about three hundred thousand people attended church during major holy days (Christmas and Easter), and that about thirty-seven thousand visited the sacred shrine of Siluva. The *Chronicle* has recently given far more optimistic figures, maintaining that some ninety percent of Lithuanians are baptized, at least eighty-five percent receive First Communion, and sixty-six percent practice Catholicism.

It is obvious that information concerning religious practice cannot be easily verified at present and that it is sometimes difficult to define a "believer" and "religious practice" in contemporary Lithuania. But the various sources do make it possible to posit some trends. It seems logical to think that the majority of the population in the countryside, which tends to be older and ethnically Lithuanian, is still religious or theistic and fairly closely connected to Catholic tradition and that there are fewer practicing Catholics in the cities. On the other hand, a few recent visitors from Lithuania maintain that religious practice is actually greater among urbanites who can more easily practice their faith under conditions of anonymity. In any case, it must be remembered that part of the decline in overall religiosity in Lithuania over the last half-century may be a natural result of secularization and modernization, the consequences of which are not unfamiliar to the Church in the West. With this in mind, the situation of the Catholic community in Lithuania should not inspire as much pessimism as some would have. It is also obvious that Catholicism still has appeal to the young, contradicting the image of some in the West of Lithuanian churches only sparsely attended by old peasant women. The Polish example reveals that the vitality of the Church depends on its relation and relevance to the society at large, not its acceptance by the regime. The future will tell whether Lithuania's Catholic Church can fulfill the spiritual needs of the Lithuanian people in their present environment.

CHAPTER 10

The Catholic Church and the Lithuanian Emigrants

The Lithuanian people have proportionately one of the largest emigrant populations of Europe. Over a million people outside Lithuania trace their roots back to the homeland, although many of them have now abandoned the speech and customs of their forefathers. Emigration occurred in several large waves over the last century and was destined primarily for North America. This chapter provides a summary of the important role played by the Catholic Church in this historic migration, particularly in tending to the Lithuanian communities in the countries where Lithuanian immigrants settled. Before proceeding with such a survey, it would be useful to review the major stages in the history of Lithuanian emigration.

The Huddled Masses

The first people from Lithuania came to America before the nineteenth century. However, we cannot properly speak of a Lithuanian community in the New World until the flood of European emigration that began in the last quarter of the nineteenth century. In Lithuania, this period marked a massive exodus, primarily of the peasantry, who swarmed into the industrial centers of the Russian Empire (see Chapter 6), Britain, and, above all, the New World. The reasons for emigration were varied: economic distress, evasion of the onerous tsarist military draft, political and religious persecution. It is estimated that between 1869 and 1898 somewhat fewer than one hundred thousand Jews and Lithuanians left Lithuania for the United States. More reliable figures have been available since 1899 when U.S. immigration authorities began to keep statistics on Lithuanians as such: a quarter million arrived in America between then and World War I. The 1930 census listed 439,255 Lithuanians in the United States, over half of them foreign-born; a half-century later, the 1980 U.S. Census counted 742,776 persons of Lithuanian extraction. By 1913 some fifteen thousand Lithuanians had emigrated to the United Kingdom, the majority settling in Scotland. Another few thousand of the pre-World War I Lithuanian emigrants who left the Russian Empire were divided among Canada, Brazil, Argentina, and South Africa. The last-named country was the destination of tens of thousands of Lithuanian Jews who together with their descendants numbered over sixty thousand by the mid-1930s.

Some myths have grown up around the Great Immigration to America. Except for the Jews, the majority of the new arrivals probably did not intend to stay in America permanently: the goal was to earn money in the teeming factories and mines of the New World, return home, and buy land, resuming a familiar life in the Old Country at a higher level. This explains why the largest single group of emigrants consisted of either single men, or married men who came without their families. The desire to stay only temporarily may also be a reason many of the East European immigrants initially made little effort to assimilate into the new society. In the end, most of the Lithuanian immigrants remained in America, but there were also hundreds who returned in any given year. It is often forgotten that as many as a third of the turn-of-the-century immigrants returned to Europe; in fact, the great migration of this period created an immense two-way human current across the Atlantic.

Lithuanian immigration to North America slowed dramatically after the First World War, primarily because of concern in the United States that the country was being overwhelmed by the foreign-born. This fear was effectively institutionalized in the new restrictive immigration law imposed by the U.S. in 1924, which drastically reduced the tide of ''undesirables'' from Southern and Eastern Europe. The poor of Lithuania had to find new outlets. In 1925 the Brazilian government began actively soliciting cheap labor in Europe, and during the next five years some thirty thousand hard-pressed Lithuanians, predominantly land-hungry peasants, sailed for Brazil. Another seventeen thousand went to Argentina between 1923 and 1939; Uruguay absorbed a further five thousand Lithuanians by the mid-1930s, most of them in Montevideo. Between the wars, another seven thousand Lithuanians immigrated to Canada. Of Lithuania's Jews, over ten thousand migrated to Palestine during the same period while a smaller number swelled their community in South Africa.

The emigration of the Lithuanian population raised concern back home. During the 1890s Lithuanian publicist Vincas Kudirka condemned the peasantry's "escape to America." In the 1920s and 1930s the Lithuanian government maintained consulates in such far-flung places as Chicago, Sao Paulo, Tel-Aviv, and Capetown to represent its emigrant citizens. There was increasing concern in the late 1930s for the desperate plight of many Lithuanian farm workers in South America, but the Smetona government's plans to organize their return were interrupted by the outbreak of the war.

The majority of Lithuanians who left their homeland before World War II were driven by economic motivations. The war brought a new wave of people forcibly displaced by deportation, acts of war, and the fear of Nazi Germany or Soviet Russia. As we have seen in Chapter 8, hundreds of thousands of Lithuanian deportees were deposited in the Russian North, Central Asia, and Siberia; many never returned. Tens of thousands of young people were rounded up for work in the factories of the Third Reich, most of whom did not return to Lithuania when the war ended. And, finally, over sixty thousand Lithuanians managed to flee to the West, successfully evading the advancing Red Army in the summer and autumn of 1944.

Most of the people who fled westward found themselves in Germany and Austria as the war ended. The tragic situation of these refugees, later termed DP's

(Displaced Persons), was unlike that of any previous generation of Lithuanian emigrants. Like the Afghan refugees of the eighties, the Lithuanian DP's were caught in a trap: on the one hand, they had no desire to emigrate and wished desperately to return home; on the other, they could hardly go back as long as the Soviets occupied their native land. As it turned out, of course, the refugees' fears regarding the consequences of repatriation were fully borne out by the wave of violence and Stalinist terror that descended on the Baltic States after the war. In the end, when it became clear that no military or diplomatic solution would allow an immediate return to their homeland, the majority of the Lithuanian DP's left their camps in Germany, settling in the United States (more than thirty thousand), Canada (about twenty thousand), Australia (ten thousand), and Latin America (about thirty-five hundred). A minority stayed on in Germany and in the other European states. Only a fraction ever returned to Lithuania from the DP camps.

Except for several thousand people who left Lithuania during the Jewish exodus from the USSR in the mid-seventies, there has been no systematic emigration from Lithuania since the early 1950s. The Lithuanians who have arrived in the West during the last thirty years have consisted primarily of rare family reunions, defectors, exiled political dissidents, and people who have managed to gain exit visas for various reasons only after considerable effort. Contacts between Lithuanians abroad and those remaining in the homeland have expanded steadily since the early sixties. Thousands of Lithuanian emigrants now visit Lithuania every year and there are now some limited cultural contacts and exchanges between the diaspora and the homeland. The extent of contact, however, has always been subject to Soviet political machinations and "freezes" whose purposes are often impossible to determine.

The Lithuanians and the Church in the United States

Until the First World War most Lithuanian immigrants to America consisted of peasants and unskilled laborers. During the 1870s communities of Lithuanians grew up in the Pennsylvania coal-mining towns such as Danville, Shamokin, Mahanoy City, Hazleton, Wilkes-Barre, Scranton, and Shenandoah. The last-named town, "Senadorius" to generations of Lithuanians, became known as the Lithuanian "capital" of the United States. During the town's heyday in the twenties and early thirties, the Lithuanians formed the largest single group in Shenandoah (over ten thousand persons) and dominated its politics under Mayor Casimir Magalenga from 1918 to 1932. The very first Lithuanian Catholic parishes were organized jointly with the Poles — for example, in Shamokin, Shenandoah, and New York. Between 1871 and 1906 eighteen Polish-Lithuanian congregations were established. However, bitter quarrels soon broke out between the two groups, partly a reflection of antagonisms resulting from the emergence of Lithuanian national consciousness. The Polish-Lithuanian parishes gradually disappeared when the Lithuanian immigrants proceeded to establish parishes separately from the Poles. In 1885 the St. Casimir Society was founded in Pittston, Pennsylvania. Its purpose was to obtain permission and funds to set up an exclusively Lithuanian parish; after much difficulty, a church was completed in 1889. In the late 1880s more such Lithuanian-speaking parishes were organized in the Pennsylvania towns of Mahanoy City, Hazleton, and Plymouth. These were joined by parishes outside the Lithuanian "coal belt": St. George in Brooklyn (1888) and St. John the Baptist in Baltimore (1889). In Shenandoah the large Lithuanian parish of St. George was founded in 1891.

The parishes, parochial schools, and religious orders were the backbone of the Lithuanian-American Catholic community. They formed the hubs that anchored all other Catholic organizational, social, and cultural activities. On the eve of World War I there were nearly a hundred Lithuanian Catholic parishes in the United States; by 1941 there were one hundred twenty-four. Lithuanian primary parochial schools had their beginnings during the 1890s and it is estimated that by 1924 the total enrollment was about twelve thousand. Over the years, as the children of the immigrants have assimilated into American life, the number of Lithuanian parochial schools and pupils has declined precipitously; some of them are still in operation but have lost their once-important ethnic character.

The schools were staffed by orders of Lithuanian nuns founded in the United States to satisfy the particular needs of the Catholic immigrant community. In 1907 Maria Kaupas (1880-1940) and Father Antanas Staniukynas (1865-1918) founded the Sisters of St. Casimir in Scranton, Pennsylvania; the first convent was located at Mount Carmel. In 1911 the congregation transferred the motherhouse to Chicago. Under the leadership of Mother Maria Kaupas, who headed the order from 1913 to 1940, the nuns (who numbered about four hundred) established twenty-three elementary schools, two high schools, and two hospitals. With over three hundred members today, the Sisters of St. Casimir remain the largest Lithuanian congregation of female religious. In 1922 the Sisters of St. Francis were founded in Pittsburgh and began work in Pennsylvania's Lithuanian parochial schools. In 1938 a group of the sisters headed for Brazil to minister to Lithuanian immigrants in Sao Paulo. There are now about two hundred members in the community. In 1924 Father Alphonsus Urbanavicius established the Sisters of Jesus Crucified in Elmhurst, Pennsylvania. In addition to teaching, these Lithuanian nuns perform charitable work in hospitals and homes for the aged. Their motherhouse is presently located in Brockton, Massachusetts. There is a tiny community of Lithuanian Benedictine Sisters in Bedford, New Hampshire.

By contrast, there were few Lithuanian male religious in America until after World War II. The most important Lithuanian monastic order of the time consisted of the Marian Fathers, who established the American branch of their congregation in 1913 in Chicago. Their work included the founding of the once predominantly Lithuanian preparatory school, Marianapolis, in Thompson, Connecticut, and the publication of the Lithuanian-language daily *Draugas* (*The Friend*), established in 1909 and still published in Chicago. The Marians have also been active in administering Lithuanian-American parishes and Lithuanian missions in South America.

At the same time, the Lithuanian community spawned a variety of Catholic organizations ranging from insurance cooperatives to immigrant-aid societies and cultural groups. Here again, the first societies were joint Polish-Lithuanian endeavors that were soon ended by communal bickering. One of the first exclusively Lithuanian organizations was the St. George Society established in 1877 in Shenandoah. The number of societies, usually named after saints or medieval Lithuanian rulers, grew rapidly and by 1900 there were several hundred Lithuanian organizations in the U.S. The earliest groups were the mutual-aid societies, organized to provide benefits for widowed families, the sick, and those injured in the frequent industrial accidents. Other organizations included the very popular theatrical troupes, choirs, bands, and various social clubs. Learned societies, libraries, and literacy groups were also founded. At the turn of the century, and especially during the period of the First World War, a number of politically oriented organizations emerged, ranging from the Communists (who split with the Socialists in 1919) on the left to Lithuanian-American nationalist supporters of the Smetona government on the right.

From the very beginning there were efforts to establish central organizations for Lithuanian-Americans with varying success. In 1886 Lithuanian Catholic activists established the Alliance of All Lithuanian Catholic Societies in America at Plymouth, Pennsylvania. In 1889 it was incorporated as the Lithuanian Alliance of America (Susivienijimas in Lithuanian). In 1901 a stormy meeting brought simmering ideological differences to a head, necessitating the creation of a separate Lithuanian Roman Catholic Alliance of America to represent the more conservative and Catholic-minded wing of the Lithuanian immigrant community. For its part, the nonclerical splinter group continued as the Lithuanian Alliance, or

SLA. The Lithuanian Roman Catholic Federation of America was founded in 1906 to coordinate the activities of Catholic groups; it sponsored an affiliated Catholic women's group as well as the Lithuanian Roman Catholic Workers' Association in 1915. The federation has played a key, albeit sporadic, role ever since. One of the most popular Lithuanian-American organizations has been the Knights of Lithuania (Lietuvos Vyciai in Lithuanian), a Catholic· youth group established in 1913, which is now one of the more active extant organizations representing the "older generations" of Lithuanian immigrants in America, that is, the descendants of those who arrived in America before World War II. The organization was at its peak in 1921 when it had more than five thousand members and over one hundred councils. Now a family organization, the K of L has at present approximately two thousand members. The Lithuanian Roman Catholic Priests' League, or Kunigu Vienybe, the organization of Lithuanian clergy, was founded in 1908.

The Lithuanian immigrants also sponsored a varied and vociferous press. The first newspaper, *Gazieta Lietuwiszka* (*The Lithuanian Newspaper*), was founded in 1879 but closed after sixteen issues. Gradually, both the quantity and quality of the press markedly improved. In 1896 Father Joseph Zebris (1860-1915) began *Rytas* (*The Morning*), a weekly newspaper published in Waterbury, Connecticut, and intended to offset the influence of liberal freethinkers and socialists. Of the lasting Catholic periodicals, the aforementioned *Draugas* (1909) and *Darbininkas* (*The Worker*) are the most important newspapers. One should also mention the organ of the Catholic Alliance, *Garsas* (*The Sound*), which appeared in 1917 in Brooklyn and is still published in Wilkes-Barre, Pennsylvania.

The Lithuanian-American Catholic community was fortunate to possess several outstanding personalities who provided strong leadership to an initially bewildered and uneducated immigrant flock. One of the guiding lights of the early period of immigration was Father Aleksandras Burba (1854-1898), who arrived in the United

States in 1889, one of the first members of the Lithuanian intelligentsia to immigrate to America. Burba played an essential role in encouraging Lithuanians to establish parishes separate from the Poles. In 1894-1895 he published a weekly called *Valtis* (*The Skiff*) in Plymouth, Pennsylvania. In addition, he contributed numerous articles and literary pieces, including poetry, to the Lithuanian Catholic and non-Catholic press. Another prominent pastor was Father Antanas Milukas (1871-1943), who edited a number of Lithuanian newspapers and became a well-known publisher. Milukas is best remembered for his part in propagating Lithuanian literature and culture in the Lithuanian-American community. Father Antanas Staniukynas arrived in America in 1904 where he was appointed pastor in Mount Carmel and Shamokin. Staniukynas became acutely aware of the coal miners' social and cultural deprivations and vigorously promoted the construction of Lithuanian parochial schools. In the process he founded the aforementioned order of Casimirite nuns to provide teaching personnel. Father Antanas Kaupas (1870-1913) made his mark as an editor, journalist, and scholar who wrote for Lithuanian newspapers in America and the homeland, and was a contributor to the *Catholic Encyclopedia*. Other outstanding figures in the history of Lithuanian Catholicism before World War II were Monsignor Joseph Karalius (1889-1982), the long-time pastor of St. George in Shenandoah, and Monsignor Francis Juras (1891-1983), known for his support of numerous Lithuanian publications.

The success of the Lithuanian Catholic immigrants at the turn of the century in organizing a strong and viable community came in the face of severe difficulties that have been largely forgotten, since they were unique to that period. Not the least of these was the indifference and even hostility of some of the Irish-dominated American Church hierarchy and clergy to the specific national and cultural needs of East European Catholic immigrants. In many instances, the American hierarchy was simply stymied by the lack of qualified clergy who could speak the languages of the immigrants. Some bishops tended toward assimilationist views and were slow to understand the importance of appointing priests who could minister to their congregations in the native language. The idea of ethnic parishes gained acceptance only after a period of considerable struggle.

Lithuanian Catholics faced still another dilemma. The period of the Great Immigration was accompanied by considerable industrial unrest. The influence of socialists and other radical ideologues among the newly arrived and often exploited immigrants was considerable; the Lithuanians were no exception. For a while, socialist and anticlerical elements were strong even within the Catholic parish committees of lay trustees that usually built the ethnic churches and then administered the congregations' financial affairs. These Lithuanian committees were often in conflict with their pastors who sometimes came to be viewed as representatives of an unsympathetic American episcopate. In Shenandoah, a period of prolonged contention between the pastor Monsignor Karalius and the parish trustees had to be resolved by the courts in 1937: the priest won. The disputes between radical parish councils and the clergy frequently erupted into bitter argument and, in a number of instances, into violence: there were shootings, assaults on priests, and bombings of rectories. Mutual suspicions were heightened when in 1915 Father Joseph Zebris was murdered in New Britain, Connecticut, by two Lithuanian criminals with leftist associations.

In the long run, however, the waning of leftist influence within the Lithuanian-American community and the increasing irrelevance of the Communist element during the 1930s led to the assertion of the clergy's authority in the parishes, putting an end to this violent period in Lithuanian-American history. The Communist and radical element also lost out because of its hostile attitude toward the newly independent Lithuanian state to which the majority of Lithuanian-Americans gave their moral and financial support. Historically, it was this common enthusiasm for the national cause that allowed liberal and agnostic Lithuanians to cooperate with the Catholic

244

wing despite their differences. Thus on many occasions Aleksandras Burba was able to work together with the anticlerical freethinker Dr. Jonas Sliupas, since they both were dedicated to the Lithuanian national movement.

Another oft-forgotten episode that reflected the tensions of the time was the formation of the National Lithuanian Church, an autonomous religious community that rejected papal jurisdiction and certain Catholic doctrines. The Lithuanian independent church grew out of the struggle between the pastors and the parish committees described above, particularly the fear of Lithuanian parishioners that the American bishops would ultimately expropriate Lithuanian church property. The first two "independent" parishes were established by the Rev. Vincas Dilionis-Petraitis in Baltimore (1898) and Waterbury (1902). At least fifteen such parishes were founded in the United States before 1929. The movement owed much to the somewhat erratic leadership of the Rev. Stasys Mickevicius who was ordained a bishop in the new church in 1917. Only two small congregations remain: one in Scranton and another in Lawrence, Massachusetts.

The success of the Lithuanian-American Catholics in America in overcoming obstacles and founding a relatively stable community meant that the thousands of postwar Lithuanian Displaced Persons, or DP's, who arrived in the United States during the late 1940s and early 1950s encountered an institutional infrastructure of ethnic parishes and organizations. The new arrivals — the majority of whom were well educated, steeped in European ways, and eager to preserve the Lithuanian language — were markedly different from the "old" immigrants. As political refugees, many of the DP's still harbored dreams of returning to the Lithuanian homeland. They encountered a largely Americanized and, to a considerable degree, linguistically assimilated Lithuanian community that sometimes had little understanding of the concerns of the DP's and their reasons for resisting American ways. For their part, the "new" immigrants sometimes gave the impression that they considered themselves culturally superior to the "old" Lithuanian-Americans. Unfortunately, the intense efforts of the former at preserving the native language and keeping alive the struggle for Lithuania's independence sometimes immunized them against the realities of American life and their new country's political culture.

Despite some problems and tensions, it can be said that, on the whole, Lithuanian-Americans welcomed the DP's and, to a considerable degree, the two communities complemented each other. At a time when assimilation and the postwar flight to the suburbs threatened the foundations of ethnic life and culture, the new immigrants reinvigorated some of the old parishes and institutions, and even created new ones, thus assuring the continuance of Lithuanian culture in America. The task of integrating the postwar refugees was facilitated by the presence of people who were comfortable in both the "old" and the "new" immigrant worlds, and were familiar with the intricacies of American politics. This kind of experience was crucial during the mid- and late forties when political and social leadership was essential but the DP's were only beginning to organize. One such leader was the American-born Monsignor Jonas Balkunas (born 1902), who excelled as an organizer, initiating cooperation between both the "old" immigrants and the postwar DP arrivals. Another such Catholic figure is Juozas Laucka, born in the United States in 1910 but educated in both Lithuania and America: he worked both as an American government official and as a leader of Lithuanian-American Catholic organizations.

For Catholics, the arrival of dozens of refugee priests from Lithuania considerably expanded pastoral work. Lithuanian monastic orders, banned in Lithuania, acquired new homes in the United States. The Franciscans established a monastery in Kennebunkport, Maine, in 1947 and another house in Brooklyn. They took over the publication of the popular newspaper *Darbininkas*. For a time, the order operated St. Anthony High School, a small secondary institution for Lithuanian-American boys that closed in 1969. The Franciscans then established the Zidinys (meaning the "hearth"), a complex in Brookyn that now serves as a cultural center for Lithuanians in the New York area. The Lithuanian Jesuits settled in Chicago where they have become particularly prominent in Lithuanian cultural work and education. The Jesuits provided the initiative for founding and then administering the Lithuanian Youth Center, a complex of buildings in Chicago that houses archives, libraries, and classrooms, and serves as the major center for Lithuanian cultural activities in the United States.

The Sisters of the Immaculate Conception established a convent and farm in Putnam, Connecticut, which grew to include a girls' dormitory (now defunct), the Archbishop Matulaitis Nursing Home, and a printing press. The Putnam development also houses the Catholic Lithuanian-American Archives (Lithuanian acronym: ALKA), which were built largely on the initiative of Monsignor Francis Juras. The nuns have been particularly active in their work with Lithuanian children: they now run a popular youth camp called Neringa in Marlboro, Vermont. In 1952 the Sisters of St. Casimir opened Maria High School for girls, which initially had a large Lithuanian-speaking student population from among the new immigrants. In 1957 the Lithuanian Roman Catholic Federation of America established Camp Dainava, a 228-acre complex west of Detroit, which has become a major center for youth and cultural activity as well as a model for similar sites in the U.S. and Canada.

Among the DP's who came to America there was a large proportion of Catholic intelligentsia, many of whom were professionals with university degrees. One of the greatest contributions of the postwar immigrants was the revival of intellectual and cultural life in the Lithuanian-American community. This was particularly noticeable in the transplanting of institutes, student and academic organizations, and scholarly journals. Perhaps the most influential "new" Catholic organization was the movement known as the Ateitis Federation (*ateitininkai* in Lithuanian), composed of high-school youth, university students, and intelligentsia. The main organs of the organization were transferred to the United States from the DP camps in Germany where the *ateitininkai* had been led by Adolfas Damusis, a prominent figure in the Resistance. In 1967 there were some three thousand members worldwide, most of them in the large Lithuanian communities of the United States. At first, the *ateitininkai* in America were led by people who had been prominent intellectuals in Lithuania. Between 1952 and 1963 Simas Suziedelis (1903-1985), former general secretary of the Lithuanian Academy of Sciences, headed the group; shorter terms were served by Juozas Girnius, Justinas Pikunas, Petras Kisielius, Juozas Laucka, Kazys Pemkus, and Juozas Polikaitis. The organization publishes the journal *Ateitis* (*The Future*) and operates a study center in Lemont, Illinois.

The Catholic community has been the backbone of the effort to maintain an organized national life among the Lithuanian immigrants in America. In addition to the institutions mentioned above, Lithuanian Catholics acknowledged the need for new forms of organization. The Lithuanian Roman Catholic Priests' League of America initiated the establishment of the Lithuanian Catholic Religious Aid in Brooklyn, which, besides providing material support for the Church in Lithuania, translates the underground *Chronicle* into English and serves as a clearinghouse for information concerning Catholic and Lithuanian affairs through its Lithuanian Information Center. It is headed by Father Casimir Pugevicius, an American-born priest with extensive experience in media. Catholics have also been the force behind the United Lithuanian Relief Fund of America (better known by its Lithuanian acronym BALF), which since 1944 has given millions of dollars in aid to Lithuanians displaced by the war and its aftermath, providing food, clothing, and other assistance to needy persons in places as distant as Siberia and Brazil.

At present there are two Lithuanian-born bishops in the United States. One of them is Vincentas Brizgys, auxiliary bishop emeritus of Kaunas. The other is the writer of the preface to this book: Paul Baltakis, a Franciscan ordained to the episcopacy in 1984 who, as titular bishop of Egara, now serves as the Bishop for the Spiritual Assistance of Lithuanian Catholics Living Outside of Lithuania. American-born Charles Salatka, archbishop of Oklahoma City, has been sympathetic to Lithuanian causes. The highest-ranking prelate of Lithuanian extraction is Archbishop Paul Marcinkus, who heads the Vatican's Institute of Religious Works in Rome, the Holy See's financial office, which has been embroiled in controversy over the last few years (although Marcinkus has now been legally cleared). In 1970 the Lithuanian Roman Catholic Priests' League of America reported some six hundred fifty members; the World Lithuanian Catholic Directory for 1986 lists over four hundred clergy of Lithuanian extraction in the United States. There are still over a hundred historically Lithuanian ethnic parishes in the U.S., although most of them have lost or are losing their exclusively Lithuanian identity; by the same token, the number of Lithuanian-language services has declined in recent years, particularly in the smaller communities. The largest number of Lithuanian Catholic parishes (seven) is in the Chicago area.

Of course, while the Catholic community is the largest single component of the Lithuanian-American population, it is not the only one. There are three Lithuanian Protestant parishes in Chicago. The Lutheran Evangelical Zion Church was founded in 1910, whereas the most active Lutheran parish (called Teviske, meaning the "homeland") was established in 1951, largely through the efforts of the Rev. Ansas Trakis (1912-1986). There are also numerous organizations reflecting various secular political and ideological currents within the Lithuanian community. The extreme left has very little of its former clout and is confined to a small group of aging Communists left over from the "old" immigration period; the moderate socialists have also lost much of their former relevance. The liberal intelligentsia of the community is represented by Santara-Sviesa, an active group of considerable cultural achievement, which includes Catholic members. The majority of the Lithuanian-American community naturally tends to be anti-Communist, though not always "conservative" on domestic issues. The occasionally vocal right-wing extremists are also dismissed as irrelevant by the majority. As with other ethnic communities, there are numerous special-interest and ad hoc groups, cultural institutions, political organizations, professional associations, and sports clubs. The Supreme Committee for the Liberation of Lithuania (better known by its Lithuanian acronym VLIK) and the Lithuanian American Council (ALT) have lobbied for Lithuanian political interests since the early 1940s, although political infighting and the aging of the leaders have weakened their efforts. For most Lithuanian-Americans of the DP era and later generations, the major political and cultural organization is the Lithuanian-American Community of the USA established in 1949 (better known simply as the Bendruomene, or the "community"). In those Lithuanian Catholic parishes that are still actively bilingual, the local chapters of the Bendruomene have often taken the leadership of Lithuanian-American affairs from the Roman Catholic Federation and the other older groups.

Lithuanians in Canada

It is estimated that in 1975 some 24,500 Lithuanians were resident in Canada, the majority consisting of DP immigrants and their children; there may now be as many as thirty thousand. More than half of the Lithuanians live in Toronto, Montreal, and Hamilton. The very first Lithuanian immigrants at the turn of the century were arrivals from England and Scotland who settled in Montreal and in Sydney Mines, Nova Scotia. Lithuanians began arriving in Canada in larger numbers directly from Lithuania after the Revolution of 1905 and additional thousands came between 1926 and 1932. As in the United States, the "old" immigrants built up their mutual-aid societies beginning with Montreal (1904), Toronto (1905), and Winnipeg (1912). The first Lithuanian Catholic parish, St. Casimir, was founded in Montreal in 1916 and the second was established in Toronto in 1928.

The arrival of Lithuanian immigrants after World War II considerably enriched the Canadian Lithuanian community. Since they eventually formed a majority, the refugees' relative impact on Canada's Lithuanians was even greater than that of the DP's in the United States. Catholic religious orders played an especially important role in parish work. The Lithuanian Franciscans established their main friary at the Resurrection parish in Toronto while the Jesuits minister to the Gates of Dawn parish in Montreal. In addition, the Franciscans founded a youth camp at New Wasaga Beach in Ontario. The Sisters of the Immaculate Conception operate convents in Toronto and Montreal and have devoted much of their work toward educating Lithuanian youth.

The two major Lithuanian-Canadian newspapers are *Nepriklausoma Lietuva* (*Independent Lithuania*) and the better-known weekly *Teviskes Ziburiai* (*Lights of the Homeland*), edited by Father Pranas Gaida; the latter paper has a considerable following among Lithuanians outside Canada. There are ten Lithuanian Roman Catholic parishes and one Lithuanian Protestant community in the country, most of them founded since the arrival of the refugees from Europe. The smaller Lithuanian colonies, such as the ones in Sudbury, Ottawa, Edmonton, and Vancouver, are served by Catholic missions.

Most of the postwar Lithuanian cultural and religious organizations (such as the *ateitininkai*) that grew up in the U.S. have their corresponding chapters in Canada, which, however, lack the massive organizational ethnic infrastructure that was built up by the "old" immigrants south of the border. Most Lithuanians living in Canada are represented by the Canadian Lithuanian Community.

Lithuanians in Australia

After the United States and Canada, Australia has the third largest Lithuanian community of the English-speaking countries. Before World War II there were probably fewer than one thousand Lithuanians in Australia; the Lithuanian Australian Society that was organized

251

in 1929 had only a hundred members. The Australian government estimates that between 1947 and 1950 about ten thousand Lithuanians arrived in the country. After two years of compulsory labor, Lithuanian immigrants were allowed to settle anywhere they wished.

Except for St. Casimir parish in Adelaide, which has been operated by the Marians since 1962, Lithuanian Catholics in Australia did not establish ethnic parishes as was the practice elsewhere; instead, Australian bishops appoint Lithuanian-speaking chaplains to minister to the faithful. Organized Lithuanian Catholic Missions are located in Sydney, Melbourne, Brisbane, and Perth. While these Lithuanian Catholic communities in Australia do not constitute actual parishes, the larger ones have Sunday schools and youth organizations. The Lithuanian Roman Catholic Federation of Australia organizes religious conferences and cultural programs. The Lithuanian Community of Australia represents most of the country's Lithuanians and it maintains schools, meeting halls, and other accommodations in the major settlements.

Approximately three hundred Lithuanians live in New Zealand, mostly in Auckland and Hamilton. Religious services in Lithuanian are held only rarely by visiting priests.

Lithuanians in Latin America

In sheer numbers, the community of Lithuanian descent in Latin America, primarily located in Brazil, Argentina, and Uruguay, is quite large. At its peak in the 1920s and 1930s, South America's Lithuanian immigrants numbered close to one hundred thousand. Brazil contained the second largest Lithuanian emigrant community; except for Chicago, Sao Paulo was the largest single overseas Lithuanian colony. However, for a number of reasons, the Lithuanian Catholic community in Latin America is organizationally much weaker than in the English-speaking countries. The immigrants' unfavorable economic conditions and low level of education promoted rapid assimilation into the Portuguese-speaking population. In addition, radical leftist influence was relatively strong among the Lithuanian communities on this Catholic continent. Finally, only a few thousand DP's came to South America; thus, unlike North America, the Lithuanians here did not receive the reinvigorating cultural influence of large-scale immigration after the war.

In 1951 official statistics disclosed almost forty-five thousand Lithuanians living in Brazil; fewer than a thousand came from the refugee camps of postwar Europe. Most of Brazil's Lithuanians live in the city and environs of Sao Paulo. During the 1930s the community was assisted financially by the Lithuanian government and the semiofficial Society for the Support of Lithuanians Living Abroad. This enabled the Lithuanians to operate a network of ethnic schools, but they were closed during World War II. The Lithuanian Catholic Community was founded in 1928. In 1936 St. Joseph church was built as the core of a large Lithuanian parish. Two years later, the Lithuanian Catholic Community and St. Joseph's invited Lithuanian nuns from the United States to help in educational work. An important figure in Brazil's Lithuanian community has been Monsignor Pijus Ragazinskas, who was appointed pastor of the new parish and has remained an active leader in Lithuanian affairs ever since. The present pastor, Father Juozas Seskevicius, came to Sao Paulo from the United States. Lithuanian Jesuits also settled in Brazil in 1963 to help in the pastoral work. The Lithuanian Salesian Fathers are based in St. Casimir parish in Sao Paulo. There are only two Lithuanian parishes in Sao Paulo, but it must be remembered that of the ostensibly large Lithuanian-Brazilian community only a minority regularly take part in Lithuanian religious and cultural activities.

Argentina contains the second largest Lithuanian community in Latin America. It is estimated that over thirty thousand persons are of Lithuanian extraction. More than half of the Lithuanian immigrants arrived during the twenties and thirties; another seven hundred fifty refugees came after the war. The community's numbers have declined in recent years due to assimilation, the emigration of many Lithuanians to North America, and the return of some leftists to Soviet Lithuania during the fifties and sixties. The largest remaining Lithuanian communities are in Buenos Aires, Rosario, and Berisso. The most important Lithuanian organizations active in recent years are the Argentine Lithuanian Union founded in 1914 and the Basanavicius Lithuanian Center in Buenos Aires. In 1939 Lithuanian Marian Fathers settled in the Buenos Aires suburb of Avellaneda where they built the church of Our Lady of Vilnius, a monastery, and a parish school. They also publish the newspaper *Laikas* (*Time*). Presently, the Marians also administer St. Casimir parish in Rosario, the other extant Lithuanian parish in Argentina. The parish schools in both places are staffed by the Sisters of St. Casimir.

Another Latin American country with a long-standing Lithuanian community is Uruguay. It is estimated that there are about five thousand persons of Lithuanian descent in that nation; most are results of immigration that occurred between 1923 and 1934. Almost all Lithuanians settled in the Montevideo area where there was an active cultural life in the twenties and thirties. Perhaps more than any other diaspora community, the Lithuanians of Uruguay have been under strong Communist influence. There was no permanent Lithuanian priest until 1953 when the Jesuit Fathers managed to build up the parish of Our Lady of Fatima, which serves as the nucleus of a small but active Lithuanian Catholic community.

Venezuela and Colombia also have small Lithuanian communities. In contrast to the three countries above, the Lithuanians of the latter two states are primarily the products of postwar immigration. Over one thousand such persons arrived in Venezuela after 1946; however, by 1964 over half of them had left for the United States and only some two hundred thirty families remain, mostly in Caracas (where there is a community facility named after St. Casimir), Valencia, and Maracaibo. The first priest to serve the community in Venezuela was the Salesian missionary Antanas Sabaliauskas, who was followed by Father Antanas Perkumas (1909-1986), another

Salesian. Several hundred postwar Lithuanian refugees came to Colombia, settling in Bogota and Medellin, where there are Lithuanian Catholic missions.

Lithuanians in Western Europe

The largest Lithuanian community in Western Europe, currently estimated at about ten thousand people, is that of Great Britain. The majority are descendants of turn-of-the-century immigrants, of whom some nine thousand resided in London in 1900; another eight thousand were reported in Scotland on the eve of World War I. About two thousand Lithuanians settled in Britain permanently after 1945. In the 1890s the first exclusively Lithuanian parishes were formed in London and Glasgow. St. Casimir Lithuanian parish in London was established in 1901 and was headed for thirty years (1905-1935) by Father Kazimieras Matulaitis. Today the parish is administered by the Lithuanian Marians, who also opened a Lithuanian Center in Nottingham in 1965 where they publish the religious monthly *Saltinis* (*The Source*). Lithuanian Catholic missions operate in Bradford, Manchester, and Glasgow. Britain's Lithuanians have maintained a relatively active cultural life: the community operates a printing house in London (Nida) and publishes *Europos Lietuvis* (*The European Lithuanian*) for Lithuanians in Western Europe.

Of the nearly sixty thousand Lithuanian DP's formally registered in 1946, only a few thousand remained in West Germany. In later years, their numbers were somewhat augmented by people allowed to leave East Prussia and the Klaipeda Territory as "Germans." The approximately six thousand to ten thousand Lithuanians in the German Federal Republic are scattered throughout the country and do not form distinct colonies. An important cultural institution is the February 16th High School established in 1951 and located near Mannheim. It is presently the only Lithuanian secondary school in the West utilizing Lithuanian as the language of instruction. The school's student body is drawn from Lithuanians in Germany and the various communities around the world.

There is a Lithuanian Catholic mission in Germany headed by Father Antanas Bunga. Bishop emeritus Antanas Deksnys (born 1906), who had been assigned by the Vatican to serve Lithuanian Catholics in Western Europe, resides at the Lithuanian Catholic Center in Bad Woerishofen. Many of the Lithuanians in Germany are Lutherans; Rev. Adolfas Keleris and the Protestant pastoral office in Bremen minister to their needs.

Of the other European states, there are tiny Lithuanian communities in France, Switzerland, and Sweden. There is a Lithuanian Catholic Mission in Paris headed by Father Jonas Petrosius, and visiting priests in the latter two countries minister to the Lithuanian faithful. The Lithuanians of Russia and Siberia naturally have little or no access to Catholic religious services. The Lithuanian Catholic community in Poland, which numbers about ten thousand concentrated around the town of Punsk and the villages of the Suwalki region, cannot be strictly considered part of the Lithuanian diaspora inasmuch as it lives on ethnographically Lithuanian territory. The Lithuanians here have a parish and secondary school in Punsk and, after long years of struggle with the Polish hierarchy, have recently acquired the right to Lithuanian-language services in the cathedral of Sejny (Seinai in Lithuanian), a town with a long Lithuanian tradition.

Despite the fact that it does not have a Lithuanian colony as do other countries, Italy (particularly Rome) has special significance for Lithuanian Catholics. The majority of Lithuanians living in Rome are clerics. In 1946 the Lithuanian bishops established St. Casimir College, a residence for Lithuanian seminarians engaged in advanced studies in Rome's theological schools, such as the Gregorian and Lateran Universities. The college accommodates dozens of priests and seminarians at any one time and has facilities for housing pilgrims and tourists. In 1956 the Lithuanian Catholic Academy of Sciences, which had been closed by the Soviet regime, was reactivated in Rome. Under its longtime president, Father Antanas Liuima, S.J., the academy has published many volumes of studies dealing with history, literature, and theology as well as the other social and physical sciences. It holds biannual conferences, usually in the United States. One of the most prominent Lithuanian scholars in Rome is Dr. Paulius Rabikauskas, S.J., a recognized authority on ecclesiastical history and the dean of the faculty of Church history at the Gregorian University. Other Lithuanian institutions in Rome are the Lithuanian desk at Vatican Radio and the Lithuanian legation accredited to the Vatican, which does not recognize Lithuania's incorporation into the USSR. The present Lithuanian emissary to the Holy See is Stasys Lozoraitis. In addition, the Lithuanian Salesian Fathers operated a Lithuanian boys' secondary school near Turin between 1952 and 1970; they still maintain a summer house in the Italian Alps as well as a novitiate and printing press near Rome.

The accession of Karol Wojtyla to the papacy as John Paul II in 1978 has given considerable encouragement to Lithuanian Catholics both in Lithuania and in the diaspora. Perhaps the only significant shadow over Lithuanian-Vatican relations has been the status of the archdiocese of Vilnius. Some Lithuanians have expressed concern at its continued inclusion within the Polish Church province, although the issue presently has more symbolic than practical meaning. The pope has made no secret of his special affection and concern for the Lithuanian Catholic Church, and his habit of addressing Lithuanians in their own language has impressed them. The Holy Father's enthusiastic initiative in celebrating the five hundredth anniversary of St. Casimir in 1984 as an almost exclusively Lithuanian affair pleasantly surprised most of the world Lithuanian community. In 1987, the Soviet government refused the pontiff's request to visit Lithuania on the six hundredth anniversary of the country's acceptance of Christianity. However, Pope John Paul II presided over the six hundredth anniversary celebrations in Rome that took place during the last week of June 1987, and which attracted some four thousand Lithuanians from around the world, including a delegation of clergy from Lithuania headed by Bishop Antanas Vaicius.

Whatever the scope and nature of activity within the worldwide Lithuanian diaspora, the focus of Lithuanians living outside the homeland remains concentrated on events within Lithuania. This has been especially true since the mid-1980s as the shifting and potentially volatile political and cultural situation within the emigrants' homeland has reignited harsh memories of the past as well as hopes and fears for the future. The elevation of Vincentas Sladkevicius, the president of the Lithuanian bishops' conference, to the College of Cardinals on June 28, 1988, has riveted attention on the Catholic Church in Lithuania. In a remarkable interview published by the Lithuanian Communist Party's daily *Tiesa* (*The Truth*) on July 15, 1988, following Cardinal Sladkevicius' return from Rome, the leader of Lithuania's Catholics candidly spoke of past suffering, present concerns, and future hopes:

Many painful wounds have remained from the recent past. We all want them to be healed as soon as possible. The [Lithuanian Catholic] Church has until recently not been permitted to assert itself anywhere. The only exception has been the propagandistic peace movement to which, as the people say, Catholic clergy were invited only for show. Priests were even prohibited from propagating temperance. Charitable work was not permitted, thus works of mercy have languished. The 600th anniversary of Lithuania's Christianization commemorated last year was, in many places, utilized not to honor the Church's contribution to the nation and its culture, but often to actually reinforce propaganda directed against religion.

It seems that the times are changing. But how are we to return what has been lost? It is not always possible to do this. This is why we all now feel a lack of charity. This lack [of mutual love] is the most painful deficiency in our society. To remove this deficiency will be very difficult. But it is particularly essential at present to foster charity, tolerance for the opinions of others, and mutual understanding. All this constitutes the ABC of democracy as

258

well. . . . What has been [allowed us] in the past are but small crumbs. We need popular religious books, but we don't have them. There is a great need for a periodical publication for Catholics. Faith does not teach a person evil. Today it is difficult not only to justify, but even to understand those people, especially the leaders, who used to look askance at and even rebuke the practicing Catholic. It is time not only to declare, but to put into practice, everywhere and in all respects, equality of rights between believers and non-believers. . . . There can be no genuine renewal of society without a moral rebirth.

We do see some changes in comparison with the recent past. New points of contact [between Church and State] will be clarified later, when the restrictions on the activity of the Church will finally be abolished. We foster such hopes . . . we see some rays of hope now. But let us also hope for a truly bright future. . . .

Suggestions for Further Reading

There are volumes of literature dealing with Lithuania and the Catholic Church in Eastern Europe. Below I have listed a few works in English that may interest readers who would like to learn more about the topics covered in this volume. The list is selective. In general, I have tried to avoid listing books of narrow, specialized interest; however, in some cases, I have included them if I felt they were particularly relevant to some of the areas covered in the book or would be of use to the general reader. Some of the works below are scholarly, whereas others tend toward the more popular approach. Not all are of equal merit regarding their level of historical scholarship, but the reader can quickly distinguish objective studies from the more polemical tracts.

Of all the works listed below, the most highly recommended and reliable regarding the situation of the Lithuanian Catholic Church in the twentieth century is Prof. V. Stanley Vardys's excellent study, *The Catholic Church, Dissent and Nationality in Soviet Lithuania.*

For those with an ongoing interest in Baltic affairs, especially Lithuania, two good quarterly journals are available: *Lituanus*, published by the Lituanus Foundation in Chicago, and the *Journal of Baltic Studies*, published by the AABS (The Association for the Advancement of Baltic Studies). The Winter 1987 (Vol. 33, No. 4) issue of *Lituanus* is dedicated to the six hundredth anniversary of the Christianization of Lithuania. The state of the Lithuanian Church is described in *The Chronicle of the Catholic Church in Lithuania.* English-language translations of the *Chronicle* are published by the Lithuanian Catholic Religious Aid, Inc., in Brooklyn,

New York, in separate issues and in bound volumes by the Society for the Publication of the Chronicle of the Catholic Church in Chicago, Illinois. There is also *The Chronicle of the Catholic Church in Lithuania, Nos. 1-9* (Chicago: Loyola University Press, 1979).

• General Histories

Chase, Thomas G. *The Story of Lithuania*. New York: Stratford House, 1946.

Gerutis, Albert, ed. *Lithuania: 700 Years*, 3rd rev. ed. New York: Manyland Books, 1969.

Jurgela, Kostas. *History of the Lithuanian Nation*. New York: Lithuanian Cultural Institute, 1948.

Manning, Clarence A. *The Forgotten Republics*. New York: Philosophical Library, 1952.

Sapoka, Adolfas. *Vilnius in the Life of Lithuania*. Translated by E. J. Harrison. Toronto: The Lights, 1962.

• Earlier Period (Before the Nineteenth Century)

Backus, O.P., "The Problem of Unity in the Polish-Lithuanian State," *Slavic Review*, XXII (No. 3, 1963), pp. 411-455.

Carstens, Francis Ludwig. *The Origins of Prussia*. Oxford: Clarendon Press, 1954.

Davies, Norman. *God's Playground: A History of Poland* (two vols.). New York: Columbia University Press, 1982.

Gimbutas, Marija. *The Balts*. London: Frederick A. Praeger, 1963.

Koncevicius, Joseph B. *Russia's Attitude Towards Union with Rome (9th-16th Centuries)*, 2nd ed. Washington, D.C.: Canorma Press, 1927.

Lowmianski, Henryk. *The Ancient Prussians*. Torun: Pomorska Drukarnia Rolnicza, 1936.

Mazeika, Rasa. "Was Grand Prince Algirdas a Greek Orthodox Christian?" *Lituanus*, Vol. 33, No. 4 (Winter 1987), pp. 35-55.

Sruogiene-Sruoga, Vanda. "Jogaila (1350-1434)," *Lituanus*, Vol. 33, No. 4 (Winter 1987), pp. 23-34.

Urban, William. *The Baltic Crusade*. DeKalb: Northern Illinois University Press, 1975.

———. *The Prussian Crusade*. Lanham, Md.: University Press of America, 1980.

———. "The Conversion of Lithuania 1387," *Lituanus*, Vol. 4, No. 33 (Fall 1987), pp. 12-22.

Zajaczkowski, Stanislaw. *The Rise and Fall of the Teutonic Order in Prussia*. Torun: Baltic Institute, 1935.

• Modern Period (Nineteenth and Twentieth Centuries)

Bourdeaux, Michael. *Land of Crosses*. Chulmleigh, Devon: Augustine Publ. Co., 1980.

Budreckis, Algirdas. *The Lithuanians in America 1651-1975*. Dobbs Ferry, N.Y.: Oceana Publications, 1975.

Danys, Milda. *DP: Lithuanian Immigration to Canada after the Second World War*. Toronto: Multi-cultural History Society of Ontario, 1986.

Dauknys, Pranas. *The Resistance of the Catholic Church in Lithuania Against Religious Persecution*. Rome: Pontificia Studiorum Universitas A. S. Thoma Aq. in Urbe, 1981.

Fainhauz, David. *Lithuanians in Multi-Ethnic Chicago Until World War II*. Chicago: Lithuanian Library Press and University of Loyola Press, 1977.

Kinsella, David and Taagepera, Rein. "Religious Incident Statistics for Soviet Lithuanian Schools," *Journal of Baltic Studies*, Vol. XV, No. 1 (Spring 1984), pp. 27-47.

Kucas, Antanas. *Archbishop George Matulaitis*. Translated by Stanley C. Gaucias. Chicago: Lithuanian Catholic Press Society, 1981.

———. *Lithuanians in America*. Translated by Joseph Boley. Boston: Lithuanian Encyclopedia Press, 1975.

Misiunas, Romuald J., and Taagepera, Rein. *The Baltic States: The Years of Dependence*. Berkeley: University of California Press, 1983.

Rauch, Georg von. *The Baltic States: The Years*

of Independence 1917-1940. Translated by Gerald Onn. London: C. Hurst & Co., 1970.

Remeikis, Thomas. *Opposition to Soviet Rule in Lithuania 1945-1980.* Chicago: Institute of Lithuanian Studies, 1980.

Sabaliunas, Leonas. *Lithuania in Crisis: Nationalism to Communism 1939-1940.* Bloomington, Ind.: Indiana University Press, 1972.

Sadunaite, Nijole. *Radiance in the Gulag: The Catholic Witness of Nijole Sadunaite.* Translated by Casimir Pugevicius and Marian Skabeikis. Manassas, Va.: Trinity Communications, 1987.

Senn, Alfred Erich. *The Emergence of Modern Lithuania.* New York: Columbia University Press, 1959.

_____. *The Great Powers, Lithuania and the Vilna Question.* Leiden: E. J. Brill, 1966.

Vardys, V. Stanley. *The Catholic Church, Dissent and Nationality in Soviet Lithuania.* Boulder, Colo.: East European Quarterly, 1978.

_____. "Human Rights Issues in Estonia, Latvia and Lithuania," *Journal of Baltic Studies,* Vol. XII, No. 3 (Fall 1981), pp. 275-298.

_____, ed. *Lithuania Under the Soviets: Portrait of a Nation.* New York: Praeger, 1965.

Wolkovich-Valkavicius, William L. *Lithuanian Pioneer Priest of New England: The Life, Struggles and Tragic Death of Reverend Joseph Zebris, 1860-1915.* Brooklyn: Franciscan Press, 1980.

_____. "Religious Separatism Among Lithuanian Immigrants in the United States and Their Polish Affiliation," *Polish-American Studies,* No. 2 (Autumn 1983), pp. 93-123.

Yla, Stasys. *A Priest in Stutthof: Human Experiences in the World of Subhuman.* Translated by Nola M. Zobarskas. New York: Manyland Books, 1971.

• Encyclopedias, Bibliographies, and Reference Works

Balys, Jonas. *Lithuania and Lithuanians: A Selected Bibliography.* New York: Praeger, 1961.

Kantautas, Adam and Filomena. *A Lithuanian Bib-*

liography: A Check-List of Books and Periodicals Held by the Major Libraries of Canada and the United States. Edmonton: The University of Alberta Press, 1975.

_____ . *Supplement to a Lithuanian Bibliography: A Further Check-List of Books and Articles Held by the Major Libraries of Canada and the United States.* Edmonton: The University of Alberta Press, 1979.

Suziedelis, Simas, ed. *Encyclopedia Lituanica* (six vols.). Boston: Lithuanian Encyclopedia Press, 1970-1978.

World Lithuanian Roman Catholic Directory. Brooklyn: Franciscan Press, 1979, 1981, and 1986.

Zinkus, Jonas, ed. *Lithuania: An Encyclopedic Survey.* Vilnius: Encyclopedia Publishers, 1986.

Our Sunday Visitor titles are available at fine religious bookstores everywhere. Titles can be ordered direct from OSV by writing or calling. When writing, include the following information: title(s), stock number(s), and quantity(ies) along with your name and address plus your payment and $2.00 for shipping and handling.

VISA and MasterCard orders may be placed anytime by calling toll-free 1-800-348-2440. From Indiana and Alaska call 1-219-356-8400. Call or write for OSV's free full-line book catalog. *Our Sunday Visitor / 200 Noll Plaza / Huntington, IN 46750.*

You will find our latest titles on the following pages.

A Celebration of Padre Pio, no. 190-7, VHS videocassette, $49.95, 58 minutes. Experience the remarkable life of Padre Pio on this new videocassette. *A Celebration of Padre Pio* includes motion-picture footage of Padre Pio working and saying Mass, firsthand accounts of miraculous events, readings from his writing, and much more.

Strangers at Your Door: How to Respond to Jehovah's Witnesses, the Mormons, Televangelists, Cults, and More, by Albert J. Nevins, M.M., no. 496-5, paper, $6.95, 144 pp. *Strangers at Your Door* gives you the background and beliefs of many evangelistic religious groups and appropriate Catholic responses to their challenges. A valuable resource for those who must explain their Catholic faith.

One of Them, by Norene Pavlik, no. 420-5, paper, $8.95, 264 pp. The moving story of Norene Pavlik's mentally retarded daughter, Jenny, *One of Them* also presents a model for life and growth within a Catholic family. Introduced by Eunice Kennedy Shriver, chairman of Special Olympics International.

The Life of Brother André: The Miracle Worker of St. Joseph, by C. Bernard Ruffin, no. 492-2, paper, $6.95, 228 pp. From the author of *Padre Pio: The True Story* comes the inspirational story of Brother André Bessette, a small, quiet, humble man who believed in and used the healing power of intercessory prayer.

I Am with You Always, by Fr. Berard Doerger, O.F.M., no. 414-0, paper, $5.95, 144 pp. Written for both the clergy and laity, *I Am with You Always* clearly explains the background, beauty, and significance of the Catholic Church's liturgical year.

The Catholic Living Bible — Four Editions, no. 218-0, Confirmation (deluxe imitation white leather), $14.95; no. 219-9, Gift (deluxe imitation white leather), $14.95; no. 220-2, Gift (deluxe imitation black leather), $14.95; no. 221-0, Gift (deluxe imitation red leather), $14.95. Give a friend or loved one the special gift of God's Word as clearly presented in *The Catholic Living Bible*.

Classic Catholic Poetry, compiled and edited by Thomas P. McDonnell, no. 494-9, casebound, $12.95, 144 pp. Dante, Chaucer, Merton, and Pope John Paul II are among the famous poets found in *Classic Catholic Poetry*. Includes explanatory notes on both the poets and their works.

Pocket New Testament — Revised New American Bible, no. 222-9, leatherette, $4.95; no. 223-7, red bonded leather, $12.95; no. 249-0, white bonded leather, $12.95, 640 pp. Take God's Word with you wherever you go with the *Pocket New Testament*. This convenient New Testament now comes in three editions: red leatherette, red bonded leather, and white bonded leather.

Stepfamilies: A Catholic Guide, by Paul J. Cullen, no. 508-2, paper, $4.95, 168 pp. Answers questions on such topics as finances, disciplining stepchildren, and interfaith marriages for Catholic stepfamilies. Includes a list of books for further reading.